[signature]

God Bless America

De Oppresso Liber

TIP OF THE SPEAR

SPEAR

THE INCREDIBLE STORY OF AN INJURED

GREEN BERET'S RETURN TO BATTLE

RYAN HENDRICKSON

CENTER STREET

New York   Nashville

Center Street

Hachette Book Group

1290 Avenue of the Americas, New York, NY 10104

centerstreet.com

twitter.com/centerstreet

First Edition: July 2020

Center Street is a division of Hachette Book Group, Inc. The Center Street name and logo are trademarks of Hachette Book Group, Inc.

The publisher is not responsible for websites (or their content) that are not owned by the publisher.

The Hachette Speakers Bureau provides a wide range of authors for speaking events. To find out more, go to www.HachetteSpeakersBureau.com or call (866) 376-6591.

Library of Congress Cataloging-in-Publication Data

Names: Hendrickson, Ryan, 1978– author.

Title: Tip of the spear : the incredible story of an injured Green Beret's return to battle / Ryan Hendrickson.

Other titles: Incredible story of an injured Green Beret's return to battle

Description: First edition. | New York : Center Street, 2020. | Summary: "The inspiring story of a US Special Forces soldier who was medically retired after stepping on an IED, and his incredible return to active duty."—Provided by publisher.

Identifiers: LCCN 2019045253 | ISBN 9781546084792 (hardcover) | ISBN 9781546084815 (ebook)

Subjects: LCSH: Hendrickson, Ryan, 1978 | United States. Army. Special Forces—Military life. | United States. Army. Special Forces Group, 7th. Battalion, 2nd. Company A—Biography. | Afghan War, 2001—Commando operations—United States. | Afghan War, 2001—Personal narratives, American. | Soldiers—United States—Biography. | BISAC: BIOGRAPHY & AUTOBIOGRAPHY / Military Classification: LCC DS371.43.H45 A3 2020 | DDC 958.104/74 [B]—dc23

LC record available at https://lccn.loc.gov/2019045253

ISBNs: 978-1-5460-8479-2 (hardcover), 978-1-5460-8481-5 (ebook)

Printed in the United States of America

LSC-C

10 9 8 7 6 5 4 3 2

To those who answered the call and didn't make it home, may we live our lives to the best of our abilities, as they would have wanted us to

CONTENTS

CHAPTER 1

TOUCHDOWN

BAGRAM AIRFIELD

BAGRAM, AFGHANISTAN

JUNE 2010

When the bulky C-17 Globemaster touched down at Bagram Airfield in Afghanistan and the rear loading ramp dropped down, I was slapped in the face by the summer heat—sticky and in the 90s. Then came the smells, which were a mixture of burning trash, raw sewage, and aviation fuel.

I wrinkled my nose, but that wasn't going to change the shit-smelling air assaulting my nostrils. None of this caught me by surprise, though. Before I left Fort Bragg in North Carolina, I heard that Kabul city, twenty-five miles to the south and the country's largest city with 3 million residents, was an open sewer, home to some of the dirtiest air in the world.

Despite the fetid smells and oppressive heat, I felt like a kid at a pizza party on this steamy June day. I had just graduated from the U.S. Army's Special Forces Qualification Course in Fayetteville, North Carolina, and this was my first time in Afghanistan and my first mission as a Green Beret. I had left the U.S. Air

Force for the Army so I would have the chance to take the fight to the enemy up close and in person. My wish was coming true. In my mind, I was a well-oiled machine ready to take on any challenge as part of Special Operations Forces.

When I graduated from Q Course, I entered an elite world as a Special Forces Engineer, which was known as an 18C—or 18 Charlie—in the SF community. Now that I was being deployed to a war zone like Afghanistan, I would have a lot of duties on the team but chief among them would be finding, removing, or detonating the number-one killer of U.S. troops in the War on Terror: Improvised Explosive Devices (IEDs), or homemade bombs and mines. While all jobs on my team were extremely important, I was trained to do something that you better not fuck up.

As an Improvised Explosive Device detection expert—and I use the term "expert" loosely—I would be directly responsible for my teammates' safety while on patrol in combat. If I let my concentration wander or missed one little detail, bad shit happened—meaning that I or any one of my fellow soldiers could lose a limb or be killed. I would have to do my damnedest to ensure that we all returned home alive and with the limbs we deployed with.

After exiting the C-17 ramp and looking to the horizon, I was taken aback by the almost picture-perfect views of the surrounding mountains. I say *almost* perfect because I would soon find out that beyond the base's security walls, anyone associated with the Taliban wanted to shoot you or blow you up with IEDs that littered the killing fields.

Carrying my sixty-pound rucksack and dragging a Tuff box full of my gear, I headed out across the concrete tarmac. Beads of sweat dripped out of my pores and drenched my beard. Special Forces soldiers blend in better with the local population if they sported full beards, so Green Berets grew out their facial hair prior to deployment in Afghanistan. I had stopped shaving a month earlier. I'd never had facial hair before, but I was pleasantly surprised that a full brown beard grew in and covered my cheeks and chin.

Each step was a reminder that I was the rookie on my team, the new guy on Alpha Company, 2nd Battalion, 7th Special Forces. My role as an 18C engineer was one of six main jobs on a Special Forces team. The others were: weapons expert, communications expert, medical expert, intelligence expert, and leadership.

My teammates had done previous tours in Afghanistan, so the brotherhood they'd formed and the bonding they'd done was something that I hadn't been part of. I was aware that I was an outsider trying to fit in with a bunch of battle-hardened Green Berets since I hadn't proven myself in combat with them. Finding my place wouldn't be quick or easy.

I didn't have to wait long to get out into the field. From Bagram, we made a few brief stops on our way to southern Afghanistan until we reached our home for the next six to nine months of our tour—Forward Operating Base (FOB) Tycz.

FOB Tycz was a large, comfortable base with the requisite security walls. The Dutch had a fire base adjacent to ours, which meant we were not alone, and the Dutch soldiers turned out to be good neighbors. The base was located in Uruzgan Province, so we were right in the thick of the fight. Like most places in Afghanistan, we were surrounded by towering mountains that gave way to dry desert in the valley below, where FOB Tycz was. We were a short drive away from the Helmand River, which was a lifeline for farming and producing huge marijuana plants, another cash crop.

FOB Tycz had what every Green Beret knows is as important as water on a hot day—a good-size gym. We didn't have to have anything fancy, but there were appearances to keep up, and no one likes a flabby Green Beret. Staying buff was the first of three rules that were taught to me while going through training. The three rules were:

1. Always look cool.
2. Don't fuck up.
3. If you fuck up, look cool doing it.

We didn't spend much time at the FOB. Instead, we pushed out to a location along the Helmand River just across the provincial border of Uruzgan and Helmand provinces. This position was pivotal to keeping the pressure on Taliban fighters operating along the Helmand River, which ran north-to-south through the Chutu Valley. Our U.S. outpost was the best location for cultivating the Taliban's drug crops.

Constant pressure was the name of the game in the fight against the Taliban. The pressure not only came in the form of U.S Special Forces troops on the ground but a relatively new strategy to the War on Terror: Village Stability Operations, or VSO.

Up to this point, the Taliban had control of the farmlands and rural villages where they could freely bring the fight to us. VSO missions would be an attempt to disrupt the Taliban's freedom of movement around the countryside and deny them safe haven, which was where Special Forces fit in perfectly.

Winning "hearts and minds" was a Special Forces soldier's

bread and butter. We trained for it and, for the most part, we believed in this mission.

When summer was coming to a close, my team, along with other detachments from our company, was tasked with entering the Chutu Valley from different locations and clearing out the Taliban to a central point, which would send the bastards running for the mountains. Working against us, however, was the fact that this was not a covert mission. Everyone up and down the valley knew we would be coming, which gave the Taliban ample time to place IEDs and prepare for us.

Finally, it was time to push into the valley. We were ready to take the fight to the enemy and not just hold ground.

One of the major concerns, besides IEDs and small arms fire from Taliban fighters, was the Helmand River. Our compound was located on the western side of the river, and the villages we planned to clear were on the eastern side.

As the 18C engineer, it fell on my shoulders to figure out a way to move men, weapons, and equipment across the headwaters of Afghanistan's longest river—which began in the Hindu Kush mountains—to where we were staging our mission.

In the bottom of the valley, the fast-flowing Helmand was probably twenty meters wide. To ford the river, I had at my disposal a Zodiac inflatable rubber raft, protective pieces of large Styrofoam blocks, and lots of lumber.

I figured I could MacGyver something up. I constructed a ramp and a platform system that would ride on top of the raft and used the Styrofoam to prevent the lumber from puncturing the rubber fabric. The platform atop the raft was designed to safely transport our gear, ATVs, and personnel during multiple trips across the river. The current was swift, and any mistake could lead to drowning or being swept away and landing in the hands of the Taliban farther downriver.

When the word was given, we set out for the Helmand River late in the afternoon of September 11, 2010—an auspicious date, for sure. I was crazy nervous because if I failed, it would be all on the new guy. The plan was to cross the river with the ATV and equipment first, then return for the next load.

When we arrived at the Helmand, it was the moment of truth—time to find out if I knew what I was doing. We loaded the first Zodiac and pushed out into the Helmand, which was fairly wide and deep. If I fell in, at least the water was warm in the summer. There was a cable across the river that we used to pull the raft across.

So far, so good, I thought. *Let's keep going.*

More than halfway to the other side, there was no turning back. We safely arrived with the first load. My amphibious contraption had worked: no ATVs or equipment ended up at the bottom of the river. I was excited with my success.

In all, we made three crossings without incident, and then we moved north about five hundred meters and staged there, waiting to kick off the operation.

Missions of this caliber with many moving parts were best left for the cover of darkness. Pushing out at night was the small advantage we had over the enemy, especially because they knew we were coming—just not the exact day or time.

The Taliban were not fond of fighting at night; darkness favored us due to our superior equipment and advanced technology. The disadvantage of moving at night was that finding IEDs would be very difficult. As good as our night vision goggles (NVGs) were, they had little to no depth perception.

It was easy to get disoriented if you were forced to run, sprint, or quickly move to cover, or really do anything besides making slow, controlled movements forward, while using NVGs. Fortunately for us, the advantages outweighed the disadvantages because having the ability to see even a little in pitch-black darkness made you better off than your enemy. One motto we believed in was: *If they can't see you, they can't kill you.*

The moon was bright as we waited in the staging area. I lay on the riverbank waiting for Ben, our detachment commander, to give us the word to move out.

Hours passed. As a slight sliver of morning light spread over the valley, we checked our gear one last time. There was still plenty of darkness, so NVGs were necessary, but the sun would soon rise, and no one wanted to travel over open ground in broad daylight. We had a good distance to clear before we got to our first village, and time was running out.

Finally, Ben made the call: "Let's move out, guys."

We slowly trudged our way toward the village of Sar Tutu in the distance. Sar Tutu was made up of several mud-hut compounds, and my group was tasked with clearing one of the sections.

Keeping strict noise and light discipline, we scanned the hillsides and the riverbank for any movement. I kept my thumb on my weapon's safety selector, ready to switch it on to engage and kill the enemy.

Taking fire from the Taliban was a risk we all knew was possible, but the more likely scenario was experiencing a catastrophic

IED explosion resulting in loss of limbs and broken bodies. All the team members were fully aware that one wrong step could change their lives forever. My job was to make sure that did not happen.

These insidious bombs could be hidden anywhere: buried in the ground, hung in trees, stashed in cooking pots, inside the carcasses of dead animals, within car trunks, or under clothing with the infamous strap-on suicide vests.

While they might have been built with fertilizer and discarded spare parts and looked like a junior high school shop class project, I never underestimated the lethality of these homemade bombs. All it took was a handful of high explosives, a few inches of copper wire, and a battery. Detonation could be triggered by compression, the weight of a soldier or a vehicle passing over the explosive charge; remote control with cell phones; or an electrical circuit from a distance. The Taliban were limited only by their imagination, which was limitless when it came to killing Americans.

The morning light took up more than half the sky, sending beautiful fluorescent colors shooting across the horizon. Even in a war zone, Mother Nature could flaunt her beauty and put on an amazing show. After moving for just over an hour, we were on the southern outskirts of the first village, and one thing was for sure: You could smell an Afghan village long before you saw it.

The odor was a combination of rotting animal carcasses and trash, mixed with the smell of wood fires used for cooking the day's meals. The smell that dominated, however, was the overwhelming stench of human shit. Given the lack of westernized sewage treatment facilities in the rural countryside, villagers usually used an abandoned room in their compound or squatted and did their business right outside the compound wall in kind of a shit trench. When the temperature rose, the feces atomized, and the noxious germs floated freely through the air, punishing my nose with each breath I took. At times the smell was so bad I could taste it on my tongue.

Moving up, we intercepted a radio transmission from the Taliban indicating that they knew we were on the move and could see us. At first, the news made my heart race. My palms got sweaty as my eyes darted around, looking for anything slightly abnormal.

I felt like I was starting to see things that really weren't there. Were my eyes playing tricks on me? Or my ears? It seemed like I was hearing all sorts of things when we stopped to get our bearings.

The guys called this hypervigilance and told me that when danger was imminent, your senses rose up several notches to high-alert status. Fueling this hypersensitivity was an overwhelming desire to stay alive.

Taking a brief moment to assess my situation, I realized there was zero chance the Taliban were unaware of who was stomping around in their backyard. Of course they knew we had arrived, but the hair-raising question was, where were they watching us from? The ridgeline? Were they hiding near the river, ready to put a burst of bullets into our chests as we walked by? Were they inside the village, hiding somewhere in the compounds? In other words, since they knew we were on their turf, what were they going to do about it?

The village was deserted when we entered. This was not

unexpected. It was no secret that we were in the valley, so the villagers had wisely deserted their homes—probably days before this assault. Whether the Taliban were hiding and waiting to spring an ambush was anyone's guess. One thing every SF guy knew was that when you enter a village and it's deserted, you better figure that you're in for a big fight or a village full of IEDs. In our minds, IEDs were a coward's way of fighting, but no one could deny that they were extremely effective.

We had to clear each compound or home, so we advanced slowly and deliberately, looking for anything suspicious or out of the ordinary that could conceal an IED. We were professional soldiers. Details mattered. A slight discoloration in the dirt, a suspicious pile of rocks, an abandoned water pail, a tree that had been tagged with a marker, a disturbance in a mud wall, or a lone person walking quickly and directly toward us—everything mattered. But we didn't see any people or anything questionable, even though I assumed that every doorway and window had a pair of eyes looking at me and my buddies.

After we hit our first planned stopping point, the team broke up into smaller elements to cover a bigger area in and around the village, including a World War I–like trench that ran adjacent to the Helmand River, one of the Taliban's favorite positions to fight us from. Each small element was made up of two or three Green Berets and a handful of Afghan fighters assisting us in clearing the village. My element consisted of myself; our team sergeant, Lance; and six Afghans—one of whom was Nick, our interpreter. Nick wasn't the man's real name, but everyone who supported our team was given an easy-to-remember nickname for ease of communication.

Our job, alongside the Afghans, was to clear the first set of compounds running parallel to the river. Once these compounds were clear, we would move on to the next set.

As I approached within fifteen meters of the first compound, I watched for everything and anything—from movement in the compounds to variations in the terrain to where I was stepping next. I stopped and turned around to check on Lance, who was behind me and several Afghans. He gave me a nod, meaning I could keep moving with the Afghans and check out the first compound.

I motioned to Nick to come closer.

"Tell your guys to move up and clear the compound," I said. "Keep your fucking eyes open." We both knew what that meant: Sweep the courtyard while watching every nook and cranny for a rifle barrel waiting to open fire.

Nick turned and relayed my direction to the handful of Afghan soldiers. Instead of moving, they stood there like statues. As precious seconds passed by, it became clear to me that they were not going to move.

What the fuck, I thought. *Do they not understand what I need them to do? Are they too scared to go?*

I whispered to Nick, "What's the problem?"

"It's too dangerous," Nick replied.

No shit. Of course it was dangerous. This was what war was all about.

I knew they were scared; I was, too. I figured they wanted the Americans to go first because they felt we had better weapons and knew we were better fighters. I kept my cool and refrained from losing my temper, but I was pissed.

This is your damn country, so fight for it.

I wanted to holler at them like a college football coach to get moving, but we needed to be as quiet as possible, and I really wondered what good it would do. Yelling at them would not make them rush into the first compound with their AK-47s ready to kill anything that moved. What I'd noticed was that Afghan men were stubborn as mules, especially the Afghan soldiers. Once they made up their minds that they weren't going in, they weren't going in.

I turned around to have a word with Lance when out of the corner of my eye, I saw Nick moving toward the front of the compound about fifteen meters from me, where a wooden door into our first mud hut was slightly ajar.

What's he doing? And why is he walking into an uncleared part of the compound without Afghan soldiers leading the way? He was my damn interpreter, not a fighter.

I knew better than to yell out to stop him since that could have invited a firefight. Even though the Taliban knew we were on the move, tactically it was best to assume the enemy did not know where we were and to remain relatively undetected for as long as possible in case Taliban fighters were inside the compound and waiting to spring a nasty surprise.

Lance grabbed me by the arm. "Get Nick away from that door!"

This wasn't the time or place for an Afghan Rambo. Even though fifteen meters wasn't a lot of ground to cover, each step was a gamble in a Taliban-controlled area.

I carefully but quickly moved up to Nick and grabbed his arm.

"Nick, don't move. Bro, we need to move back to Lance's position and regroup. This is uncleared ground."

Nick looked at me.

"We're going to back away...slowly," I continued. "I want you to place your feet over my boot prints and slowly move with me back to Lance. If you stay in my steps, you'll be okay."

Nick didn't want to retreat. "We can still get our guys inside the compound," he said.

"No, the time is not right," I reiterated. "We need to get reorganized."

The firmness in my voice told Nick that I meant business. He started to move back from the compound, and I retreated slowly as well, making sure I had my M-4 ready to rock in case someone in the compound moved around the corner and opened fire on us. My eyes were sweeping the compound as well as looking where I placed my feet. I took one slow step after another when—

—BOOM!

CHAPTER 2

BACK TO THE BEGINNING

FALL RIVER MILLS, CALIFORNIA
SPRING 1978

I grew up in the unincorporated California town of Fall River Mills, nestled between the Sierra Nevada and Cascade mountain ranges in rugged Shasta County. If you know where Redding is in Northern California, Fall River Mills is seventy miles to the northeast. It's a dinky town in the middle of nowhere, and even back then, there were pot farms tucked in out-of-the-way places. The population when I was born in 1978 was a little over 375 people, but could have been more with the boom-or-bust logging industry.

The population dropped by three when I was three or four years old. My father, Larry, my sister Wendy (older by two years), and I moved down the Sacramento Valley to Redding in search of a better and more stable life.

Life pretty much sucked because my mother, who'd delivered my sister and me into this world, was hooked on drugs and alcohol. I guess everyone has their demons, and hers came in the form of stimulants. The upshot was that she didn't or couldn't take care of Wendy and me, so Dad sent her packing when I was in preschool.

In my early years, Mom had visitation rights for my sister and me, but all that ended around the time I was in middle school. After that, I had to track her down and make the effort to see her. But at that time in my life, our relationship wasn't a top priority to me. Looking back, I probably should have made more of an attempt to have a connection with my mother, but it wasn't in the cards. I didn't know her, and consequently I grew up without a mom, which created its own set of issues.

My dad was a Vietnam veteran who did two tours as an aviation crew chief before returning to the Pacific Northwest and eventually Northern California following his honorable discharge from the U.S. Army. During the Vietnam War, my dad's primary aircraft was the DHC-3 Otter with 54th Aviation out of Vũng Tàu, but he constantly found himself flying into a combat zone in a Huey—a military helicopter formally known as the Bell UH-1 Iroquois. It was in a Huey that my father experienced the true horror of war as an M60 door gunner, using the deadly firepower at his fingertips to rain death down on NVA troops and the Viet Cong.

From what I've seen on the History Channel and read in books, my dad must have gone through things that are beyond my imagination, but he has a way of keeping everything contained and burying the demons of Vietnam deep inside. All I can do is speculate on how bad his war was.

To this day, I know very little about his tours, although he did squeak out a few stories from time to time. Like an 18C engineer sweeping for IEDs, the door gunner position was extremely dangerous because you were exposed in the open door of the helicopter as the aircraft swooped in over the enemy. My father was lucky—he lived. But what he saw, did, and experienced would stay locked away in whatever closet he used for the vilest of his demons. He was always of the mind-set that this was his issue and he was damn sure he wasn't going to let others into that part of his world.

———————

We arrived in Redding as the logging industry was taking a major hit from the northern spotted owl, which had been declared a threatened species. Before you could shout "Save the spotted owl," the entire logging industry in Northern California was in the shitcan.

Suddenly, sawmills were shutting down all over the place because the environmentalists got the U.S. Forest Service to close millions of acres of forest to loggers. Dad, who was hoping that Redding would be a place to get back on his feet, found job opportunities to be slim pickings. This figured because Redding was originally named Poverty Flats during the Gold Rush in the mid-nineteenth century once its residents realized there wasn't much gold in the foothills surrounding the town. When the Central Pacific Railroad selected Poverty Flats to be the northern terminus of the railroad in 1872, the railroad wanted a more dignified name. In honor of the land agent who bought up property so that the railroad could be built, the town was renamed Redding.

My father did the best he could picking up odd jobs, mostly in construction. It helped that Dad was good with his hands at just about everything. His talents were put in check, however, by living in a region with more than 20 percent unemployment. We managed, but regardless of how hard life got, my dad always took care of us, and he often wound up feeding other children on our block who had no food. Our neighborhood was filled with run-down, clapboard houses and families barely scraping by, so there was never a shortage of hungry kids.

I can remember a hot summer day when my dad filled our VW bus full of neighborhood kids and drove us out to Clear Creek on the outskirts of Redding, where we went for a swim and grabbed an ice cream cone on the way home. Simple pleasures like that were his way of helping where he could. A kind gesture went a long way and took the kids' minds off the shit they called life.

We lived in Redding for a few years, but then it was time to move on in search of jobs. That seemed to be the way life went for us: jobs would dry up, we'd move to a new place for work, Dad would pick up some journeyman work, he would get laid off, and we'd move on. Not a bad life, but I never got a chance to settle down in one place to make lifelong friends and develop the kind of lasting relationships I saw in *Stand by Me*, a movie that came out in the mid-1980s about four boys growing up in a small town in Oregon.

Despite moving around more times than I can remember, Dad made sure he gave us the best possible life he could, given the fact that he was a single parent responsible for raising two kids, putting food on the table, and keeping a roof over our heads. I'm sure he would have been happier out at the bars chasing some tail or following his passions, but he gave that up to raise us kids.

Before Wendy and I came into the world, though, my dad was a guy who liked his beer. He'd get drunk, and if you happened to cross paths with him in the wrong way, you would most likely be at the losing end of a fistfight. He worked hard at logging, putting in crazy twelve-hour days, but he partied even harder. When the logging industry was booming and good money was coming in, he was blowing a healthy portion of his dough on booze. You could say that alcohol and partying filled his life when he wasn't out in the woods, knocking down tall Douglas firs with his crew.

He blazed quite a path of destruction, even after he got married. One night when my sister and I were still toddlers, my dad got piss-ass drunk after a fallout with my mother. After years of built-up stress, anger, and rage, everything came to a boil. Leaving my sister and me at the house, my dad jumped in the truck and drove to my uncle Steve's place. Steve was my mom's brother and close friends with my dad.

While driving in his drunken stupor, my father thought about what his life had become. His options had slowly dwindled down over the years. With no hope and no future, he believed he was facing his last choice—to end it all. He didn't know exactly what he was going to say to Steve when he got there, but he knew my uncle would watch out for us kids if my dad turned a gun on himself. I'm not sure how much good that would have done since Uncle Steve was a drunk, too, but even in his compromised state my father knew that someone was going to have to look after us when he was gone.

Dad pulled his truck in front of Uncle Steve's house. Right as he shifted to park, a man appeared in front of the house and walked up to the driver's-side window. Dad hadn't seen him leave the house, so he didn't know how or why this man had approached his car—my uncle lived in the middle of nowhere.

"Larry Hendrickson?" The middle-aged man, dressed conservatively, had a smile on his face.

My father had never seen the man in his life. "How do you know my name?" he asked.

The man ignored the question. "Larry, you're out of chances, aren't you?" he asked.

This time, my father was too stunned to answer.

"It doesn't have to be that way," the man continued. "Jesus has a better plan for you and your life."

My dad was extremely drunk—he had to get shit-faced if he was going to follow through on killing himself—but when he heard the name *Jesus*, he immediately became stone-cold sober.

The man motioned for my father to get out of the truck and extended his hand. "My name is John Merrill, and I'm a pastor here in town. I think I can help."

In front of my uncle's house that night, my father found God. After that, his hellion days slowed to a trickle. That didn't mean he didn't get pissed off at the cards he was dealt in life, especially after he had just polished off another six-pack. But my father, like everyone else I've met, including myself, was on a journey.

Where that journey was taking him, he had no clue. Dad had grown up in Oregon and still had family there, so he moved us to Birkenfeld, located midway between Portland and Astoria, where the mouth of the Columbia River meets the Pacific Ocean. Birkenfeld, a tiny hamlet along the Nehalem River, was miles from the nearest city. There was a store, a café, a tavern, a garage, and a church, and that was it.

We lived out in the woods in a house that had no running water due to damaged pipes and limited electricity, so the place was cheap. But that was all my father could afford since he had such a hard time finding steady work.

Shortly after we arrived, my father got so sick that he couldn't get out of bed. Wendy, then seven, and I had to tote metal pails to the river and fill them up so we could boil water on a wood stove for cooking and drinking. Somehow, we survived on hot dogs and boxes of Kraft Mac & Cheese.

Once my father got back on his feet, it was clear that he couldn't even afford a home with running water or steady electricity. His only option was to have us move in with his mother, who lived in Colton, Oregon, one hundred miles to the southeast. Colton was even smaller than Birkenfeld, but my grandmother could help provide the necessities of life while my father got his feet under him and attended a Bible college. He wanted to become a preacher.

We were poor, and I knew it. I was teased at school because of my hand-me-down clothes, worn-out sneakers, and free school lunches. Most of that ended when I learned how to fight. Poor or not, I wasn't going to be trampled over.

After my father got ordained as a preacher, his first pastorate was at a small church in Lincoln City on the central Oregon coast. He seemed happy, and we as a family were happy. Although we were still poor, it didn't matter because life was good.

My dad being a preacher didn't lift us out of poverty—actually, just the opposite happened. We had to live in a tent for several months while we waited to move into the upstairs parsonage. Tent living wasn't bad, but it did get embarrassing when other kids saw our living conditions and teased me at school. I never felt like I was good enough when I was around other kids my age. I always felt this need to prove myself, and there was a chip on my shoulder that I carried for years.

Regardless of our bleak situation, my father refused to let me feel sorry for myself. One of the ways he did that was to keep me busy. He had me working and earning money basically since I learned to walk. From a young age I learned the value of a hard day's work and came to understand how quickly one can go from riches to rags.

After the tiny church in Lincoln City couldn't afford to keep its doors open, we were forced to pack up and move again. This time we settled in the sleepy logging town of Lowell, Oregon, twenty miles southeast of Eugene and populated with one thousand residents.

Located on the north shore of Dexter Reservoir, Lowell's most prominent attractions were several historic, wooden-covered bridges that spanned the reservoir and the Middle Fork of the Willamette River. Nice little town for sure, but the loss of logging money left its scars.

My dad did his best to keep us in one spot until I could finish high school and move on with my life. I guess having four years in one place is why I say that Lowell is my hometown.

I was always an active kid, preferring to wander around the foothills of the Cascade mountains or play sports rather than sitting on my butt, watching movies, or doing nothing. I'm sure I was hell to raise for my dad, but he instilled in me the idea that I should set the rules for my life, not let life set the rules for me.

At Lowell High, I gave everything I had to our football and wrestling programs. I was never the most talented athlete, but every coach said I was the toughest kid they had ever trained. That was when I first heard the saying, "That boy's too stupid to quit." A backhanded compliment for sure, but I wore it like a badge of honor.

School work? I wasn't into my studying that much. Somehow I maintained a low C average, which wasn't going to win me any academic scholarships. I knew college wasn't in my future, but Dad didn't want me getting comfortable working at a gas station down the road and never leaving tiny Lowell.

One day, as we were kicking around my future, he told me a story.

"There were two old men sitting on their porches staring out into the abyss. They didn't know each other, but they had one thing in common—they were waiting on Death," he began.

I leaned in closer. Dad could always tell a good story, but this was different. He meant business.

"One old man was miserable," he continued. "He had let life's chances pass him by, and now thoughts of opportunities long gone were replaced with haunted ideas of what could have been. The other old man was totally fulfilled by the life he had lived. He had done everything there was to do, and now he could sit back and relish his golden moments and wonderful memories because he had lived life to the fullest.

"So there you go, son. 'I wish I would have done this or done that' statements are a prison of misery for the mind. You want to go through life and be perfectly content with the life you've lived. You want to do everything there is to be done. Right or wrong, you do it and never regret a decision you made."

This from a man who'd been off to war, fought for his life, seen the world, given life, taken life, loved, and had his heart broken. He had made mistakes, taken chances, and failed and succeeded many times.

"Good or bad, I can sit back and reminisce on my life and feel good about it," he said. "When God tells me it's my time to go home, I will leave this earth fulfilled because I've done it all, and I want you to feel the same way. So let me leave you with this thought: What kind of old man do you want to be, son?"

"I don't want to ever have any regrets, but I'm still figuring it out," I replied. But I was midway through my senior year of high school, and decisions needed to made.

My father looked me in the eye and basically cut through the bullshit. "You can go to college, but I don't have the money to support that. Or you can join the military. Every man should serve his country for at least four years. What you do is up to you, but you can't stay here in Lowell. There's no future here. If you stay, you will get sucked into small-town life and never get out and see the world. I highly recommend you serve your country and see what life has to offer."

I thought long and hard about what he said for the next few weeks. Given my lack of options, I felt like I was destined for military service. I decided to check out all four branches of the military.

The first person I talked to was an Army recruiter, which my dad really pushed for because of his time in the Army. This was in 1997, a relatively calm time for the United States. The Gulf War had been over for a few years, and 9/11 and the War on Terror were four years off. Because there were few skirmishes around the globe, there weren't a lot of job opportunities in the Army or Marine Corps.

The same went for the Air Force—not a lot of job options. I didn't even contemplate the Navy, but that changed when a Navy recruiter visited my school to talk to my best friend, Zac, who was extremely smart. All the service branches wanted him.

Sitting in the school's office, I was letting everything the recruiter said go in one ear and out the other until he showed us pictures of all the countries that U.S. Navy ships visited. Zac still wasn't biting, but I could feel the hook setting in my mouth. Then the recruiter said, "Do you want to see the world and have the Navy pay for college? I've met beautiful, exotic women all over the world, and you can do the same."

Now he was really talking my language—and playing on the priorities of testosterone-rich eighteen-year-old guys!

"Where can I sign up?" I heard myself saying.

And that was what I did that day—signed on the dotted line and committed to joining the Navy as soon as I finished high school.

I felt good about what I was doing—going into the military. As a kid, I was always playing little Army Man Ryan, running around the countryside in whatever made-up war I had in my head.

My father congratulated me but also reminded me that up until now, my life was a book with blank pages. "It's up to you what you fill those pages with. Will your life be worth reading about when everything is said and done?" he asked.

I didn't know, but I was going to find out.

CHAPTER 3

BOOT CAMP

RECRUIT TRAINING COMMAND
GREAT LAKES, ILLINOIS
APRIL 1997

Given my options, joining the military was a no-brainer for me. When wrestling season was over at the end of the winter quarter, I had enough credits to graduate early. I decided to take my high school diploma and leave for Navy boot camp in April 1997. Man, did I ever get slapped in the face when I left home at eighteen to see the world and be on my own.

My flight to Recruit Training Command, the unit responsible for Navy basic training, in Great Lakes, Illinois, was my first time flying in an airplane. I was full of anticipation, a smidgen of fear, and tons of excitement. I had no idea what lay in store for me, but I felt like I was writing the first pages in my life's book.

I was picked up at O'Hare and loaded onto a white Blue Bird bus bound for the Great Lakes training facility. It was dark, so I decided to close my eyes and get a bit of sleep. I didn't know how long the drive would be, so I figured what the hell.

I viewed myself as a tough, hard-working farm boy and was

still a bit cocky from a good senior year in football and wrestling. I figured the world was mine to conquer and no one could touch me.

No one except for the first person I would meet when the bus came to a stop.

A stern-looking, muscle-bound black dude wearing a starch-white Navy "crackerjacks" uniform stepped onto the bus.

"Welcome to Great Mistakes," he shouted. "Now get the fuck off my bus! Move, move, move!"

All hell broke loose. His booming command sent a couple of dozen green recruits jostling for their duffle bags and hustling out the front of the bus.

"Get your ass in gear! What the fuck are you looking at? Fucking move! Grab your shit and go!"

This drill instructor would prove that it was possible to fill a sentence with as many cuss words as actual words.

When I exited the bus in darkness, there were four more drill instructors waiting to get in our earholes.

"Move your asses, ladies!" one screamed. "Line up! You're too slow! Move faster, dumbasses. Get in line, shortest to tallest. MOVE!"

We immediately scrambled like a bunch of Keystone Kops, attempting to get everyone lined up in the right order. I'm sure we looked like a bunch of assclowns. A couple more drill instructors got in our faces.

"You're taking too long! Move, move, move!" yelled one at the top of his lungs.

"C'mon, ladies!" another DI teased. "Let's go!"

It's hard to accurately describe the chaotic scene that unfolded. I was a kid from a small Oregon town surrounded by guys from different small towns and big cities all over the United States, each of us trying to obey the screaming voices in Navy uniforms telling us what to do—and all of us were getting it wrong. Within the mass confusion, I was in a state of shock.

Just a few weeks earlier, I was a hot-shot high school senior. Now I felt like the scum on the bottom of these naval drill instructors' shoes.

Boot camp was an eye-opener for me, and I grew up a lot, but it was all I needed. I met all kinds of people and started to see exactly what my father meant about broadening my horizons. Before I knew it, boot camp was over and I was assigned to my first duty station in Groton, Connecticut, home of Naval Submarine Base New London.

For some reason, I had decided during boot camp that submarines would be a good fit for me, but it took exactly two seconds on board a sub for me to realize that I didn't do well in tight spaces. I needed room to move, so I opted out of submarine duty. The Navy was accommodating because it's in everyone's best interests to find out sooner rather than later who isn't cut out for sub duty.

When I joined the Navy, I had big aspirations and set my goals high. I had seen movies about the Navy SEALs and had dreams of giving it a shot one day. All that had to take a back seat once I settled into life in the fleet. After declining submarine duty, I was sent to the "Needs of the Navy," as it's called, which basically meant I would be assigned to whatever ship needed sailors. What would I be doing? I didn't know. Nobody told me a thing until I was commanded to report to my new duty station.

My first assignment was to the USS *Shreveport* stationed in Norfolk, Virginia, as a boatswain's mate, mainly in a maintenance and general deckhand role. My ship wasn't at its home station, however; it was out at sea en route for Istanbul, Turkey. I jumped on a long flight to join the *Shreveport* in Turkey.

The seaside port city of Istanbul was different from anything I had ever expected, but I had nothing to really base my assumptions on. The Byzantine churches, Ottoman mosques, Turkish and Arabic languages, and melting pot of European and Asian cultures were all a first for me. Besides a mission trip to Mexico during high school, this was the first foreign country I'd ever been to.

The ship was anchored out in the bay. I was shuttled from a small boat to the *Shreveport*. I had no idea how big the ship was until the utility boat pulled alongside and I looked up. My first impression was that the ship had to be fifteen stories high and way longer than a football field, making it a massive ship, but to my surprise, I was told that the *Shreveport* was only a medium-size ship and about half the length of a Nimitz-class aircraft carrier. Classified as an amphibious transport dock or landing platform/dock, the USS *Shreveport* was a warship that transported elements of a landing force for expeditionary missions. In other words, our mission was to bring combat-ready Marines anywhere around the globe.

The excitement and adventure would soon wear off when I got out to sea. Being on board a ship with nine hundred other sailors and Marines—all male on this deployment—was a major culture shock and not for the faint of heart, especially for lower enlisted sailors like me. Working sixteen- to eighteen-hour days and doing maintenance duties like keeping the deck equipment in good condition, loading and unloading cargo, shining brass, busting rust because of the salt water, and painting bulkheads (walls) and passageways the same battleship gray sucked. What little free time I had was spent in my coffin rack trying to get some much-needed sleep.

The racks—glorified cots—were stacked three high and faced another set of three bunks, which meant zero privacy. If you were a big guy, half of your body would hang outside your rack while you slept.

If I got a chance to steal any moments of privacy, I tried to take them during the early mornings or twilight. Sunrises and sunsets out at sea were something that could only be re-created in a masterpiece painting. At times, the yellowish-red glowing ball of the sun would take up my entire field of view, sending colors into my eyes that I never saw on land. They mesmerized me like the mythical siren sea nymphs who lured sailors to their death with a bewitching song.

Some of the most beautiful views happened only at sea: the moon shining bright on the water while dolphins danced in the ship's wake; the stars dotting a canopy of black ink in the middle of wide-open ocean; and the glow of oil fires in the distance while traveling through the Persian Gulf. In these moments, I was at peace and able to reset my mind.

While a sailor's life out at sea was hard, the payoff was worth every bit of it. After deploying with both the USS *Shreveport* and the USS *Camden*, and being stationed in two different parts of the United States—Norfolk, Virginia, and Bremerton, Washington—I had circled the globe and seen the world. I never dreamed that I'd get to visit so many foreign lands like Portugal, Spain, Italy, Romania, Turkey, United Arab Emirates, Bahrain, Thailand, Singapore, and Australia.

I was serving my country with the benefit of seeing the world. Life out at sea was hard, but I was willing to pay the price to have all these incredible experiences. I was living the life my dad pushed for, and writing the pages in my life's book.

Most of my time in the Navy was peaceful. Entering the Persian Gulf was the exception. We would get the usual harassment from Iran whenever we passed through international waters that they considered their territory. The other hot spot was Iraq because Saddam Hussein, Iraq's dictator, continued to rattle swords with the United States following Operation Desert Storm in the early 1990s.

In February 1998, while docked in Romania, the USS *Shreveport* was called to the Persian Gulf to be part of a military build-up and assist with Operation Southern Watch, which was maintaining the establishment of no-fly zones over northern Iraq to protect the Kurds, and over southern Iraq to keep the Shiites from harm. The *Shreveport* had nine hundred Marines on board, one of many ships ready to invade Iraq, but that never happened because Saddam would always cooperate enough to delay an attack.

When Iraq repeatedly violated the no-fly zones and the brass's patience wore out, however, orders came down from Washington to give Saddam a reminder of American air superiority. I can remember walking out on the flight deck of the *Shreveport* one night and witnessing multiple Tomahawk missiles blasting off from different ships in the Persian Gulf, each warhead headed for Iraq. An awesome display of American naval power.

In December 1998, after our deployment, Saddam Hussein kicked out the United Nations' weapons inspectors, prompting a stiff response from U.S. Armed Forces. A four-day bombing campaign ensued, aimed at military and security targets in Iraq that were instrumental in that country's ability to produce and maintain weapons of mass destruction.

Two years later, I would get my first experience with American bloodshed at the hands of a radical Islamic extremist group that wasn't very well known in the United States at the time: al-Qaeda. On October 12, 2000, a fiberglass boat carrying C-4 explosives and two suicide bombers pulled alongside the USS *Cole* while it was refueling in Yemen's Aden harbor. A trigger ignited a massive explosion that ripped a forty-by-sixty-foot gash in the ship's port side, killing seventeen American sailors and injuring thirty-nine. This would be the deadliest attack against a United States naval ship since 1987.

At the time the USS *Cole* was bombed, I was on board my second ship, the USS *Camden*. We were within twelve hours of Yemen. When the distress call came out, we sailed full steam ahead through the Strait of Hormuz, along with the USS *Donald Cook*. We would be the first American military personnel to arrive and assist the *Cole* crew in saving the ship and pulling bodies from the wreckage.

I'll never forget the smell of burning human flesh when I stepped on board the *Cole*. For the next week, we teamed up with *Cole* crew members to keep the ship from sinking and recovered the remains of all seventeen heroes killed that day. I had witnessed the first salvo in what would become known as the War on Terror, and our rescue-and-recovery effort with the USS *Cole* would impact my life in the years to come.

In the spring of 2001, my four-year commitment to the Navy was up. I was ready for something else. I had gotten married to an Army woman named Sara, whom I met while I was stationed at Norfolk. We agreed that I would get out of the Navy, which made me a military spouse of sorts. I would wait for her to finish her time in the Army, and then we'd figure out what we'd do next.

While searching for a path in life, I tried my hand at various jobs like construction, landscaping, and even being a waiter, but strangely enough the one that stuck was working as a bartender. I was no Tom Cruise in *Cocktail*, but I could spin bottles of vodka with the best of them. But like in the movie, bartending opened a door to a world that a young married man should never be a part of.

Civilian life had its ups and downs, but it wasn't the right fit for me. In my mind, I had a higher calling and a bigger purpose. What exactly that was, I did not know. After traveling around the world in the Navy, I had turned into a man who could only be fed by excitement and adventure. Life wasn't fulfilling as a civilian, which was becoming clear to me. I needed adventure, a fair amount of risk, a sense of belonging, and a purpose for living.

And then that dreadful day happened: September 11, 2001. I was living near Fort Lewis, Washington, when the same shitheads who carried out the strike on the *Cole* eleven months earlier masterminded a terrorist attack that took down the Twin Towers in New York City and scored a direct hit on the Pentagon. Another plane, United 93, avoided crashing into the White House due only to the courageous passengers aboard.

In the aftermath of 9/11, I felt an agonizing urge to do my part. What my part was, I didn't know. I was also trying to save my marriage, which complicated matters. As the days went by and America geared up for war, my dilemma tore at me. I needed to be a part of what was about to happen and wanted to exact revenge for what those cowards did to us—the worst terrorist attack in American history, an attack that killed 2,977 people.

My convictions urging me to be a better man and save my marriage outweighed a return to military service, however. I decided to stay the course and remain in civilian life.

One day in early 2002, I received a phone call out of the blue.

"Hi. Is this Ryan Hendrickson?"

"Yes, who is this?"

"Your big sister, Chris. Remember me?"

Barely, I thought. Our family had been separated when I was still in diapers. I had two older half sisters—Paula was five years older and Chris was eight years older. I also had a half brother who was ten years older than me and lived with us periodically. His name was Robbie.

Both my dad and his first wife were heavy drinkers. One night, she swept up my older siblings and disappeared. I had memories of them, but I was so young I did not really have a grasp of what happened or who they were. And now this phone call out of the blue.

"I'm not going to lie. Not too well," I said. I was standoffish because of the strangeness of the call, but after talking for some time, I was happy to hear from my sister.

We talked for hours about my childhood and how she used to take care of me when things got bad at home. We caught up on what everyone was doing and my military career. When I was finished, she cautiously asked me, "How's Dad? What's he doing now?"

When I told her that he was a pastor for a small community church, it was like the air rushed out of the room. There was stark silence. At first she did not believe me, but after reassuring her about how my father had changed the direction of his life, she was floored.

"How could a man who was so bad be a pastor now?" she asked.

"Because he's not the same father you once knew," I said.

We talked for a bit longer, and when we hung up, I felt like I had the other half of my family back in my life. Over the next couple of months, I spoke on the phone with my half sisters and half brother many times and even met them in person when my dad and I drove to New Mexico for a long-awaited reunion. We healed wounds that came from growing up in a broken family. In our own way, we started over again.

Life seemed to be on the upswing for me, but I could never shake the feeling that I should be doing something more with my life, something bigger. As America plunged deeper into the War of Terror, I wasn't completely detached from the U.S. Armed Forces because I was part of the Naval Reserves, doing my one weekend a month plus two weeks a year.

I wasn't living the life of a glamorous battlefield warrior that I had envisioned for myself when I was a little boy, but I was still playing a part. Each drill weekend, I hoped my unit would be activated to support the war, but it never happened.

Then an unexpected opportunity came up. As a Naval Reservist, I could attend the Basic Underwater Demolition School (BUD/S) at the Naval Special Warfare training complex in Coronado, California, near San Diego. BUD/S, a six-month training class, was the first part of Navy SEAL training, so if I ever wanted to become a SEAL and a member of the Naval Special Operations community, the Basic Underwater Demolition School is where I had to start.

My wife, Sara, knew that being part of Special Operations had always appealed to me. Now this opportunity was sitting right in front of me. I had undergone training as a rescue swimmer in the Navy, so I assumed I had the swimming part down. When I was approved to attend the six-month BUD/S course, visions of becoming a SEAL danced in my head.

I quickly found out how tough it was during the first phase of training—a pre-BUD/S training course that lasted around three weeks. From there, I went on to phase one, which consisted of eight weeks of grueling exercise and conditioning topped off by "Hell Week." Typically, more than half of the recruits wash out; sheer fatigue and sleep deprivation cause every candidate to wonder what his limits are.

The nonstop beating that our bodies took from some of the hardest training the military has, followed by long stretches of being wet, cold, and miserable, with no time to recover, took its toll. When my body broke down from a leg injury and severe pneumonia, I was dropped after three months of training. I could have tried again after I recovered, but I couldn't bring myself to go through all that shit again.

For the first time in my life, I experienced a major setback. Becoming part of an elite unit was something I wanted with every inch of my being, but I couldn't make the cut, which prompted a series of questions:

Why did I fail?

Why wasn't I good enough?

How come my body broke down?

Was I that weak?

I had no answers and I came up with every poor-me excuse in the book. You'd think that for a guy who was raised the way I was, excuses would be the last thing on my mind, but they were my crutch. I slowly but steadily turned myself into a victim. *If only I didn't grow up in a broken family . . . if only the world and everyone in it weren't against me.* That wasn't just about BUD/S, but me not making it through brought my buried demons to the surface.

When Sara finished in the Army, we decided to move to her home state of Minnesota. This would get her closer to her family, and I would get to live in a new place. A fresh start where no one knew me seemed like a great idea. Everything was perfect except for one major problem: I could not overcome my immaturity and my sense of being a victim.

When I refused to take responsibility for my actions, I drank, partied, and ran my marriage into the ground. I used whatever excuses I could find, starting with how my mother was never there for me, how other women treated my father like shit when I was a kid, or how I was sexually abused when my father was away at work, experiencing things that no little boy should have to go through.

I had a long list, and it pulled me further away from reality. I hid behind these excuses and believed that the world owed me a solid because of the bad things that had happened to me in my past.

After a year in Minnesota, my marriage was at the breaking point. Sara and I agreed a change was needed and that I should go back into the military to get some structure in my life. We discussed me going into the Army, but she didn't want to live as an Army wife, so we quickly dismissed that idea. The Navy was out, so the only answer left was the Air Force. I didn't know if the Air Force had the excitement I was looking for, but the service branch provided a military career and I would be serving my country again. Something in me wanted to take the fight to the Islamic terrorists who attacked America.

I looked at Air Force Special Operations Combat Control and jumped feet first into training. I buried myself in every aspect of the course until a medical review of my records showed I had taken depression medication while in the Navy.

A lot of people need prescription antidepressants, and depression ran in my family. Antidepressant medication and counseling helped me through a very dark period in my life, but this detour came back to bite me. The Air Force decided that I was not medically qualified for Special Operations and put me in a job where they needed bodies. I was told that I would become an Ammunition specialist or AMMO troop.

An Air Force career in Ammunition basically meant loading bombs and bullets on aircraft that were used to kill enemies of the

United States. The job description sounded interesting enough, and the fact that we were at war in Afghanistan and Iraq meant that I could have a direct impact on the battlefield even if I wasn't the one pulling the trigger.

So that was the route I took. I finished Ammunition training in Texas and was stationed in Mountain Home, Idaho, as my first base in the Air Force. I loved Idaho, and I worked in what was probably the tightest-knit career field in the Air Force. AMMO troops were family; we took care of and looked out for one another. True, there were shitbags, but we were tight, and I loved what I did. As much as I relished my new career in the Air Force, something was still missing. I couldn't put my finger on it, but I thought I was coasting a bit too much. I needed to do something more exciting or challenging.

While stationed in Idaho in 2004, I got deployed to the Middle Eastern country of Qatar. Other than sitting on a ship in the Persian Gulf and making a few port calls at United Arab Emirates and Bahrain, I did not see a lot of the Middle East on that deployment.

Qatar, a desert land located on the eastern side of the Saudi Arabian peninsula and on the Persian Gulf, was certainly different, but all in all, my deployment was a nice change. I also felt that what I was doing actually impacted the war in Iraq. It seemed like we were loading U.S. military aircraft with bombs and bullets every night. A couple of hours later, they would fly over Iraq, and every night they would return empty. The munitions we loaded were killing an enemy that hated the West and particularly America.

After I returned from a four month–long deployment in Qatar, Sara had enough of the games and overall bullshit. She filed for divorce. I don't want to get into the details of our ill-fated marriage, but suffice it to say I don't know how she lasted as long as she did, and I take responsibility for the problems in our marriage.

The following year, 2005, I had my first deployment to Iraq, which was a good thing. After the divorce, I needed to get out of Idaho and clear my mind. This time around, I would *not* be loading planes with bombs and bullets. Instead, I would be pulling security. Not exactly what I wanted to do, but this was my chance to get boots on the ground in Iraq and do my part.

I was stationed at Kirkuk Air Base, arriving in the torrid summer. I had never felt heat like that before; temperatures routinely hit 110 degrees Fahrenheit and above. It was so brutally hot that it was difficult to even move around the base during the daylight hours.

Kirkuk Air Base was hit daily with rockets or mortars from insurgent forces, but nothing crazy and nothing close to what other soldiers were experiencing around Iraq in 2005. The terrorists were smart and used the sizzling summer heat as a weapon. For instance, they would fill a mortar tube with ice, then place a mortar round on top of the ice at night. As the sun would melt the ice during the day, the mortar round would drop and eventually hit the firing pin and launch toward our base. By the time the rounds were incoming, the terrorists were miles away, safe from retaliatory strikes by our Quick Reaction Force. The enemy, expedient and smart, was finding different ways to strike us without dying every time they picked a fight.

Iraq was the first place that I was exposed to the U.S. Army Special Forces—the Green Berets. These bearded, shaggy-haired men seemed to play by their own rules. We would see them walking by, and later that night when the rest of us were hanging out after dinner, the stories of what we thought we knew about these guys would spill out.

Most stories were tall tales or rumors that a friend of a friend said he'd heard. I would see these Green Berets in the gym or in the chow hall, but I never had anything to say or the stomach to go up and start a conversation. If I tried, I knew how it would go down:

Uhmmmm, hi. My name is Ryan. I'm just some airman pulling security on a bunch of Iraqis. That's the extent of my hard-core life. Can you please tell me some of your war stories? That would be really cool.

I mean, let's get real. Unless one of them was from my home state of Oregon, I had nothing in common with them. That would all change, however, when I was working out at the gym late one night.

"Hey brother, could you spot me?"

I looked over from my bench and spotted a Green Beret named John ready to bench-press.

"Sure, I got you."

This was all I needed to fill this guy's ear holes full of questions. John and I must have talked for a couple of hours. I was in awe, listening to him explain what he did and the cool parts of his job, which was completely different from my job—or anything I had ever done, for that matter. As I soaked in his stories, I imagined myself doing the same stuff.

We talked about a few missions they had done in northern Iraq and what he did before going into Special Forces. The entire time I thought, *It would be so awesome to have his badass job someday.* John was easy to talk to and did his best to answer questions that cropped up in my mind, like the type of training they did and how difficult it was to become a Green Beret. To an outside observer, I must have looked like a jackass firing questions at him nonstop, but John didn't seem to mind.

Days later, he introduced me to more guys on his team. One guy in particular, a dude named Gary, was in the Air Force before going into the Army. This got the wheels in my head turning. *What if I tried to become a Green Beret? Could I do it? Do I have what it takes?*

My failure at BUD/S was never far from my mind when I contemplated my future. One thing was for sure: I did not want to be an old man sitting on my porch, wondering about what might have been.

When it came to the life I wanted to have and the setbacks I'd suffered along the way, I still had some unfinished business to take care of.

CHAPTER 4

TAKING LEAVE

MOUNTAIN HOME AIR FORCE BASE

SOUTHWESTERN IDAHO

SUMMER 2006

After my deployment to Iraq, I needed to take a break and free my mind. What better way to do that than go on a poorly prepared, underfunded trip to Vietnam?

I was now in the Air Force and stationed at Mountain Home Air Force Base in the middle of Idaho. I went through the proper channels and somehow got my command to sign my leave form for an eight-day vacation, what they used to call R & R back when my father was fighting in the Vietnam War.

Since my dad served two tours and fought in that horrible conflict, I was naturally drawn to checking out the places he had told me about. I wanted to see some of those locales with my own eyes. There was also a beast within me that craved adventure. Though I had only a few weeks to prepare for my impromptu trip, I made my escape to Vietnam with just $750 to my name.

I decided that Ho Chi Minh City would be the launchpad for my travels. Once I landed, I spent the day getting situated and

acclimated to my new surroundings. Early the next day, I sum-
moned the all-too-familiar tuk-tuk, which was a three-wheeled
motorcycle pulling a row of passenger seats in the back—like a
motorized rickshaw. I directed my driver to head north up High-
way 1 to Nha Trang. I wanted to hit as many picturesque beach
villages as I could.

My journey north was like the video game Frogger. I would
pass a little beach village or something I wanted to see, pull over,
pay the tuk-tuk driver, and take in the sights. After a bite to eat
or a cold beer, I'd flag down another motorbike taxi and continue
north. I was on my own time and had no one to answer to. I was
in heaven.

Once I arrived in Nha Trang, I felt like I had discovered
Southeast Asia's hidden gem. I didn't have the money to live like
a king, but I did have enough dollars in my pocket to get a good
taste of it. The long, curvy stretch of beach along Tran Phu Street,
the amazing foods served by street vendors and in restaurants,
the modern cable cars to Hòn Tre Island—everything about this
coastal city of four hundred thousand blew my mind.

Then I jumped on a ferry and visited Vũng Tàu, nearly four
hundred kilometers to the south. Vũng Tàu was one of many
locations where my dad was stationed in Vietnam and was also
the battlefield where he fought for his life during the Tet Offensive launched by the NVA and Viet Cong against U.S forces.

Then I returned to Ho Chi Minh City, where I did the usual
touristy stuff: visiting the War Remnants Museum, touring the
Củ Chi Tunnels, and taking in a Mekong Delta day cruise. I
would have set out on more adventures, but I ran out of money
and days off. Nonetheless, I had the time of my life.

What I couldn't get over was how the remnants of a war that

happened not that long ago were everywhere. It didn't matter where I went—whether I was in a city or out at a tiny village, the scars of war were all around me. Trinkets, from silver Zippo lighters that were carried by GIs during the war, to sets of U.S. dog tags, were peddled everywhere.

My week in Vietnam flew by, which was great because I was able to completely leave my life behind and concentrate on experiencing as much I could. At each place my dad told me that he had spent some time, I wondered if I was stepping in the same footsteps my father had made so many years back. After squeezing in as much as I could into an eight-day trip, I was ready to head home and back to the life I had run away from.

When it came time to check out of my hotel and head for the airport outside Ho Chi Minh City, I didn't have the money to pay my hotel bill. I mean, I thought I had enough, but upon checkout, I got socked with a $300 phone bill charged to my room.

It was bogus, but the hotel staffers behind reception were insisting that I had to pay up. I kept asserting that I didn't owe them an extra three hundred bucks because I never placed any calls from my room. It slowly occurred to me that I was stranded in a communist country with no money. *I'm fucked*, I thought.

The next thing I knew, I had three Vietnamese soldiers with AK-47s detaining me, threatening this dumbass American with jailtime for coming to Vietnam, spending all his money, and having no way of paying his hotel bill. This was the making of an episode on the new hit TV show called *Locked Up Abroad*, and I was going to be the star.

Just when I thought all hope was lost and I was going to jail, three young European ladies were walking by the front of the hotel when they witnessed what was happening. They approached me and asked if I needed help.

"It seems that I owe the hotel $300 for phone calls I never made, and now they're threatening to throw me in jail unless I pay up, but I'm out of money and all I have is my debit card, which is drained," I said.

These three young ladies talked among themselves, then offered to pay my bill. For no reason except for understanding that I was in deep shit, they stepped up to pay $300 for a man they had never met and would never see again. To this day, I believe they were angels sent from heaven to bail me out of a terrible predicament.

I thanked them profusely. I promised that I would send them money when I returned to the United States. For all they knew, I was full of shit, but I knew my word was gold. (As soon as I returned from Vietnam and was paid, my first stop was to Western Union where I wired them $450—$150 extra for helping a stranger out.)

I grabbed my bags and left the hotel as quickly as I could. My flight wasn't for another twelve hours, but I didn't have any cash for a cab to get to Ho Chi Minh International Airport, which was more than twenty miles away. Once again, I was up shit creek without a paddle. If it wasn't one thing, it was another.

I found a bench in the middle of Ho Chi Minh City near the main traffic circle and sat down next to my suitcase. I had no idea what I was going to do. Then I remembered a coffee shop down the road from my hotel. When I first arrived in Ho Chi Minh City, the owner and I had talked for a couple of hours while I sipped one of her coffees. This Vietnamese woman, who spoke excellent English, gave me some great advice about things I should do and places I should visit.

Not sure what to say to her—and knowing full well that at this point I was a beggar—I walked into the coffee shop.

"Mr. Ryan, why do you look so sad?" she asked. I was surprised she remembered my name.

I told her my hard-luck story about the hotel, and she was instantly upset about what had happened. Without a care in the world, she reached into her purse and handed me $50 in U.S. currency.

Once again, I was blown away by the generosity of strangers. Except for the dirtbags at the hotel, the people of Vietnam were warm and caring toward me. If they still hated the Americans for the war, I never saw it.

Because I was fresh off a divorce, everything I did and saw upon my return to Idaho reminded me of what a screw-up I was.

I had purchased a little RV trailer to live in while I worked at nearby Mountain Home Air Force Base, but after getting home from Vietnam, I fell into a funk and returned to my all-too-familiar state of depression. I loved experiencing a different part of the world and couldn't wait for my next adventure, but part of me was running from my problems. I picked up where I left off before Vietnam, drowning my sorrows in booze. Once my paycheck was wasted on drinking, I would bum alcohol from friends until my next paycheck, all the while sliding further into a deep depression.

Because my AMMO crew was so tight, my shop chief saw the hell I was putting myself through.

"Ryan, you need to get some help, man. What can I do, brother?"

"I need to get out of Idaho, boss. This place is killing me," I said.

"You want to go to Korea? A new rotation is coming up and they need bodies. What do you think?"

I didn't have to think long. "Korea? Sure, sounds good. I'll go."

"Ryan, I got your back. Just do me a favor. Get your shit straight. I don't like seeing you like this."

Korea was not a glamorous assignment, but it would get me away from the hellhole that I had created. Before leaving for Korea, I had thirty days of leave to burn through. Since I still had this major itch to travel, what better idea than picking up and heading out again, even though I was still short on money and had no real idea where to go? I decided that I would just use these thirty days to see where they took me in the world.

At Mountain Home, I had made a good friend named Janna. She was in the Air Force with me and was currently stationed in Germany.

Germany? I'd never been to Europe, but I had heard how easy it was to do the backpack-and-hostel thing, traveling by train. I said, *Screw it, I'm going to Germany.*

I flew into Frankfurt in December, was picked up by my friend, and the adventure began. Jumping train to train, Janna and I ran all over Europe. We started with a train ride to the Benelux countries—Belgium, the Netherlands, and Luxembourg. Then we swung into Paris, checked out the Swiss Alps and nearby Lichtenstein, and stayed in Vienna, Austria, during a celebration of Mozart's birthday. My favorite city by far in Eastern Europe was Prague in the Czech Republic.

We did it all on the cheap—sleeping on trains, staying in rundown youth hostels, and picnicking on food from local grocery stores. On a whim, we flew to Dublin, Ireland, because having a pint at the Gunnies Factory—the home of Guinness Brewery—was a must-do for me.

This time around, I used my new credit card, which I got after the Vietnam snafu, and decided that I would worry about the financial hole I was digging for myself later. For now, I was having a blast and didn't care.

When the monthlong trip was over, I was broke again, but my brain was overflowing with many stories and great memories. Then reality hit: Ten days after I arrived back in the United States, I was on my way to Osan Air Base in the city of Pyeongtaek, South Korea, around forty miles south of Seoul.

My year tour in Korea turned out to be the best time in my military career. The Asian-Pacific environment was just what I needed to get my life back on track. Just like in Idaho, AMMO lived up to its reputation as a tightknit group. We worked our asses off but partied even harder. Once it was quitting time, the name of the game was booze and girls.

One day while walking to the gym, I passed a group of guys playing rugby. I knew some of them, so I stopped by to say hi. One thing led to another, and I was invited to try out. Since I played football in high school and had a knack for contact sports, rugby turned out to be the perfect match for me. I fell in love with rugby, and I was actually pretty good at it. They invited me to join the team. Even better, the guys liked to drink a lot.

I had no idea that playing rugby for Osan Air Force Base would turn into a chance to travel. Not only did we run around Korea playing rugby, but we also entered a Rugby 10s tournament in Phuket, Thailand, which was another fantastic travel experience.

Before arriving in Phuket, we decided to spend a few days in Bangkok, which was out of this world. Bangkok wasn't just another city—it was almost like being on a different planet. The atmosphere was alive, and there was never enough time to see and do everything you wanted to do. My eyes and brain at times could not make sense of what I was seeing, hearing, touching, or tasting. Everything felt like an out-of-body experience.

One day, I would have to face my demons and try to fix my life, but for now, I was happy running on the rugby field and away from my past.

My unquenchable thirst for adventure was laying the groundwork for some major decisions in my life. Like my dad had said, I was writing my story and putting memories away to be brought back out when I was that old man sitting on my porch.

Halfway through my year in Korea, I was given two weeks of leave. My dad and I spoke on the phone about what I should do.

"Son, home will always be here. Go see the world while you have the chance," he said. While most servicemen and servicewomen flew back to the United States to visit loved ones, that was all the reassurance I needed to head back to Southeast Asia.

The first thing on my bucket list was seeing the Great Wall of China. I figured if the Chinese all those centuries ago built a humongous wall to repel Mongolian invaders, then I might as well take it in.

While in China, I met people who were backpacking the world

like I was. We were all from different places but shared one thing in common—adventure. In Beijing, I met two girls from Florida who were going to see the Great Wall but were on their own. We exchanged plans over a few beers, and just like that, we were a threesome traveling around China.

Then I headed back to Bangkok to see what I missed on my first trip to Thailand.

I visited the Temple of Dawn, trekked in a jungle atop a gray elephant, and ate fried scorpion from a street vendor. I also hit the bars, drank until the wee hours, and got very little sleep. I figured I could suck it up. *You can sleep when you're dead*, I thought.

After a few days in Bangkok and another out-of-this world experience, I wanted to see something else. I went to the Bangkok International Airport and checked out airline tickets for anywhere cheap. I didn't care where I flew; I just wanted a new adventure. At the ticket counter, two girls from Italy asked me if I knew anything about Cambodia.

"No, I don't. Is that where you're going?"

"We heard the Angkor Wat temple is interesting," one of the Italian girls said.

We talked some more, and when they said they didn't like traveling alone, I volunteered to go with them. The next thing I knew, we were buying cheap plane tickets to Phnom Penh, the capital of Cambodia. Just like in China, I had linked up with new travel buddies.

The flight was sketchy. We touched down in the middle of a monsoon or close to it—I guess commercial flights didn't have weather restrictions in this part of the world—but ten minutes after we landed, the weather turned sunny and humid. We waved down a tuk-tuk and were taken to our hotel.

Since my dad served in Vietnam, I had heard about the Khmer Rouge and Pol Pot and seen the movie *The Killing Fields*, which describes the genocide of Cambodians by members of the Khmer Rouge in the 1970s.

Visiting the Genocide Museum, which had been the infamous S-21 Prison, and the Choeung Ek Genocidal Center—a former orchard and mass grave of victims that were better known as the Killing Fields—were sobering examples of how ugly and brutal humans can be to each other.

One area at the Killing Fields stood out to me. There was a large tree in the middle of the camp where the Khmer Rouge soldiers would either toss babies into the air and bayonet their bodies or smash their heads against the large tree so as not to waste bullets. I could not comprehend how a human being could do such evil acts.

Cambodia had a rich history apart from the genocide, and I wanted to experience it. The Angkor Wat temple complex, the largest religious monument in the world, was only an airboat ride up the Mekong Delta.

Hell, the temple is on the Cambodian national flag, so I knew it must be important. The next day, we had our airboat tickets and were on our way to the city of Siem Reap in northwest Cambodia. This was the rainy season, so taking a bus was a risk due to flooded roads and something more sinister—bandits. During the rainy season, they would use the washed-out roads as a choke point to stop the buses, which were known to have tourists. Then they would rob everyone on board. No, thank you. I wasn't in the mood to lose what little money I had.

Heading up the Mekong Delta was an adventure. We passed floating villages, floating markets, incredible vegetation, and beautiful wildlife—it was impossible to take it all in, but I snapped picture after picture in an attempt to capture it all. Throughout the day, we visited the massive 402-acre temple known as Angkor Wat.

With my leave days flying by faster than I wanted, I finished my trip to Southeast Asia with a few days in Laos. The capital city of Vientiane had a surprisingly slow pace compared to the hectic streets of other crowded major cities in Asia. I got tired of walking everywhere, so I rented a moped that seemed to break down every time a monsoon rain storm hit, leaving me stranded and soaked.

Since the city was known for its many golden temples, I made the most of my time in Vientiane going to the famous Buddha Park, the Great Stupa (known as the most sacred monument in all of Laos), the Patuxai Victory Monument, and the Vientiane Night Market.

As with all good things, my time in Southeast Asia came to an end, but I had plenty of interesting experiences to write about in my book of life. My experiences in this mysterious, majestic, and beautiful part of the world helped me feel happier than I had in many years.

I returned to South Korea refreshed and ready to get back to work and train with my rugby team again while enjoying my last six months at Osan Air Force Base.

While in Korea, I started a relationship with Jessica (not her real name), an Air Force girl who worked on base with me. We were both in our late twenties, we both had explosive pasts, and we both were trying to find happiness, or something close to it. I guess there was a void that I needed to fill after I divorced my first wife.

From the start, I knew I had no business trying to get serious with anyone, especially after what I went through with Sara. But South Korea had a funny way of warping your mind into thinking a bad situation could work. What's the worst that can happen?

But when you take a bunch of military personnel away from family, send them halfway across the world, cram them into a military base, and add alcohol, a perfect storm is created for many weak-minded guys like me. As much as I told myself to keep my distance and not get attached, I slowly let myself slide back into an ill-advised relationship.

Fueled by partying, booze, and an attitude of not giving a fuck, I was hooked. Jessica and I had more downs than ups and fought nonstop, but we stayed together. Maybe I needed the feeling of having someone there. Maybe there was a boost to my self-esteem in having a pretty girl on my arm. Maybe I was just a dumbass who loved getting his heart shredded.

I don't know, but here I was again, thinking I was in a position to settle down and fall in love, when deep down I hated myself for the mistakes I had made. I still hid behind excuses that held me down. Not helping my case was that I drowned everything with alcohol and blamed my problems on whatever excuse I could find. The big question that followed me like a lost puppy was, *When am I going to grow up and take responsibility for my life?*

Near the end of my tour, I was told that I had orders for Hurlburt Field, the home of the Air Force Special Operations Training Center. Hurlburt Field is located in the Florida panhandle, near the towns of Mary Esther and Fort Walton Beach. I was excited to go to the Sunshine State, my first time except for a short stint at Rescue Swimmer School in Jacksonville while I was in the Navy.

On the other hand, Jessica had orders dropped for North Dakota. If given the decision between North Dakota and the beaches of Florida, most people would choose Florida. Jessica was no different, but the only way she could get orders to Florida was—you guessed it—if we got married.

Yes, feelings were there, but not the true-love-until-death-do-we-part component. It didn't take a fortune-teller to predict that this new marriage was destined to be on the rocks within a short year of living together in Florida.

If I could step back in time and open my eyes, I would have seen that I met a girl, got married so she could come to Florida with me, and tried to force love. What the hell did I think was going to happen? Instead of learning a valuable life lesson and working hard to make positive changes in my life, I found myself looking for something different, a new challenge, a place where nobody knew me. In other words, for the hundredth time in my life, I was looking for a fresh start. It never occurred to me that I was the problem, not the other people in my life.

The inevitable breakup happened in 2007, when I'd been in Florida for about a year. We decided with some ugly exchanges of words that our sham of a marriage wasn't going to work.

Divorce proceedings started. In many ways, I felt like I was back at square one, thinking, *What do I do now?*

At Hurlburt Field, I was submersed in the Special Operations environment. Not only did this development get the gears turning in my head, but being there gave me a better idea of "who was who in the zoo" when it came to the different Special Operations units.

The Army Special Forces had always piqued my interest, mostly because my dad had spent his time in Vietnam attached to Special Forces teams as a helicopter crew chief. After years of hearing my dad's stories and bullshitting with some of the SF guys who I met in my first deployment to Iraq, I wondered if I had what it took to become one of the military's elite.

I could daydream as much as I wanted, but I was in the Air Force, not the Army. I had to face the music: Going from the Air Force over to Special Forces did not give me a high chance of passing the fourteen-months-or-longer series of demanding courses and training necessary to become a member of Special Forces.

My other consideration was that most of the guys trying out for Army Special Forces were coming from a combat-related job such as an Infantry unit or Ranger battalion. Boil this all down, and most of the guys trying to join Special Forces had a leg up on me: They had the basic weapon skills, land navigation skills, and just overall Army experience and expertise that were needed to even consider becoming a member of Special Forces and an elite Green Beret.

I was never exposed to this type of training while I was in the Navy or Air Force. I would have to learn everything from the ground up as a twenty-nine-year-old with nine years of different experiences in the military. The task looked nearly impossible to me.

Then there was another aspect—where I was in life. I didn't see how I could go much lower. I felt like I was at the bottom looking up, but I was desperate enough that I was ready to completely dedicate everything I had to accomplishing something huge.

I needed a win—a big win. I was never the type to give up, but with two blown marriages, a failed attempt at becoming a Navy SEAL, and a feeling that I hadn't found my calling in life, I was just settling and letting life run me ragged. I needed to reset my failures with a major victory. That was when I decided that there would be no more losing. It was time to start winning again.

My chance came in the form of a recruiting poster. I needed to update my Air Force promotion file at the base personnel department. I walked into the Air Force Career office and saw a life-size cardboard cutout posted at the entrance. The cutout was of a military man standing at attention. He was dressed half in an Air Force uniform and half in an Army uniform. The tagline said, "Go Blue to Green."

At the time the Air Force was overmanned in certain jobs, AMMO being one of them. The Army had a shortage of soldiers in certain career fields, so the Air Force was offering a direct transfer to the Army.

I had just gone through the realization that I needed a change—a big challenge—and the Army had a few jobs that would help me do just that. All I had to do was contact the phone number on the recruiting cutout.

I spent a few days talking with family and friends about what I was thinking about doing. I wanted to hear their perspective about trying out to become a Green Beret. This would mean giving up everything I had worked for in the Air Force and leaving a good AMMO job with great people for an opportunity where there was a high probability that I would not even make it through the first month of training. Once I left the Air Force, there was no going back.

One thing my dad had told me years earlier kept nagging me: *If you don't try, you will never know, and if you never know, it's because you didn't try.*

The answer was clear. I wasn't going to live a life of regrets, even if the high risk of failure was there. After clearing my head, I decided to jump in head first, eyes closed, into the unknown.

CHAPTER 5

NEVER LOOK BACK

FORT BENNING ARMY BASE
FORT BENNING, GEORGIA
SUMMER 2008

Move, move, move! Get off the fucking bus. Now! Get lined up!"

Holy shit. Was I back at Great Lakes?

No, I was at Fort Benning outside of Columbus, Georgia. I lined up and checked out the new kids, who looked scared out of their minds. I hoped they were reading my body language, which said, *Toe the line just like me.*

The privates got in somewhat of a formation as several drill sergeants created chaos, yelling and screaming:

"Fall in!"

"Tallest to shortest!"

"Move! Move faster!"

"Don't be stupid! Un-fuck yourself!"

One soldier who made eye contact with the drill sergeant immediately wished he hadn't.

"You eye-fucking me, private? See something you like?" the DS growled. "What's your name, soldier? Actually, I don't care. Your name is Private Dumbass."

"Yes, Drill Sergeant," yelled the rookie.

The new recruits were on the receiving end of what the Army called an "intimidation walkthrough." From my vantage point, it was working. Drill sergeants moved so close to the recruits' faces that the brims of their stiff Military Campaign Hats nearly touched their noses. Another torrent of verbal commands spewed forth:

"Stand at attention!"

"You call that attention, shit-for-brains?"

"Arms at the side!"

"Legs together!"

"Eyes straight ahead!"

The green recruits were taking a long time to get into formation. Once we were standing at attention and fairly lined up, the lead DS barked, "Right face!"

Three other guys and I knew exactly what this meant and obeyed as commanded. Our correct movement caught the attention of the lead drill sergeant, who made a beeline for me. A clipboard was tucked in the crook of his right arm.

"What's your last name?"

"Hendrickson, Drill Sergeant," I replied.

The drill sergeant glanced at a typed-out list on his clipboard. As he looked down the sheet of paper he motioned for me and the other three guys—they must have been prior service like me—to step out of formation.

"Look, I know you have all been through boot camp before,

but this is Infantry Basic, a whole different beast," he said. "You four will not have to play the fuck-fuck games like the recruits, but you will be a part of every training event and formation. I'm talking PT, chow, ranges, field exercises—everything. Clear?"

"Crystal clear, Drill Sergeant," I said. The others repeated their affirmation.

"Welcome to Fort Benning, gentlemen."

I had decided in June 2008 to give up everything and jump into the unknown world of Special Forces. I had packed a bag, locked the door to my house in Navarre, Florida, and vowed to never look back.

I didn't know what lay ahead of me. In my mind, only one thing was for sure: It was now or never. Transitioning from the Air Force to the Army had been a painless process, but there was one more thing I had to do before I arrived at Fort Benning. When I had reported to the Military Entrance Processing Station (MEPS) in Montgomery, Alabama, a few weeks earlier, my divorce from Jessica was not final.

I didn't want to join the Army until I was single and nothing was holding me back. Shortly after arriving at MEPS, I scheduled a telephonic court hearing with the judge back in Fort Walton Beach. The timing was perfect. During my phone appointment with the court, the judge approved the divorce due to our "irreconcilable differences." All it took was twenty minutes, and I was no longer a married man. I walked back into the In-Processing office when I was done and said, "I'm single. Let's get this started."

My first step was to attend a Warriors Transition Course (WTC) at several different training sites in New Mexico. Once again, the pieces were falling into place. Not only would I finally start training to become part of Special Operations, but I'd be near family: My dad and sister Wendy had picked up and moved to New Mexico a couple of years earlier to be closer to my older sisters, Paula and Chris.

My older brother, Robbie, still lived in Seattle, but at least my three sisters and my dad were together again. In a way, I was starting to fill in the gaps after being apart from my family for many years. My dad, after going through another divorce with another ill-matched wife, had chosen to work at a ranch way up in the mountains of Artesia, New Mexico. The quiet life suited him perfectly. He was on his own with no more drama and nothing but miles to roam. The man had been through a lot in his life. Some time to relax was just what he needed.

After WTC, I arrived at Fort Benning for Infantry Basic, which was my second boot camp. Not sure what to expect, I was surprised. I loved it. Nonstop weapons training, field training, infantry tactics, and everything else that goes into being in the infantry was awesome. The constant training kept my mind off the bullshit I had just been through with my divorce, and I found out that I was actually good at soldiering. We were training hard, and I was gaining confidence.

Since I was catching on to everything we did, I was waking up excited for the day for the first time in a long while. Infantry Basic was everything I needed and more.

With Infantry Basic finished, I moved on to the next phase of training—Airborne School, better known as Jump School. If I was going to fall from my cloud nine, at least I'd have a parachute on.

Airborne School taught the basics of parachuting by the use of a static line, which allows soldiers to jump from low altitudes because the parachute opens automatically due to a fixed cord attached to the aircraft.

For the first two weeks of Jump School, we trained on everything that an Airborne soldier needed to know so that no one would get killed or hurt while conducting static-line airborne operations. Parachuting boiled down to basically five Points of Performance, or steps:

Step 1: proper exit, check body position, and count
Step 2: check canopy and gain canopy control
Step 3: keep a sharp lookout for other jumpers during the entire descent
Step 4: prepare to land
Step 5: land

These steps entailed many days of practice landings while jumping off five-foot stands; sitting in a parachute harness for hours learning how to steer the canopy; and all the little to-dos in between. Most feared were the three 255-foot jump towers, which looked like looming metal giants keeping watch over Fort Benning. Each trainee was hoisted to the top by a cable and released to descend by parachute. This was the final step before we would have to exit the aircraft.

Lots of information was crammed into my head for what I assumed would be an extremely dangerous event—jumping out of an airplane. After two weeks of training for the five qualifying jumps needed to graduate, the day came to put everything to the test.

After donning our chutes and going through prejump inspections—called a JMPI, or Jump Master Personnel Inspection—we stepped onto a C-130 Hercules. I lined up with more than a dozen guys for my first parachute jump and was assigned to be second off the plane. Nervous and sweating profusely, I prayed to God my legs wouldn't give out on me before I even got to the paratroop door.

I wasn't a fan of heights and probably showed it. I silently hoped that everyone behind me wouldn't see my legs shaking uncontrollably. We didn't look that high off the ground, and we weren't—1,200 feet, to be exact. The ground below zipped by rapidly.

Holy shit, the Army wants me to jump? Just land the plane and I'll walk off. There's no need to jump. The plane is not going to crash.

"One minute!" the jumpmaster yelled over the wind noise, which was repeated down the line. Inside the aircraft, the sound of wind passing by made it seem like we were caught in a jet-powered wind tunnel. As the countdown continued, I was a hot mess. My shaky right hand grasped my static line tightly while nervous sweat poured into my eyes, stinging them.

"Thirty seconds!" the jumpmaster screamed.

I'm jumping to my death, I thought. I was thinking that I could quit and call it a day, but then I looked behind me: there was a 120-pound female soldier looking like she was ready to kick some ass and take names. If she was jumping, then I was jumping, even if I was going to die.

The jumpmaster yelled out, "Stand by!"

Oh shit, here it comes!

I focused and kept repeating to myself:

Feet and knees together.
Feet and knees together.
Feet and knees together.

"Green light, go!" the jumpmaster commanded. Before I knew it, I followed the guy in front me and stepped out of the C-130, certain I was plunging to my death.

One thousand, two thousand, three thousand, four thousand… if I counted past *four thousand* and my main parachute didn't deploy, then I was to activate my reserve.

A split second later, I received a spine-jolting shock as my parachute unfurled.

Hot damn, it worked! Then I remembered my Points of Performance. After I checked my canopy and gained canopy control, things were looking good.

When I was over a thousand feet in the air, I felt like I was just floating. *Okay, this isn't so bad.* With the hard part out of the way, all I had to do now was execute a proper landing. How difficult could that be?

As I got closer to the ground, the green field started coming at me extremely fast. *Damn, I'm coming in hot.*

"Face into the wind," one of the safeties on the ground screamed over a bullhorn. *Okay.* I grabbed my riser and turned my direction into the wind. Faster and faster the ground was coming up on me.

Feet and knees together. Remember, you're landing.

A proper landing fall is a technique used by hitting five points of contact to help disperse the shock of hitting the ground. The five points of contact were the balls of your feet, your calves, your thighs, your buttocks, and your pull-up muscle known as the latissimus dorsi muscle. This was how we were taught to land to reduce the chance for injury.

Ten feet, five feet…I closed my eyes and slammed to the earth like a two-hundred-pound bag of flour thrown from the top of a two-story building.

Instead of executing a proper landing like I had been taught, I hit the balls of my feet, then my head, back to my feet, then I face-planted. I tumbled along the ground like I was in a washing machine and came to a final resting spot, spread-eagled and with my face in the ground.

My first landing was not over, however. The wind sweeping across the drop zone caught my parachute and started dragging me down the field. When I finally came to a stop, I struggled to get to my feet.

Thank God my face broke my fall, I joked to myself as I tried to figure out where I was. Nothing was broken, but I was in pain. Hell, I was glad I was alive. Just then one of my jumping buddies ran up to me.

"Dude, how did you survive that landing? You ate shit, man."

"I don't know. Yeah, that really hurt," I said.

"Just think, man. Four more to go before we can graduate."

That was not what I wanted to hear at that moment. After that hard landing, four more jumps would surely cripple me—if I survived.

I continued to feel that way every time I stepped out of the aircraft. Each jump left me literally shaking in my boots.

I should have relaxed. Over the years, millions of soldiers had attended Airborne School and lived to tell their grandchildren about the experience, so it was proven to be a very safe school.

But that didn't change my fear of heights or the way I thought about jumping out of an airplane. To this day, my team calls me Bambi because my legs and knees shake like crazy before I exit the aircraft.

Jump School wrapped up, but that wasn't the end of me donning a parachute. I was seeking a job where jumping every three months was mandatory.

Well, I told myself, at least I had two months and twenty-nine days to stew over my next opportunity to jump to my death.

Before I joined the Army, I was offered several different jobs by the recruiter. I could have gone in to do the same job I basically did in the Air Force, which was AMMO. I was also offered Infantry and a couple of different MOS (Military Occupational Specialty) options. But one job opportunity sounded like my calling. It was an 18X contract (also known as an X-ray program), which was part of Special Forces Candidate Jobs.

Basically, an 18X meant taking a guy coming from a different branch of the service—or straight off the street—into Special Forces. Many soldiers in the Army had different opinions about guys joining Special Forces through the 18X program because they lacked Army experience. I felt that if someone had what it takes to make it through the rigors of the Special Forces pipeline and was a mature adult who knew how to work through stress and adversity while putting the mission above himself, then why not give him a chance to be one of the best? Regardless of people's opinions about the 18X program, the job was there for the taking, and I was going to grab it—experienced or not.

The 18X training pipeline consisted of Infantry Basic, Infantry Advanced training, Airborne School, Special Forces Selection Preparation Course, Special Forces Selection, and, if selected, Qualification Course (Q Course). All total, it was around eighteen to twenty-four months of training from start to finish.

Once I had Infantry Basic, Infantry Advanced training, and Airborne School under my belt, it was time for the SF Prep Course. What the hell was a preparation course for Selection like? I didn't know, but I was told that I would be on my way to Fort Bragg to find out.

After arriving at Fort Bragg near Fayetteville, North Carolina, and checking in to my new command at the John F. Kennedy Special Warfare Training Center and School, I was shown the barracks where I would be living for the first phase of the pipeline—the SF Selection Prep Course. I soon met other soldiers and made friends while we all waited for our training date to arrive.

There were thirty of us who were either transitioning from a different branch of the service or coming over straight from civilian life. Those of us who passed the Preparation Course would move on to SF Selection and integrate with around two hundred or more soldiers seeking the elusive approval to move on to the Q Course. We didn't have to wait long to get started. Within a short week of arriving at Fort Bragg, we began training.

The 18X Preparation Course was extremely hard and pushed me to my limits. I'm talking nonstop physical training, twelve hours per day getting beat down. The intent of the prep program was not only to get a soldier ready mentally and physically for Selection, but also to weed out the weak.

In a way, this course gave us a major advantage over the regular Army guys just showing up for Selection. Even though we lived on Fort Bragg, we would spend many days at Camp Mackall because the base had a larger training area and, more important, being there got us in the right mind-set and familiar with the terrain we would be in during Selection. We would come out of Prep Course in top physical shape because for thirty to forty-five days prior to our Selection date, we were getting run through the wringer.

Although extremely difficult, the 18X Preparation showed me what I needed to pass Selection and be successful in the Q Course. Most of all, it kept my mind off of all the personal shit that led me up to this point. In other words, I was feeling that life was great.

After what seemed like months going through the 18X Selection Preparation Course, it was time to prove myself for Special Forces Selection, the first key step in becoming a Green Beret. If I wasn't selected, I'd be sent where the Army needed me in something other than Special Forces.

From what I heard, those who washed out were put on a direct path to the 82nd Airborne Division at Fort Bragg. I'm not saying that the 82nd was a bad job, but I came to the Army for one reason and one reason only—to become a Green Beret.

On an early October morning, just before sunrise, the cool crisp North Carolina air had settled in as a trio of white Blue Bird buses pulled up to the barracks, ready to pick up us 18Xs for a short forty-five minute ride out to Camp Mackall and the start of Special Forces Selection.

This was do-or-die time, an eighteen-day gut check to pull out all the stops. There was no way I would accept failure because I didn't think I could handle another fuckup in my life. This was most likely my only chance, and I was going to make it happen. Everything that I had been through, all the hard work I'd put in... everything led up to this point—Selection.

As soon as we stepped off the buses at Camp Mackall, it was game on. We started with the usual Army PT test—a readiness assessment also known as the Army Physical Fitness Test. To my surprise, some soldiers showing up for a shot to be the best failed the first PT test and were gone on day zero. That first day quickly turned into night, then day, then back to night with a battery of different physical events and tests.

Time was flying for me, and I was killing it. Regardless of whether it was a ten-mile run along sandy backwoods roads, a 10K rucksack march with sixty pounds on my back, a twelve-mile land navigation course, Rifle PT, Log PT with telephone poles, or the dreaded Team Week events that broke the will of most of the trainees, I was speeding through. As excruciating as everything was, I was amazed at how well I was doing.

The 18X Prep Course lived up to its name. Those of us who were part of 18X were more prepared for Selection than 90 percent of the soldiers showing up from regular Army units. From long runs, rucks, and just overall movements, there was always a group of 18X studs in the front.

We were constantly on the move, eighteen to twenty hours a day, whether it was a ballbuster PT session or hustling from one event to another. Shuteye came in snatches, and meals were always on the go.

Not getting enough food for the number of calories I was

burning took its toll after the first week, but I didn't care. While the lack of calories depleted my energy and strength, that—combined with the lack of sleep—was all part of mentally and physically breaking down a trainee.

Even when we were not training, the Selection instructors would have us form up in a large gravel lot next to our sleeping tents, which we rarely used anyway, and stand there for hours listening to lectures between training events. I would see guys' knees buckle and hit the ground because they were so tired. I was more drained than I had ever been in my life, but I was going to remain upright.

Whenever we would form up, we would fall in before the infamous whiteboard, which listed our next event or what we were going to be doing for the next few hours. That whiteboard became a source of anxiety. It could have 10 MILE RUN or RUCK MARCH written on it—but it rarely told us that we could rack out for a few hours.

Most of the time we would be dragging ourselves back to the whiteboard after some hellacious event, praying we could get some chow or sleep, only to find 10K RUN IN 20 MINUTES or something worse written in big letters. The whiteboard was extremely effective at getting into our heads. The instructors could have told us about everything we'd be doing that day, but the mind-fuck came in the form of never knowing what was coming next. I was always wondering if I was following the directions exactly as they were given.

I would hear different trainees say there was no way the instructors would have us do anything more until they let us get some sleep or a chance to eat, but then we'd return to the whiteboard and see another gut-wrenching training event on the schedule. Many soldiers crumpled and quit because of the commands written on that whiteboard.

The Selection Cadre—a group of instructors in charge of our fates—did not yell or scream at us. They didn't have to. Yelling and screaming were not needed to weed out the weak. The events they put us through were designed to *induce* stress; it was up to us to follow instructions and perform to the best of our abilities. When no verbal instructions were given, it was on each trainee to take and execute all written guidance from the whiteboard that more or less said, *Can you follow instructions and pay attention to detail?*

Selection was designed to be rigorous and extremely difficult. The mental strain prompted many trainees to quit. For any given event or exercise, one or more of the Cadre would be with your group and constantly evaluating everyone, notebook in hand. This practice was most prevalent during Team Week, when the Selection class was broken up into twelve-man teams and evaluated on any number of events.

Whether it was carrying three twenty-foot-long telephone poles for five or more miles, moving five-hundred-pound sandbags multiple miles, or enduring some other torturous event, everything was done as a team. Team Week gave the instructors a good look at who was a team player and who wasn't, and who was a good leader and who lacked the necessary leadership skills to become a Green Beret. Most of all, the instructors were looking for those who wouldn't quit when the task was impossible. Team Week claimed most of the SF trainees.

If the Cadre opened his book and started taking notes while we completed our tasks, the stress level went through the roof.

What is he writing?

Did I fuck something up?

I know I'm getting dropped now.

All these thoughts made me think about running and grabbing his notebook just to find out my fate.

As the days turned into weeks, our bodies were breaking down. Still, I pressed on. As we neared the end, the final, major obstacle in my way would be a long ruck march. We weren't supposed to know the distance of the final trek, but every Selection class got the scoop from guys who had gone before: We would be going between twenty-five and thirty miles.

Each trainee would have a sixty-pound ruck, basically a military backpack, along with our weapon. No Nikes in this group; we'd have to cover all those miles on sandy roads throughout Camp Mackall in combat boots and a full uniform.

Oh, and we were told one more thing: We would have twelve hours to complete the march—for how many miles, we didn't know. Even though my body was spent, beat up, and bruised, I had been preparing for this marathon-or-longer ruck march.

The instructions from the lead instructor were clear: "Gentlemen, you will move for an undetermined distance. You have twelve hours to complete this task. If you're injured or cannot move anymore, set your ruck down on the side of the road and wait for a vehicle to pick you up. Trainees are not to talk to one another. If you are caught talking, you will be dropped. Follow the lane markers and do not get off course. You are always being assessed. Stay hydrated and good luck."

When we took off, it was every man for himself. Underneath

all that weight in my ruck, I felt like I was struggling early and thought I was falling behind. In reality, I passed many of my counterparts. Nonetheless, I decided that I needed to step up my pace and max out my effort. I hurt with every hill and wondered if I could keep up the energy-zapping stride I set for myself.

I got so tired! I wanted so much to take a break and lie down for a quick nap, but if I did that, my dreams of becoming a Green Beret were over. I never thought it was possible to fall asleep while walking with sixty pounds on my back, but one time I found myself in the middle of several bushes about fifty feet from the main road.

Holy shit, I'm sleepwalking.

Other times I would see things that just weren't possible—like rain puddles jumping up at me as I walked by. Thank God I wasn't the only one having issues with being dead tired. I walked up behind another guy stopped in the middle of the road. When I reached him, I noticed that he was sleeping standing up. I didn't even know that was possible! I didn't dare talk to him because of the warning we received before we stepped off, so I made sure to bump him as I walked past so he would wake up and keep going.

"Thanks, brother," he whispered.

It turned out that our march was *more* than thirty miles. We had to do two extra miles as a cherry on top—one last mind-fuck. The instructors knew we all had the lowdown about how long it was supposed to be, so they decided to add a little extra to the march. They were asking us one more question:

Do you really want to be here? Don't you want to quit?

I wasn't going to quit—no way and no how. I worked my arms and legs as never before and crossed the finish line with twelve minutes to spare. I had cut it close, but I made it. My feet were swollen and blistered, and I couldn't remember when I felt more exhausted.

Making it under the cutoff time didn't mean I was an automatic lock to be selected. Even though I went hard from day one and had the strength to be standing in the end like I did, if I didn't possess what they were looking for in a Special Forces soldier, then I wasn't going to be selected. That would be a kick in the balls. All that hell just to come up short.

After hitting the finish line, we gathered in a large conference hall to hear who got selected and who didn't. I could barely put one foot in front of another, but at least I walked in under my own power. Those left standing after the dust cleared looked like they had spent years as POWs. Most of the guys hobbled and limped their way into the conference hall, beaten down and on edge.

As I took a seat, my tired head was filled with questions:

Will all this physical and mental effort be for nothing?

Did I give it the best I could?

Do I have what they are looking for?

After a wait that seemed like days, the Selection Cadre entered the hall to call off the roster numbers of the guys selected. I was roster number 049 out of 185. As he went down the list, he reached those in the 040s. I held my breath and closed my eyes.

"Roster number 049, selected."

I melted into my chair as the relief spread over my body. Out of 185, only fifty men or so were selected—a little more than one out of every four. I was one of them. But I wasn't there yet.

I still had more hurdles in front of me. Out of the fifty of us who would advance to the Qualification Course, less than half would become Green Berets.

Those concerns didn't matter much to me at that point, however. For now, I savored my accomplishment. I was on my way.

***

The Q Course, barring injury or failing a certain portion, usually lasted around fourteen to fifteen months. If you were set on becoming an 18D, a Special Forces Medic, it was going to take a hell of a lot longer. I wasn't going that route. Before starting Q Course, I had chosen to become an 18C, a Special Forces Engineer.

The Q Course was an ever-changing beast. That meant the Q Course was broken into training phases—known as "training gates"—that needed to be completed for graduation. The phases were aligned a certain way one year but could completely change the following year.

After I passed Selection and was given a few weeks to recover—my blistered feet needed every minute—I started Q Course with a Special Forces Professional Leaders Course. Next in my training pipeline was Small Unit Tactics, followed by Survival, Evasion, Resistance and Escape (SERE) training. I am not at liberty to discuss what this training involved, but in general I was taught how to survive off the land if I was separated from my unit, and how to respond to a captivity situation.

I had attended an Air Force SERE "C" course in Spokane, Washington, so I had a good idea of what to expect. I thought that would give me an advantage in the Special Forces version, but nothing can ever really prepare someone for Special Forces

SERE. This course was on a whole different level from what I experienced in the Air Force.

Due to the highly secretive nature of the course, I cannot go into many details about our survival, evasion, and resistance training. What I can say is that I went without food for days and wound up feeling so tired that I couldn't form a logical thought. There were times when I had to remind myself that this was a training course because everything felt so realistic.

Upon completion of the SERE course, I had three months of language instruction in Spanish. Why Spanish? Before Selection, I was given a Language Aptitude test. My score determined the difficulty of the language that I would learn. Well, let's just say that Ryan Hendrickson's test results were modest at best and I would not be learning Arabic or Mandarin Chinese.

Spanish, a language lower on the difficulty scale, was a good fit for me, but I still struggled with the basics. "I can barely speak American, let alone Mexican," I joked with guys in my class. They watched me struggle daily to conjugate verbs and learn my vocabulary, but somehow I passed.

After Language training, the Q Course got more in my wheel-house. When I said I wanted to become a Special Forces Engineer, 18C, that meant Demolitions. Getting to blow things up was a dream that 90 percent of young boys have growing up—well, at least I had. Working with demo during the 18C course was fun, exciting, and a great learning experience.

What the SF Engineer course did *not* prepare me for was the rigors of equipment accountability and the supply-sergeant aspect of the job. Sounds easy enough on paper, but when you're accountable for almost a million dollars' worth of team equipment and one little item goes missing, all hell breaks loose.

This aspect of the job would take up the majority of an 18C's life on a team when not deployed. Why would anyone want to be a Special Forces professional supply sergeant, you ask? Because blowing shit up when training or on deployment made up for the not-so-glamorous side of the job.

Now that my MOS training was under my belt, I had one last hurdle to pass. Known as "Robin Sage," this was a series of unconventional warfare exercises and would be the final test after more than year of training. The Robin Sage exercises were intended to force us to analyze and solve problems to meet the challenges of a "real-world" military operation.

We—meaning twelve prospective Green Berets—were given a scenario to fulfill: We would have to infiltrate the fictional country of Pineland, which happened to be in Western North Carolina and surrounding states. Over a period of three weeks, we would plan, infil, train, advise, and assist a resistance movement that, on some level, backed the United States and was seeking to defeat the occupying repressive forces in Pineland. This would be, by far, the most realistic military exercise to prepare men for what we could actually encounter while deployed.

I went through Sage in the winter of 2009 during an extreme cold snap with lots of ice and snow. It got so cold at times that I'd start to take a drink from my canteen only to find out that my water had turned into a block of ice. The amount of snowfall that year plus the freezing temperatures made for a really shitty time, but it was still very rewarding.

I was grateful that I made it through the entire course without having to retake any part of the course or getting hurt. This was an accomplishment on its own. The chances of making it from start to finish without a hiccup or an injury were not good.

When times were hard and I needed to pull strength from somewhere, anywhere, I would see someone in the course who I thought had no business being there. Someone who was riding the coattails of others, performing only when the spotlight was on him. I would pick these guys out and think, *I'm not going anywhere if this guy is still here. I'm better than this shitbag and will outlast him no matter what.*

Then that guy would fail out or quit, and I would target someone else that I knew I was better than. I would use their weaknesses to make me stronger. In a crazy way, I fed off their failures. Bad, good, or indifferent, this was the mind-set I used to keep pushing myself.

From the moment I joined the Army, I had listened closely to my instructors, worked my ass off, and performed well in everything that was thrown at me. For eighty-four weeks—that's twenty months—from start to finish, my tired and broken body performed at levels that I didn't think were possible. I pushed myself to my limits and through to the end.

After I went from Infantry Basic training to getting selected and all the way through the Q Course, I walked across the graduation stage as a Green Beret.

I was elated—and humbled—to realize that of the four hundred or so guys who had started in my Selection class, only fifty five went to the Qualification Course, and of those fifty-five, twenty-three became Green Berets. This means from the original class of four hundred guys, only one out of every sixteen was able to don the green beret.

As a guy who'd served in the Navy and Air Force, with no

combat arms background in the military, I stood tall. I had accomplished what I had not thought was possible just twenty months prior when I was sitting inside a MEPS office in Montgomery, Alabama.

Life had dealt me some major blows, and no one knew better than me that I had dug a hole for myself that was damn near impossible to get out of. Despite how much I had fucked things up, I had pulled myself out of the pit, started something, and seen it through to the end, leaving nothing behind.

I had given this everything I had and succeeded.

Now I was a Green Beret, ready to write the next chapter of my life.

CHAPTER 6

THE NEW GUY

CROWN COLISEUM
FAYETTEVILLE, NORTH CAROLINA
MARCH 2010

I felt proud to be welcomed into the brotherhood.

Seated among sixty or seventy soldiers, each of us outfitted in Army Class A dress uniforms and surrounded by family and friends, I listened to a retired Green Beret sergeant major address us—the graduates of the U.S. Army's Special Forces Qualification Course—inside the Crown Coliseum in Fayetteville, North Carolina. It was a cool afternoon on March 10, 2010, and we were about to receive our graduation certificates. We were now the newest members of the Green Berets.

"Gentlemen, you are all from different walks of life, and each of you has a different background, but today is a special day," the sergeant major began. "Today, you have successfully navigated your way through the trials and rigors of the toughest and finest training the Army has to offer. Regardless of the path that led you here, you are now crossing over into a brotherhood of warriors with a tradition and history written with the blood of our forefathers. You will be required to go above and beyond what you ever thought was possible, and you will be asked to perform at a level higher than most men ever will. You have proven you have what it takes because you are sitting here today. Congratulations, and welcome to the best of the best—the U.S. Army Special Forces."

When my name was called and I walked to the front to receive my graduation certificate, I thought about how my long road to becoming a Green Beret was finally over at the age of thirty-one. After completing five phases of training in Q Course—unconventional warfare, foreign internal defense, special reconnaissance, direct action, and counterterrorism—I had finished what I started. I couldn't help but feel amazed by my accomplishment, even though it was long in coming. I had earned the right to wear the green beret that I coveted so much.

I was acutely aware that the Green Berets' purpose and mission weren't as sexy as other Special Operation units like the Navy SEALs, which seemed to get more publicity back home, especially after Marcus Luttrell's book, *Lone Survivor*, came out in 2007.

We did things differently. Green Berets lived with indigenous peoples, learned their language and customs, gained their trust, and molded them into fighters to defeat our mutual enemies. Doing all these things was a slow, long-term process that fit the type of wars we'd been fighting since Vietnam in the sixties. That's why we were known as the "quiet professionals." We had a motto in the Green Berets: *De Oppresso Liber*, which was Latin for "To Free the Oppressed." Our call to duty was not one that just any military force could live up to.

When the graduation ceremony was over, I had a few days

to decompress and visit with family and friends who had made the trip to Fayetteville to witness my graduation. Afterward, I returned to nearby Fort Bragg to check in with my new unit, 2nd Battalion, 7th Special Forces Group. As I pulled into the parking lot that morning, I did my best to calm my racing mind. Training was one thing, but I was in the big leagues now.

I headed across a large quad to the headquarters building, a long, one-story structure that was the home to 2nd Battalion, one of the three operational battalions in the 7th Special Forces Group. I was initially taken aback by how old the building looked; it reminded me of a relic from World War II. In the crook of my left arm was a folder filled with the necessary paperwork to process me into my new unit.

After entering the 2nd Battalion HQ, I was told to wait outside the office of the command sergeant major until he could see me, whenever that was. On the wall outside his office, I spotted his picture and a brief write-up describing who he was and where he was from. The first thing that caught my eye was that his home state was Oregon, where I had grown up. Having this little bit of familiarity put me at ease and helped calm my heart, which was practically beating out of my chest. I was reading more of his bio when I heard a stern voice mutter, "New guy, get in here."

I stepped into his office and popped to attention. "Staff Sergeant Hendrickson reporting for duty," I said.

"At ease," the command sergeant major said. "You're making me nervous. Where are you from?"

"I was born in California but raised in Oregon," I replied.

"No shit? Well, I won't hold California against you. Are you a Duck or a Beaver?"

I smiled. In Oregon, you pledged allegiance to either the

University of Oregon Ducks or the Oregon State Beavers. The two schools clashed in the "Civil War" football game every fall.

"I'm a Duck," I proudly replied.

"Good man."

I don't know who was the bigger Duck fan, me or my new command sergeant major. After twenty minutes of talking about living in Oregon, he turned to more serious matters. "You're going over to Alpha Company. They got back from Afghanistan five months ago. They're going back to war in a few months and need all the bodies they can get. You're an Oregon boy, so I know you'll do well."

There were three companies in 2nd Battalion: Alpha, Bravo, and Charlie. Within each company were six teams, or detachments, each with a dozen members. Every elite detachment was not only trained to support conventional Army operations, if needed, but they were also the best the military had to offer when it came to guerrilla combat, sabotage, and subversion techniques.

After finishing my meeting with my new command sergeant major, I exited the 2nd Battalion headquarters and walked toward the building that I would call my new home, Alpha Company. My first stop was the front office.

"Who the fuck are you?" the guy behind the counter asked.

"Staff Sergeant Hendrickson. I just graduated Q Course and was told to report to Alpha Company," I replied.

"Okay, hold on." Turning around to an open office door behind him, he said, "Sergeant Major, we have another new guy."

The sergeant major for Alpha Company walked out and shook my hand.

"So, you just graduated the course?"

"Roger, Sergeant Major."

"Let me see your paperwork."

He flipped through several pages. "Okay, you're the new 18C I've been waiting for. I'm assigning you to ODA 7215."

I knew the 7 stood for 7th Special Forces, the 2 for 2nd Battalion, the 1 for Alpha Company, and 5 for the fifth team in the company.

Now I was getting somewhere. Each ODA team, small and versatile, consists of twelve men and is the heart and soul of a Special Forces company. ODA stands for Operational Detachments Alpha, or A-Teams, and there were six in Alpha Company.

"You'll find 7215 down the hall," the sergeant major said with a jerk of his head. "I hope you have thick skin because you'll need it on that team."

I headed down a long hallway paved with faded white linoleum flooring, unsure what he meant by that. I passed doors—7212, 7213, 7214—until I reached the second-to-last one on the left.

I knocked on the door. A tall and stocky team guy a few years younger than me took one look in my direction and said, "Who the fuck are you?"

Was this Alpha Company's way of saying hi?

"I'm the new—"

"Stand in the hallway until someone invites you in!"

He quickly turned his back on me and closed the door in my face. Before the door shut, though, I caught a glimpse of my new team sitting at desks along the perimeter of the room, laughing and joking as the workday ended.

My new teammates were fully aware I was standing in the hallway, but they couldn't have cared less. Since I was the latest addition to 7215, that meant someone would have to show me the ropes—and not a single guy wanted to get stuck with that duty this late in the day. So, I stood there and didn't say anything. I *couldn't* say anything…because I was another cherry-ass new guy coming into a company that had just returned from the battle-fields of Afghanistan. They didn't have time for rookies who wanted to play Army.

During Q Course training, I had heard about initiation rituals like this, and now it was happening to me. I waited outside the team room for an hour or so, and then I left when everyone else departed—but no one made eye contact with me. I definitely felt like the odd man out.

I returned the next morning but was ordered to stand in the hallway until I was called upon to answer any quick questions they had. Then I was directed back out to the hallway to wait again. Finally, after the third or fourth day, I heard a voice inside yell, "New guy, get in here!"

My nerves kicked into overdrive. The days of waiting to be invited to become part of my new detachment were over—I hoped. I knew the spotlight would be shining on me and my teammates would be forming impressions of me.

I was nervous stepping into the team room, but I wasn't going to let the other guys see that. Weakness was like blood in the water to a school of sharks, and I wasn't in the mood to get ripped to shreds right off the bat.

Besides, how bad can it be? I thought. After nine years in the military, I had a good idea what I was walking into. I looked quickly around the room and sized up the other Green Berets, knowing that every eye was on me, judging and analyzing. I knew what they were thinking:

Is this new guy battle-tested?

Can he be trusted in combat?

Does this dude think he's good enough to be on our team?

Out of the corner of the room came the first shot across the bow.

"Don't just stand there. Tell us who the fuck you are," one of the senior operators commanded.

"Staff Sergeant Hendrickson." I didn't use my first name. This was business.

"Yeah, no shit. We can see your name tag. What's your first name?"

"Ryan," I replied.

"Hey, new guy Ryan, what's your job?" asked another guy.

"I'm the new 18C."

"Oh, shit, this is our new engineer, everybody," he announced. "You have big shoes to fill. Don't fuck it up."

I knew my job as an 18 Charlie wasn't for the faint of heart. While patrolling in enemy-held areas in Afghanistan, I would find myself up front—the tip of the spear, one might say—with three to five Afghan counterparts who specialized in counter-IED operations and were very good at finding them. We would be exposed to Taliban snipers or any run-of-the-mill dumbass wanting to take a shot at us. The worst part of being the man up front was that I would be the first soldier to encounter the IEDs. I'd rather be in a firefight with the Taliban any day of the week than deal with IEDs, which were a nasty but very effective way to fight a war.

One of the more senior guys back in a corner spoke up. "You got a lot to learn in a little bit of time. Sit down and listen, but most of all, keep your mouth shut and your eyes open. This will be a fire hose."

I guess the introductions are done, I thought. I figured nothing would be easy as the new guy on a Special Forces team that had done tours together in Afghanistan.

For the next couple of months, I worked my ass off trying to prove myself, staying late at the office to get every aspect of my job crammed in because Alpha Company, 2nd Battalion was on its way back to Afghanistan in just four short months—sometime in June 2010, to be exact.

Even though I felt like I was soaking in everything like a sponge, every day was a test. I could be the smartest and the hardest-working soldier in the Army, but until I proved myself with bullets whizzing past my head, the guys would still have reservations about my abilities.

Training for several months in anticipation of the mission was intense but fun. Learning the different aspects of team life, along with how we would operate together in combat, was something different, exciting, and new. I had spent four years in the Navy and five years in the Air Force before joining Special Forces, so this type of soldiering was an adrenaline rush and completely different than performing ship maintenance or loading bombs on fighter planes. I had taken a leap of faith and given up a good job in the Air Force to see if I had what it takes to become one of the military's best.

If you look at the U.S. military as a whole, 90 percent of the armed forces support the remaining 10 percent—the boots on the ground, the warfighters. Less than *1 percent* of that 10 percent make up Special Operations: the Green Berets, Army Rangers, Navy SEALs, Air Force Commandos, and Marine Corps Force Reconnaissance.

I had made the cut. For the first time in my military career, I was part of that 1 percent and proud of my accomplishment. On top of that, I loved belonging to a combat unit that was one of America's top responses to global unrest.

While training at Fort Bragg one afternoon, three UH-60 Black Hawk helicopters suddenly appeared overhead.

This is different, I thought. It sure didn't look like part of our training. We were dressed in full gear: body armor, ballistic helmet, and weapons—everything we needed to successfully train for a combat deployment.

On this particular day, we were conducting Close Quarters Battle training. I was in my zone, soaking in everything, when the beat of the rotor blades started to get louder.

"What's going on?" I asked one of my new buddies.

"Fuck if I know."

Our team leader interrupted my thoughts. "Everyone form up with the rest of the company."

Probably fifty Green Berets joined up and quickly stood shoulder to shoulder, talking among ourselves about what could be going on as the Black Hawk helicopters touched down.

"Company attention!" the company commander called out.

While standing with my body stiff and straight, I saw officer after officer step off the Black Hawks and form a welcoming committee next to the side door of one of the UH-60s. A tall, trim, bespectacled naval officer wearing a khaki uniform with gold shoulder tabs displaying four stars stepped out of the chopper. Salutes snapped and handshakes were exchanged.

"Holy shit, that's Admiral Mullen," one of my team members said.

"What's he doing here?" I asked.

"Beats me. I guess we'll soon find out."

Admiral Mike Mullen was no ordinary commander. He was the highest-ranking military leader in the country—the chairman of the Joint Chiefs of Staff who advised the president of the United States, the secretary of defense, the Homeland Security Council, and the National Security Council on military affairs.

Admiral Mullen made his way toward us and then walked the line of Green Berets, shaking each hand and thanking every man for his hard work and service to America. Then he stepped back and addressed us as a unit.

"Gentlemen, soon you will be deployed to Afghanistan to take the fight to the Taliban. You will be deployed to one of the most dangerous places in Afghanistan, an area that needs U.S. Army Special Forces now more than ever. Before you leave, I want you to know that you have the full support of the United States of America backing you, and if any man is wounded or killed in action, I also want you to know that I will personally look after you and your situation."

Admiral Mullen's pep talk impressed me because he did not have to be there, let alone shake every man's hand, but he felt it was his duty to do just that. Being the new guy on the block, I didn't really understand the *Oh, shit* impact that his arrival had on the senior guys, but their faces told me this type of visit didn't happen very often.

While I appreciated Admiral Mullen's promise to personally look after every man wounded or killed during this deployment, I brushed off his comment, figuring this was what all high-ranking officers would say. Nevertheless, hearing him make that statement was a bit unnerving. His words were a grim reminder that I could return home in a flag-draped coffin or missing one or more of my limbs.

When I landed at Bagram Airfield and was smacked by the smells of shit and jet fuel, I was well aware that our C-17 Globemaster had landed during the fighting season—summer time.

I was mindful that I was entering a land that hadn't been conquered by a foreign force since the days of Alexander the Great and Genghis Kahn. From what I could see beyond the outer perimeter of the base, the Hindu Kush Mountains in the distance gave way to miles of green farmland spotted with small mud-hut villages.

Afghanistan, a South Central Asian country bordered by Pakistan, Iran, a bit of China, and three "stans"—Turkmenistan, Uzbekistan, and Tajikistan—looked like a land untouched by time. Officially known as the Islamic Republic of Afghanistan, the landlocked country is about the size of Texas and has a population of more than 30 million people, mostly comprised of Pashtuns, Tajiks, Hazaras, and Uzbeks.

Before deploying, I carved out time to read up on the people of Afghanistan and the enemy I was fighting. It didn't take a genius to quickly figure out that Afghanis were tribal people who had been fighting each other and foreign invaders since Alexander the Great and his Greek troops stormed into the countryside around 330 BC.

Alexander and his tens of thousands of fighters didn't last long, nor did the Indian emperor Ashoka, or a group of sun-worshipping Zunbils who were thrown out just before Muslim Arabs arrived in the seventh century wielding the sword of

Islam. In more modern times, the British were defeated at the Khyber Pass in the mid-nineteenth century, the Russians in the 1980s, and now we were here.

What made our deployment especially treacherous was that we were heading to Southern Afghanistan's Helmand Province, which was the most dangerous region in Afghanistan in 2010.

The Helmand was known for holding many Taliban fighters itching to kill Americans. Not only did Taliban fighters want to annihilate infidel American soldiers, but they were inspired to protect the single source of money keeping them in the fight— opium. Helmand Province was a drug haven because vast fields of papaver somniferum, commonly known as the opium poppy, produced bundles of pungent, jellylike opium that could be used to produce morphine and heroin. The Taliban would run the drugs north and across the borders for distribution around the world.

Opium, which didn't spoil or rot, was an ideal cash crop for the Taliban. Since they lived in remote areas with poor roads, it was hard to mount an attack. The Taliban knew they couldn't beat us in a head-to-head fight, so they used their weapon of choice—the IED—to protect their crops and their defensive positions.

If American forces were able to take over the Helmand Province, however, we could block such a vital lifeline for the Taliban and stem the flow of cash funding the insurgency against the United States and our allies in the fight against terrorism. That was a big task since the province was believed to be the world's largest opium-producing region, responsible for around 42 percent of the planet's total production. This gave the Taliban even more of a reason to protect their opium trade and hold the ground at all costs.

After the U.S.-led invasion of Afghanistan in late 2001, NATO armed forces, mainly the British, attempted to clear the province of the insurgents. The Taliban, along with local tribes and drug-financed militias from as far away as Chechnya, fought back ferociously. They were not willing to give up power or their cash cow—the opium trade—without a major fight. Following four years of intense combat, with some of the most brutal fighting the British Army had seen since the Korean War, the Brits reached a standstill with the Taliban. They had made little progress, "liberating" less than five hundred square kilometers of the province. Without more support, the Helmand was a lost cause.

When the British wore thin, the Taliban moved back in, stronger and more determined than ever. Within months, the Taliban doubled and then tripled the size of their forces. Opium harvests grew tenfold within a year. That was when the bigwigs at the Pentagon knew they could no longer ignore the growing threats festering in Helmand Province and began drawing up plans to stop the Taliban in their tracks. Fast forward a few years, and the U.S. forces were still at a stalemate with the Taliban. That was where my company came into play; that was where Alpha Company would make its name.

We weren't in Afghanistan to conquer but to kill the shitheads whose warped ideology helped bring down the Twin Towers in Manhattan on September 11, 2001. In areas where Afghan government troops had little or no presence, the idea was to put American Special Ops troops on the ground, win the hearts and minds of the villagers, and then train them to stand against the Taliban and protect themselves. To successfully conduct Village Stability Operations, we had to have a basic understanding of the Afghan people in the different areas around the country, but religious and cultural differences in Afghanistan made every aspect of the U.S. mission extremely challenging.

The facts in Afghanistan were simple and hard. Islam was practiced by 99.7 percent of its population. The Afghans were poor; the average yearly income for an Afghani was less than $300. The literacy rate was abysmal, right around 31 percent of the population of those fifteen years and older, but the number of people who could read had increased by 50 percent since U.S. Coalition Forces entered the country.

I knew that women were forced to cover themselves in public with head-to-toe burqas, which had to be unbearable in the heat. Families conducted "honor" killings of women, often after an arranged marriage went south, and these types of murders were legal and widespread because the power and influence of the central government in Kabul basically vanished once you left the capital city. The cold, hard truth was this: Winning the hearts and minds of Afghans boiled down to U.S. dollars and support.

On our way to Forward Operating Base Tycz in southern Afghanistan, I resisted the nagging urge to take pictures because I didn't want to lose what credibility I had gained with my team. Looking like an excited kid at Disneyland wouldn't be cool and would open me up to ridicule from my teammates. I was supposed to act like this was no big deal…been there, done that. The reality was that this was my first time in Afghanistan and I wanted to soak it all in. What better way to do that than busting out my camera and snapping a few photos? Pictures are worth a thousand words, right?

I had family and friends back home who would have loved to hear from me. I knew that my father and my siblings were eager to receive news and pictures about my adventures. I had a new girlfriend who was looking forward to hearing from me as well. But staying in touch with the home front was secondary. As a newly minted Green Beret, I needed to be focusing my energy on our mission—dealing death to the Taliban.

Throughout history, the conquerors and countries who tried to win wars through eradication of a population or changing the way the population did things never ultimately succeeded. With the safety of the Afghan civilian population foremost in the U.S. and Afghan governments' minds, a different approach was needed. Our mission would require the expertise of the Special Forces regiment known for operating outside the box and experienced at winning over the villagers to achieve the greater good.

I understood the VSO mission, but at that point in my brief Special Forces career, all I cared about was that I was finally in the fight. Every man needs to find out exactly what he's made of, a thought that lurked in the back of my mind. In addition, every combat soldier has nagging questions bouncing around his brain:

How will I act when someone is trying to kill me?

If it's kill or be killed, can I do it?

Will I win?

Questions like these can be answered only in combat—life-or-death situations—and I needed these questions answered.

The summer of 2010 would turn out to be the deadliest year for Special Operations in Afghanistan. Things were about to get ugly fast, and all my questions would get answered in ways I never expected.

CHAPTER 7

THE ALAMO

HELMAND PROVINCE

SOUTHERN AFGHANISTAN

SUMMER 2010

When we landed at Bagram Air Base, my team fell smack-dab into the middle of a military surge in Afghanistan, which was keeping everyone on their toes. The U.S. military was going after any known Taliban safe haven to deny freedom of movement and prevent more attacks by the enemy. These safe havens were in remote places that hadn't seen an invading military force since the Russians occupied parts of Afghanistan from 1979 to 1989.

Upon our arrival at FOB Tycz, I was told that we would be tasked with holding ground in and around the Uruzgan and Helmand provinces in an attempt to deny the enemy their freedom of movement. No one knew when our first mission was going down, but we had to be ready to go at a moment's notice.

The call came quickly. We had been in-country for only one week when we learned that we would be heading out for a ten-day mission at "the Alamo"—the nickname for a mud-hut compound along the Helmand River. We would be relieving a Special

Forces detachment that had been in-country for nine months and would soon be heading back to the States.

The news that we were on the move excited me. This would be my first time "outside the wire" of our compound, and I was ready to go.

After loading up the vehicles, we departed the safety of FOB Tycz and made our way toward an area that we called the West Bank (the Alamo was located on the west bank of the Helmand River).

We had just crossed the Helmand River when we started hearing radio traffic saying that our guys at the Alamo were in a major firefight with the Taliban.

Oh, shit. Not only was I on my first mission as a Green Beret, but I was walking into a live combat situation. This wasn't a video game. Real 7.62-caliber bullets would be flying. This caliber of bullet would easily rip a hole the size of a silver dollar through a man's torso and tear his internal organs to shreds. We wore body armor that gave some protection to our chests and upper backs, but when a bullet penetrated the chest cavity, nine times out of ten you were dead.

I was driving the lead vehicle when our convoy arrived at the last stopping point, around one thousand meters from the Alamo. A call came over our vehicle radio communications: "All vehicles stop! Stop!"

During our pre-mission brief that morning, I remembered being told that we would have to make a mad dash over one kilometer of open ground to reach the safety of the Alamo, so we needed to be prepared for that.

The Alamo was surrounded by a U-shaped ridgeline. A fingerlike natural rock structure that ran toward the Helmand

River was our last cover before a kilometer of open, uphill terrain that would lead us to the main entrance of our compound. All one thousand meters were in range of the Taliban machine-gun crews high up on the western ridgeline, where they waited for our vehicles to make a run for it. I was told to drive like a bat out of hell when we crossed into the open. *Roger that*, I thought.

Then the call came over the radio: *All vehicles move!*

I hit the gas on my RG-33 mine-resistant vehicle and started covering ground. Within seconds, a Taliban machine-gun crew started sending rounds our way. I heard pings from the bullets hitting our truck. Thank God our RG-33 was armored.

Sprays of dirt and dust from incoming bullets engulfed our vehicle. My senses shot up to overdrive and adrenaline pumped through my veins. Even though I was scared, I had never felt so alive as I concentrated on keeping the heavy vehicle moving forward.

Then a *crack*—we'd been hit! The front windshield split in a hundred different directions, like a spider's web.

Crack, crack—two more rounds hit my windshield. I didn't know how many more rounds this windshield could take.

"Drive!" my captain yelled from the front passenger seat. "We got to get the fuck off this open ground!" I jammed the gas pedal to the floorboard and pushed the RG-33 to the limits.

An RG-33 weighs around thirty-eight thousand pounds, so maneuvering such a large bullet magnet over one thousand meters of uneven, rough terrain was no easy task. I managed to rumble to safety through the Alamo's single-entrance gate and into a large courtyard. The other two vehicles arrived safely as well. Almost as soon as my RG-33 stopped in the courtyard, I jumped out and ran to the nearest elevated position in the compound. I toggled the selector switch on my M-4 carbine from Safe to Fire and started sending rounds downrange toward the enemy.

For the next few hours, we exchanged sporadic gunfire, but I have to admit that it was hard to think clearly—adrenaline had really taken over my body. At that point, training kicked in and I reacted with muscle memory that been honed through hundreds of hours spent training for combat.

When my first battle experience was over, I couldn't get my hands to quit shaking. My nerves were tingly as well, but I felt good. The question of how I would react when bullets were flying had been answered.

That evening, some of the guys looked at the damage on my vehicle. We could see where the rounds hit even though the bullets hadn't made holes. But there were indentations everywhere.

"Damn, one more round hitting your windshield and it was gone," one of my teammates said. "You would have been fucked up."

"You got that right," I said.

"Looks like you got your CIB, bro," joked another buddy.

The CIB, or Combat Infantry Badge, was awarded when an infantryman or Special Forces soldier was in direct contact with enemy forces.

All wisecracking aside, I was jacked. Combat was a rush that I'd never experienced before, and that skirmish set the tone for our rotation. Each morning, the Taliban would wake up, send rounds our way—almost like they were clocking in for a job— and we would return fire. After a few hours, we'd call in air strikes, and then all would be quiet.

It was almost like they were playing a game—a game that came with a warning:

Don't get comfortable. We're here to kill you.

⎯⎯⎯

We were told to expect a ten- to fourteen-day rotation at the Alamo. We would be mentoring and training the local Afghans to defend themselves against the Taliban while also going out on patrol and seeking to build relationships with villagers in the region—that is, during the times when we weren't getting shot at. You never knew if there was a bullet in the air with your name on it.

The Alamo consisted of a large, single-story mud-hut building containing around four rooms of equal size that were used for storage of equipment and food, and a little privacy for a shitter. We would be sleeping outside in the courtyard, however, because the heat made it impossible to sleep inside.

Surrounding the Alamo was an eight- to ten-foot-tall mud wall that served as our security barrier from Taliban hordes wanting to swoop in and chop off our heads at night. We'd heard stories about what these Islamic extremists did to their enemies and knew if the Taliban captured a U.S. soldier, they would have him kneeling in front of a camcorder with a sharp blade to his throat. The thought of being decapitated sent shivers through all of us, but the biggest risk came from a sudden night attack in a hail of bullets, mortar fire, or rocket-propelled grenades (RPGs).

The security wall was layered with sandbags for added protection and piled high enough to give us good fighting positions. From our vantage point, we could keep tabs, for the most part, on the Taliban moving around the Chutu Valley or changing positions on the ridgeline. The Alamo was situated on a hill about two hundred meters from the Helmand River, which allowed us to see down the river on both sides from our elevated perch.

At nighttime, the courtyard looked like a gypsy camp with cots and mosquito nets spread around. During the day, however, we had to stay somewhat under cover because the Taliban liked to fire at us from the ridgeline above the Alamo to the west. The possibility of landing a few rounds in the courtyard was something that happened often. Nobody wanted to be the recipient of a lucky shot.

My bed consisted of a medical stretcher used for moving wounded guys off the battlefield. At night, I wrapped myself in a small blanket because I like being covered while I sleep, but this wasn't actually necessary in the incessant heat and humidity of Afghanistan. Surrounding my medical stretcher bed was a mosquito net that barely covered my body, but something was better than nothing.

We joked that if the Taliban didn't kill us, then the bugs and creepy crawlers that came out every evening were up to the task. We all believed the bugs were a weapon used by the Taliban to completely fuck with us. Most of the nasty-looking insects hid in the darkness of the mud-hut rooms during the heat of the day and ventured out at night to warm up on the hot ground. I was sure the favorite gathering spot for the Taliban bugs was outside my mosquito net, where they would watch me squirm all night in fear. I was afraid they would eat a hole in the net and then start gnawing on my face, neck, or arms. I had some bad dreams to that effect.

Taking care of our personal hygiene in a mud-hut compound

with no electricity or running water made for some interesting adjustments. Showers were taken using baby wipes and lots of scrubbing, but that got old, so every now and then we would go to a part of the Helmand River that our Afghan counterparts controlled and jump in for a soap-and-suds swim. We always made sure that at least two guys stood guard while the others lathered up and rinsed off.

We should have known that the villages upstream dumped their raw sewage into the river, but we didn't and I'm not sure that would have stopped us from washing up anyway. No skinny-dipping around the Afghans, though, because if a village woman saw us naked, she would be beaten for looking at us. We kept our shorts and shirts on, but damn if that cool water didn't feel good on our sweat-caked, dirty skin roasting in the summer sun.

Taking a shit consisted of an ammo can, a plastic bag, and a private corner. After you did your business, you tied up your bag and threw it into the fire pit, which was outside the compound wall. Being the new guy and the 18C, guess who was told to burn the trash and the shit pile every night?

I learned quickly that 90 percent of a deployment was sheer boredom followed by 10 percent of heart-racing terror and excitement like I experienced on my arrival.

Each rush of combat left me craving more. There was something about the kill-or-be-killed aspect of fighting that gave me a high—a high that was dangerously addicting.

We conducted multiple foot patrols down along the Helmand River and up on top of the ridgeline to get a better idea of the enemy's "pattern of life," and of where they were setting up attacks.

By the base of the river, towering rows of marijuana plants stood more than six feet tall. Patrolling through pot fields in the summer heat was an extremely humid and sticky business. Breathing alone was an aerobic workout, and every breath I took felt like I was inhaling the gooey resin of pot leaves that hung in the air.

Afghanistan's blazing temperatures were unbearable, but when you add walking around with body armor, weapons, and ammunition, life sucked. Adding to the misery index were the hummingbird-size bugs that lived in the pot fields and the giant Afghan shepherd dogs—known as Kuchi dogs—that the Taliban loved to leave behind in the fields as a nasty surprise for sweat-soaked soldiers patrolling through. Every soldier had heard horror stories about someone who had been bitten by one of these dogs, and no one wanted to face that pain—not to mention the rabies shot that would follow.

It seemed like almost every time we left the relative safety of our compound we got into a fight. Some of the skirmishes were basic and light, while others were hair-raisers that led me to believe that the enemy had us surrounded.

Besides trying to keep American soldiers away from their marijuana and poppy fields, the Taliban were using the Chutu Valley to move men, weapons, and equipment to staging areas outside of Kandahar, Afghanistan's second-largest city. This war matériel would then be used to launch attacks on Kandahar and further disrupt the Afghan government.

The Alamo's location gave us a strategic advantage of being able to keep a close eye on our little section of the valley and keep the enemy on their toes. The Taliban's main route to Kandahar ran through us. We also benefited from being in close contact with a somewhat friendly village south of our compound from which we conducted VSO.

Before we controlled the Alamo, the Taliban could move as they pleased, with no worries about us dropping a bomb on their heads. Now they had the American obstacle to bypass, and their freedom of movement was disrupted. They couldn't poke their heads up without getting shot at.

There was a friendly village—which we named Graham because that was what it sounded like when the local Afghans pronounced its real name—that didn't like the Taliban because of the taxes imposed upon them as well as extremely harsh cultural rules. Girls couldn't go to school, and women were treated like second-class citizens. They were forced to wear burqas and were rarely able to leave the confines of their homes for risk of being seen by a man. To top it off, regardless of how sick a woman became, she was forbidden to see a male doctor. The imposition of sharia law made life unbearable for everyone. A villager who spoke out against the Taliban was handed a death sentence.

Because of this situation, we could conduct Village Stability Operations. By gaining trust through our interaction with villagers—mostly the village elders—we were able to give them medical aid and military training so they could stand up to the Taliban. The locals knew as long as we were there, the Taliban were not a big threat. Regardless of whether or not they liked Americans, the villagers saw us as a better alternative to the Taliban.

We experienced most of our success because of the money and firepower we brought to the fight. The villagers, for the most part, just wanted to be left alone. As long as we were a benefit to them, there was less chance of being hit by enemy forces coming from the south.

The problem with the Alamo was that it could turn into a real-life Alamo massacre at any given moment, meaning that we were *way* outnumbered. Most of the time, we had six to eight Green Berets in the compound with a few dozen Afghan fighters. In contrast, there were hundreds of Taliban soldiers running around the valley looking to kill us, to the best of our knowledge.

Strategically, not only did the Taliban control the high ground above our compound, they had freedom of movement around the northern part of the river because of their trenches and sophisticated tunnel system. This allowed the Taliban to move somewhat undetected along the river and launch attacks. Since our compound was surrounded on three sides by enemy fighters, anyone arriving or leaving the security of the Alamo was quickly engaged by pesky Taliban PKM machine-gun crews hidden on the ridgeline several hundred feet above us.

With the ridgeline to the west, the Helmand River to the east, and Taliban-controlled terrain and villages to the north, there was one way in and one way out—from the south. That was ground that we had to hold.

To this day, I have no clue why the Taliban didn't launch an all-out attack on our compound one night and take us down. They must have figured we had more troops in the valley, never knowing there were only six to eight guys and their Afghan counterparts operating out of the Alamo. Nor did they know that we were just holding ground until the planning was finished for a major assault on the valley a few months later.

During this holding pattern, the fighting was intense whenever we locked horns with the Taliban. Hours went by like seconds. Thousands of rounds were fired, and every moment was exhilarating.

When nothing was happening, however, we got bored. Seconds passed by like hours in the astonishingly hot Afghan summer sun.

One thing about bored Green Berets is that we always came up with things to do. Besides the daily task of eating and turning food into shit, we had to look for ways to occupy our time. Reading got us only so far, so we ginned up some excitement by triggering a few carefully placed shots across the valley to the trenches or ridgeline.

If we got a response or thought we had a bead on a Taliban outfit, we could call in an air strike, or close air support, which basically meant asking for U.S. military aircraft to drop some bombs on the bad guys.

I was surprised to learn how little effect this had on the enemy. The dust would clear, and just when I thought there was no way someone could have survived explosions like that, they were sending 7.62-caliber rounds right back at our heads, almost as if to say, *Is that all you got? Better pack a lunch, boys, because it's going to be a long fight.*

Maybe antagonizing the enemy because we were bored wasn't the greatest idea, but it was damn sure fun.

Even though the Taliban seemed to be immune to our air strikes, they hated the A-10 Warthog and its 30 mm cannon sticking out the nose of the aircraft. The slow, low-flying A-10 was my favorite close air support aircraft and had a distinct way of swooping in and dealing death from above. A burst from that

30 mm cannon, and the Taliban were crawling into whatever hole they could find to survive the lead rainstorm the A-10 would bring.

One night, we received a call over the radio from our Australian counterparts just down the river from us at FOB Coyote. They were on patrol and needed a place to stop and get some rest.

Hell yeah, I thought. *Visitors.* It would be great to have new faces and someone else to talk to other than my teammates. I was growing sick and tired of smelling their asses and stinky feet all day long.

The Aussies, dressed in jungle green camo, worked their way through the dense marijuana crops that I hated so much and moved up the hill toward our compound. As they approached under the cover of darkness, a full moon lit their way. A night patrol in the marijuana fields was not a place you wanted to be because the Taliban and local farmers sometimes booby-trapped the crops to keep Americans and thieves away. The booby traps could be trip wire, tilt rods, motion-initiated—the list went on and on. The Taliban would arm the IEDs around a village at night and disarm them in the morning because they knew that was when they were most vulnerable to our attacks. Luckily, everyone arrived safely.

The next day we got to talking with our new Aussie mates, and the topic of discussion was all the firepower we had at the Alamo now. This would surely take the Taliban by surprise, so how could we let it go to waste?

"Do you want to get into a fight today?" one of our guys asked the Aussie commander.

The commander was a bit taken aback by the question, but he

responded in typical Down Under fashion. "Are you kidding me? Fuck yeah, I do, mate," he said.

That's all our team sergeant, Lance, needed to hear to come up with a plan and put it into motion. We decided that we would do a quick foot patrol down by the Helmand River, which was guaranteed to cause a fight. One thing was for certain: We didn't have to walk far to hear from the Taliban.

Leaving the Alamo, we got across no-man's-land without incident and walked under the cover of the dense foliage toward the Helmand River. We had been moving for around twenty minutes when the first shots rang out.

Zip, then *crack*.

The *zip* meant the 7.62 round was close, but the *crack* meant you better get your head down and put some lead downrange because the next one could be deadly. No question about it, the Taliban had us in their sights.

After the first burst of Taliban machine-gun fire, I heard the craziest sound ever—the sounds of cheering, screaming, taunting, cussing, and all-out savage war cries coming from the Aussies.

These Australian soldiers were absolutely and intensely excited that they were in a fight and loving every minute of it. If I were the enemy, I would have turned tail and run away because of the amount of firepower we unloaded on them. It didn't take long for the Taliban to realize they were in a shit storm and needed to retreat fast.

Intercepted radio communications revealed that the Taliban fighters thought we had three hundred to five hundred soldiers on the ground and the valley was about to fall, when in reality all this action came from about forty-five really pissed Aussie and American soldiers who had talked about getting into a little fight that morning.

Once again, I experienced the adrenaline rush of combat, addictive as hell and stronger than any recreational drug. I guess in one crazy way of thinking, the Aussies were at the Alamo to get their combat high, and they sure got it that day. So did we.

Once the Taliban got tired of getting their asses kicked, they collected their wounded or dead and faded back into the villages to the north to lick their wounds. Our side got through without taking casualties, so luck was with us.

The fight was over, for at least that day.

Even though I understood and believed in the concept of VSO, most of the time it felt like I was a French Legionnaire holding on to a remote outpost in the middle of the desert. Holding ground wasn't usually a Special Forces mission, but adapting to any environment was our job, not to mention the best way to stay alive.

Green Berets, I was learning during my first few months in-country, were masters at adapting and overcoming anything the enemy could throw at us. We might not like it and might bitch a lot while doing it, but there was no one on Earth who could do it better.

During my first three months in Afghanistan, my detachment saw combat and got caught up in several intense firefights, but we didn't take any casualties. For the rest of the men of Alpha Company, 2nd Battalion, however, 2010 was proving to be one hell of a deadly deployment. Two men on a different detachment were killed in action, including one of our Air Force counterparts, and more than a dozen were wounded. Normally, a deployment to Afghanistan resulted in four or five wounded guys and maybe one fallen soldier, but our company more than doubled or tripled that amount.

One afternoon, our team leader approached me to tell me that a friend of mine named Jason had been killed in action that day in a different part of Afghanistan.

"Jason died when his vehicle hit an IED," he said. "Damn man, shit sucks. Are you going to be okay?"

I absorbed the emotional blow. "Yeah, I'm good," I said, even though my chest was closing in.

I hadn't known Jason that long, but we had gone through a large portion of Special Forces training together back at Fort Bragg. It's through training that you really get to know someone.

I knew I could always count on Jason for help. There were times when I felt like a fish out of water, coming over from the Air Force to the Army, but Jason took the time to help me whenever I got hung up on whatever part of training I was stuck with. Jason was someone I looked up to. I admired how everything was easy for him. He was smart, in great shape, a super dad to his kids, and an amazing husband to his wife. But just two months into his first deployment as a Green Beret, he was dead.

In the past, I had heard about guys from a different battalion or unit dying in Iraq or Afghanistan, but this was the first time I knew someone personally. Death in combat was not just something I saw on the news—now it was personal. Jason was my friend, and this was the ugly reality of war.

I tried my best not to think about Jason's death too much, which was difficult. I knew full well that Afghanistan was not the place to mourn the death of friends. There would be plenty of time back in the States to think about that and try to come to terms with it.

I still had a job to do—make sure no one on my team stepped on an IED—and a promise to myself to fulfill: I would do whatever it took to make sure my teammates returned to their families in one piece.

In 2010, though, Afghanistan was not getting safer, and the real fighting had yet to begin.

CHAPTER 8

FIGHT OF MY LIFE

HELMAND PROVINCE

SOUTHERN AFGHANISTAN

SEPTEMBER 2010

When summer was coming to a close, my team, along with other ODAs from our company, was tasked with entering the Chutu Valley from different locations and clearing out the Taliban to a central point, which would send the bastards running for the mountains. Working against us, however, was the fact that this was not a covert mission. Everyone up and down the valley knew we were coming, which gave the Taliban ample time to place IEDs and prepare for us.

We weren't under any illusion that our actions would completely clear out all Taliban factions anyway, or that they would come crawling to us with white flags of surrender just because we were in the house. To the best of our knowledge from all the fighting we'd done in the previous three months, there would be a lot of bad guys waiting for us. None of that mattered much at this point, though. We were ready to go and only an act of God would keep us from mounting an offensive.

Finally, it was time to push into the valley and take the fight to the enemy. The date was September 10, 2010. Each of us was carrying different equipment for the mission. Besides my body armor and M-4 rifle, I was toting a sixty-pound assault pack on my back filled with ammunition, demolition matériel, food, water, extra batteries, and whatever else I would need for three days. My average fighting weight was two hundred pounds, but with the body armor, weapons, ammo, and my assault pack, I probably tipped the scales at 280 pounds.

My plan to traverse the Helmand River and get all of our equipment across using a Zodiac amphibious beach-landing craft went off without a hitch. Once we reached our staging area, it was a waiting game.

I took a moment to look up at the moon, whose light created shadows over the river. The stars gleamed off the glistening water, and for a brief moment I almost forgot that very soon I would be facing Death and asking it to dance with me and my buddies.

While waiting to kick off the mission, each member rechecked his equipment to ensure everything was in order. Each guy reviewed the plans for entering the first village on our list, named Sar Tutu, and plans for best-case and worst-case scenarios.

During our final pre-mission checks, I had time to let my mind wander.

What will be waiting for us out there?

Do they know we're coming?

How hard will it be to find the IEDs?

How will I react when the bullets start flying?

All these questions plagued my mind as I lay there watching

the river flow in the light of the moon until it disappeared into the darkness.

This seemed like a good moment to take out a small pad of paper from my assault pack and write a quick note for my family in case the worst happened:

Dad, Wendy, Paula, Chris, and Robbie,

I hope I made you proud. If you're reading this note, I did not make it. Death doesn't really scare me because I'm doing what I believe is right and just. I guess that's really all you can ask from a man.

Death comes to everyone at some point in life, so there's no use fighting it. When it's your time, it's your time, and there is nothing you can do about it. I believe I lived as good of a life as possible, and I'm asking you not to stay sad very long. Very soon you all will be joining me in heaven, and we will again be together. I'll keep the beer cold for you all. I love you.

Ryan

I don't know why I chose to write this note. Maybe it was the fact that I was a new guy and had no clue what would happen on my first patrol far from the Alamo. Maybe I had seen too many war movies and figured this was a good idea. Maybe deep down I really believed that this mission was destined to have a terrible outcome.

Whatever the reason, I chose to write down exactly what I felt at that moment because I wanted my family to hear from me one last time if the worst happened. I folded the note, placed it in a

Ziploc bag so it wouldn't get damaged if it got wet, and stuck it in my right front uniform pocket where, God willing, someone would find it and pass the letter along to my family.

———

So there I was, outside the compound, urging Nick to follow me back to the group and away from the uncleared ground. I retreated slowly, making sure I had my M-4 ready to rock in case someone in the compound opened fire on us. My eyes were sweeping the compound as well as looking where I placed my feet. I took one slow step after another when—

—BOOM!

A deafening explosion pounded my eardrums at the same instant as a hot, searing brighter-than-midday flash of light enveloped me. The blast shattered the silence across the valley, sending birds into the sky as they flapped their wings and screeched. The concussive explosion knocked me to the ground like a blindside hit from a linebacker.

In an instant, I landed on my back just outside the compound entrance. The foul, ammonia-smelling air clogged my lungs and choked my breathing. I instinctively rubbed the grit from my eyes and waited for the dust to settle, trying as hard as I could to breathe. But I could only manage the barest of breaths. As I fought for air, a yellow-brown cloud swirled around me. I couldn't see my hands in front of my face because of all the dust in the air.

I shook my head and yawned a couple times, trying to squelch the high-pitched ringing in my ears, but that didn't work. Then I opened my mouth to scream for Nick, wanting to make sure he was okay, but nothing came out. The thickness of the dust, mixed with the overwhelming smell of ammonia in the saturated air, made it impossible to yell or take a full gulp of air.

I'm not sure what just happened, but if I don't get fresh air I will suffocate and die.

In those first few disorienting moments, I didn't feel any pain, so I had to be okay.

I tried to stand, but then I fell back over in a heap.

Damn.

I tried again, but I couldn't stand up. What the fuck!

What's happening to me?

I was having trouble thinking clearly. Then a moment or two later, I suddenly realized what happened: I had stepped on an IED.

Now what?

The dust was still thick, and I was sucking in dirty air. Both of my eyes were watery, but I was regaining my sight, which allowed me to regain my bearings. As my mind clicked back on, I had the presence of mind to do an inventory of my limbs.

First, I checked my hands by clenching a fist. Good news. Both hands worked. Then I counted the fingers on my hands: 1, 2, 3, 4, 5, 6, 7, 8, 9, 10. Ten digits, attached to two hands, attached to two arms, attached to my shoulders.

So far so good.

Wait a minute. How come I wasn't getting some help? How come no one was coming to help me? Then my training kicked in: If an IED goes off in your vicinity and a buddy goes down, *do not* run to his aid. The reason for this was elementary: If one IED goes off, most likely there are more in the surrounding area.

I suddenly became aware of the pain. It was slowly creeping in, like a snake squeezing its victim to death. I reached down for my left leg and wiggled it. The leg was still there—bloody, but still there.

When I tried to move my right leg, however, the pain was unbearable. Waving the sand and dust away with my hands to get a better view, I could see that my right combat boot was bent at a weird ninety-degree angle. It was like my combat boot made a T at the end of my leg.

It didn't seem possible that my leather boot could be twisted like that, so I grabbed my right leg behind my knee and lifted the leg to get a better look. As I raised my right leg up a tad, my right foot flopped off to the side of my leg.

Oh shit. The only thing connecting my foot to my leg was stringy, bloody red muscle tissue and ragged skin. What was more disturbing was seeing stark white bones poking out of my leg. I was amazed at how glistening white they were in contrast to my bloody leg.

Oh God, this was bad.

"I'm hit, I'm hit, I'm hit!"

This time the words poured out of me like a gusher.

My mind went on autopilot and I recalled my training again: Apply a tourniquet to stem the bleeding until my team could safely reach me.

I somehow managed to find the tourniquet in my body armor, but I couldn't muster up the strength to wrap the tourniquet around my lower right leg.

I looked down and saw bright red blood leaking out of my stump where my leg had been minutes before. *You're bleeding too fast*, I thought. *If you don't put on a tourniquet, you're going to die.*

I felt helpless as reality set in. What had happened was a lot worse than I expected. An IED had nearly blown my foot off, which hung at the end of my leg. The bloody mass of muscle tissues, lacerated skin, and pearly-white bones poking out of my leg nearly caused me to faint.

Despite the bloody gore, I was having difficulty believing what had just happened to me. I reached over and moved my foot in an attempt to align what was left of the appendage with the stump at the end of my leg. The incredible pain was too much to handle, however. It felt like someone was jabbing a hot poker into my flesh while smashing my bones with a hammer; on a scale of 1 to 10, I was at a full 20. I had never experienced pain like that before in my life.

I distracted my mind from the searing pain by hoping that if I aligned my boot with my leg, then I would somehow magically wake up from this nightmare all in one piece.

But the reality was staring me in the face—my right foot was nearly blown off and hanging by a thread. One thing was for sure: I had stepped on an IED and I might not survive. Thinking of my mortality scared me shitless.

Nick, our interpreter, was lying on the ground about twenty feet away. The blast had thrown him to the ground, but he didn't seem to be seriously wounded. He wasn't moving, though, either because he was unable or unwilling to risk stepping on another IED in the area. I saw cuts on his face and arms from the blast, but something told me he was going to be okay.

Just then I heard Team Sergeant Lance yell, "Don't move, Ryan."

"Where the fuck do you think I'm going?" I screamed back at him in my pain.

Of course, I knew we had been trained to limit movement

after an explosion due to secondary IEDs, but I also knew that many IED strikes were followed by an ambush. The Taliban had learned some nasty tricks and loved to use them. *That* was why no one came to my immediate aid.

I was going into shock. I stopped and tried a second time to apply the tourniquet but was unsuccessful. I couldn't summon the strength to do anything because I was losing so much blood. Then I heard Lance yell, "Medic!" I knew the medic was farther down in the village. Why Lance didn't use the radio I will never know, but he might have been in shock from what he had seen.

The seconds stretched by like hours. I had never been in so much pain or felt so alone; it was like I was the only person in that village. I lay on my side in the dirt, waiting for the bright light everyone says you see before you die. Lance was the closest American to me, but I knew he couldn't rush to my aid because I had walked right into an IED-filled area. Chances were that he would be next, and then what?

In that moment, it was impossible to think clearly. *This is it. I'm going to die in this shithole village in Afghanistan.*

As I lay there for what seemed like hours, I prayed harder than I had in years. This was serious; I felt like I was on the cusp of eternity. I'd always heard there were no atheists in foxholes, and I guessed they were right. I was a Christian who had accepted Jesus Christ into my heart years ago, but I had strayed from the path of righteousness since then, to say the least. Nonetheless, I made my peace with God and figured He understood.

The mistakes I had made in my life came back to me, but so did the things I had done right. I asked for forgiveness for my sins and for the people I had hurt. In the state of mind I was in, I felt this could be my last chance to make things right.

Suddenly, I felt a calm come over me that I couldn't explain. The pain lessened as I felt like I was fading into a deep sleep. I thought of some of the good times I had had in life. Fourth of July barbecues with loved ones, watching the fireworks without a care in the world. Traveling around the world and all the amazing experiences that brought me. But most of all, I was thinking about my family and how much, at that moment, I missed them.

I hoped I made my family proud. But I also felt a strong sense of nagging guilt from letting my team down. No Green Beret wants that to happen, but it did. I fought back tears because I felt like I had failed my team.

Five minutes or so after stepping on the IED, I knew I was hanging on for dear life. I could feel myself slipping away. I'd heard many say that your life flashes before your eyes just before you go, but that wasn't happening. I didn't know if that was a good thing or a bad thing.

"Stay awake!" Lance yelled. "Don't pass out, Ryan! We're moving!"

I nodded, but it was all fading. I imagined what it would be like reading my own obituary:

Staff Sgt. Ryan Hendrickson, 32, assigned to Alpha Company, 2nd Battalion, 7th Special Forces Group based at Fort Bragg, North Carolina, was killed by an improvised explosive device while on combat patrol in the village of Sar Tutu, Chutu Valley, Helmand Province, Afghanistan.

SSG Hendrickson, a 7th Special Forces Green Beret with extensive training and nearly twelve years of military experience, is survived by his father, brother, and three sisters.

And so it would go. I knew they'd print my Army photo alongside the obit. I'd be in my dress uniform, positioned in front of an American flag, staring into the camera lens like a true warrior with a shit-eating grin on my face. We called those pictures—which, by regulation, every soldier must take—"death photos" since everyone knew the only time anyone would ever see them would be after your demise on the battlefield.

I didn't want my "death photo" to be published. I wanted to live.

I fought to stay conscious. I could hear my team close by, or maybe they were around me, but God almighty, I was feeling tired. Losing all that blood and slowly dying was freakin' exhausting.

I lay on my back, and my team surrounded me as they worked to save my life. I watched a hawk circling above me in the azure sky full of daylight. It reminded me of lazy summer days when I was a kid growing up in Oregon, hanging out at the lake with my friends.

The thought warmed me and helped me escape to a place where I wasn't fighting for my life. It was peaceful. I was at peace. I thought of my past and wondered about my future.

I took a couple of deep breaths and closed my eyes.

I felt a sharp slap across my face. And another. And another. Each one harder than the last.

What the fuck!

I opened my eyes and found myself still lying in the dirt of this pissant village in the Chutu Valley. My teammate Jorge screamed, "Stay awake! Ryan, keep your eyes open!"

The pain shooting up my right leg was very intense. It felt like my foot was stuck in a hot bed of coals while someone with a handsaw slowly sliced through my leg.

I felt myself losing consciousness again when Jorge's hand quickly connected with my face.

THWACK!

Okay, okay. I got the message.

I opened my eyes, wanting nothing more than to slug Jorge as hard as I could, especially if that would make the excruciating pain go away. But I couldn't summon the strength or the will. I couldn't do much of anything.

I forced myself to take a series of deep, slow breaths. The smell of burned flesh mixed with blood and dust was potent in the air. Slowly, things came into focus as I started cutting through the fog of war long enough to realize that Jorge had risked his life and limbs by running through a field of hidden IEDs to come to my aid.

Most people want to believe that soldiers in battle are fighting to protect lofty ideals of patriotism, our nation, and the American way of life. All of this is partly true; in fact, every soldier takes an oath to protect and defend the U.S. Constitution against all enemies, foreign or domestic. In reality, though, soldiers on the battlefield are fighting to protect their fellow brothers in arms. It's difficult to explain the incredible bond between those who've experienced the horrors of warfare together. Only in combat will one ever witness the true meaning of brotherhood and what a man will do to ensure his teammate goes home to his wife and kids, even if that means he will never see his own family again.

Jorge stayed by my side, encouraging me, keeping me awake while trying his best to keep my body in line and stable in case I had spine damage. The rest of the team quickly established security and cleared a narrow pathway through the field of IEDs. They did this so they could move me out of the area and away from any possible Taliban small-arms fire to a selected landing zone (LZ), where I'd be extracted by a Medevac Black Hawk helicopter.

The pain was so intense. I needed a morphine shot and a fentanyl lollipop, which was an opioid analgesic. Every Special Forces operator carries them in their individual medical kits.

During World War II, GIs were given morphine syrettes— a small device for injecting liquefied morphine through a needle, similar to a syringe except that it had a closed flexible tube (like a toothpaste container) instead of a typical rigid tube and piston—with their medical kits. We had basically the same thing along with fentanyl lollipops, tourniquets, gauze, and ACE wrap bandages.

The key with the fentanyl lollipop is to stick it under your tongue and let it do its work. Well, in the disoriented state of mind I was in, I chewed up the lollipop the instant our medic gave it to me, which basically made it useless. At the same time that I was gnawing on the fentanyl lollipop, my medic administered a morphine shot. The second he hit me with that morphine needle, I broke out in hives all over my thigh—a clear sign that I was allergic to morphine. A helluva time to find that out.

This meant I had no painkillers in my body at a time when I needed meds desperately. But the medic couldn't give me any other painkiller without taking a chance of something even worse happening to me. Meanwhile, my body was crying out for some sort of relief from its suffering.

My medic did have an array of flexible splints for broken arms, legs, and ankles at his disposal, but there was nothing for a nearly severed foot. My buddy Shane, one of the two medics on the team, stepped in and fashioned a splint using the buttstock of my M-4 and carefully placed my just-about-detached foot—which was still hanging at a ninety-degree angle—in line with my shattered leg.

Shane wrapped the whole bloody mess in field bandages. It was the best he could do, and it wasn't perfect by any means, but his ministrations did help to reduce the pain a bit.

After stabilizing me to get me ready to move, it was time to get out of there. Another buddy, Kyle, who was a strong dude, lifted me up and hefted me over his left shoulder—the fireman's carry. Then he started hustling me toward the LZ we picked, figuring it was the safest place to establish a Medevac pickup. The number of IEDs in the area as well as the threat of the Taliban shooting down the helicopter made it impossible for a helicopter to land where I was injured.

Kyle couldn't move fast because of his body armor and gear, along with carrying a two hundred-pound man over his shoulder. Since the LZ was a long way, more than five hundred meters—or the length of five football fields—the team took turns carrying me while keeping security high. The Taliban knew I was hit because our Afghan interpreter monitoring their radio traffic could hear them celebrating and laughing about hitting me.

With each jolt from being carried, however, I don't know who cursed more: the guy who kept complaining how heavy I was, or me because I was feeling a sharp, piercing pain from every rock and bump he hit. Not only was my leg killing me, but I had taken shrapnel right in my nuts—*and that was painful!* Each time I bounced, my scrotum took the full frontal brunt of his shoulder grinding into my lacerated sack.

After what seemed like an eternity, we finally made it to the LZ. Kyle carried me last and carefully put me on the ground as we waited for the extraction. I didn't know where the hell I was going, but I didn't care. All I cared about was ending the throbbing stabs of pain from my dangling foot and my balls.

Someone please stop the pain.

My team immediately set up defensive positions at the LZ in case the Taliban got ambitious and used the situation to hit us at our most vulnerable point. Evacuating casualties always created a perfect opportunity for the enemy to use the chaotic situation to move on our position and ambush us.

The team was amped up and ready for anything; they were taking no chances as their eyes scanned the horizon. Time passed by slowly until we heard the familiar *THUMP-THUMP-THUMP* of the titanium-core Black Hawk rotor blades beating the air into submission.

The Black Hawk came in so damn hot and fast that I could feel the ground vibrating underneath me. At the last possible moment, the chopper pulled up, spun around 180 degrees, and softly landed no more than twenty feet from where I lay in the dirt. Sand and rocks kicked up from the Black Hawk's rotor wash, but I didn't care. I was grateful that I was leaving that shithole village.

I knew things would move rapidly now. I was quickly loaded onto the floor of the helicopter with my medic and the crew chief hanging on to me.

The huge twin General Electric T700 engines revved up with their distinctive ear-piercing screams, and we were suddenly airborne, leaving the rest of my team in the distance. As I looked out, I could see my buddies getting smaller the farther away we flew. I couldn't escape that overwhelming feeling that I had let my guys down. I should have picked up that Nick wasn't in the right place or stopped him from advancing closer to the compound altogether. Now they were down a man and missing a vital position for clearing the village. What happened on the battlefield was ripping at my heart.

Lying in the back of the Black Hawk, being tossed about in every direction by stiff winds whipping down from the mountains, the actions of the flight crew were professional but sadly routine—like they had done this way too many times during their deployment. They had undoubtedly seen the faces of injured and dead U.S. soldiers on their helicopter way too often. To them, I was just another severely mangled body in what was likely another long tour of duty.

Because the side door of the Black Hawk remained open, I focused on the terrain we were flying over and not the pain in my body. As I looked down, I saw the tops of pine trees speed by along with the rocky and hilly terrain of southern Afghanistan. We were flying to Tarinkot, the first stop on the way to Kandahar Air Field (KAF).

Tarinkot, or TK as we called it, was the FOB that had a Level 1 trauma center, meaning they had the lifesaving capabilities and equipment to make sure I didn't go home in a pine box. As I looked out the window, I wondered if in the next few minutes, hours, or days anyone from my team would be joining me in the hospital. After all, there had to be a shitload of IEDs back in that village. Where there was one, there were sure to be many more.

In the cockpit, the pilots kept their heads forward, their eyes constantly shifting between their instruments and the moving ground below. Not once did they look back at the medic, the crew chief, or me. I later learned it was an unspoken rule that Medevac pilots never looked around at the horrors unfolding behind them. Their job was to fly the bird and not get emotionally involved with the severely injured, sometimes dying, soldiers they were transporting.

These pilots drove their helicopters harder than other helo jockeys in the Army. They knew they were literally in a race to save lives, and seconds counted. Conventional wisdom said that the first hour after a soldier was wounded was the most critical. If I could make it to a field hospital in less than sixty minutes, I stood a good chance of surviving, which is why this was called the Golden Hour. Every minute over sixty, though, and my odds of survival dropped precipitously. Unfortunately, in my case, the Golden Hour had passed. My team had had to carry me five hundred meters to a safe area where a helicopter could land. By now, it was probably eighty or ninety minutes since I'd taken that fateful step, but in the chaos of everything unfolding I couldn't be sure.

I could tell, though, that these Medevac pilots were pushing this helo to the max, right up to the turbine-gas limit. If they flew over that limit, even by a few degrees, the metal components in the engines would melt and another Medevac would have to be sent out to pick up the body parts.

After only a few minutes in-flight, the dim outline of TK appeared off to my left. The chopper approached the LZ at an alarming speed, but I didn't give a shit. In seconds, I felt the back wheels of the Black Hawk touch down, followed by the front wheel, in a hard but controlled landing.

I looked out the side door and saw a half-dozen soldiers, each wearing blue rubber gloves and medical scrubs, emerging from behind stout HESCO walls and crouch-sprinting to the Black Hawk. Within seconds, they maneuvered me out of the chopper and double-timed me across a small concrete tarmac toward TK's field hospital. Before I was even inside the bay doors, I heard the helicopter's engine whine; the Medevac had already been called to pick up another wounded warrior. Sadly, the crew's day was a long way from being over. I caught a glimpse of the Black Hawk lifting and making a sweeping turn toward the battlefield.

As the medical team whisked me into the forward operating trauma center on base, everything hit me: The road map of my life had changed the split second I triggered that IED.

All my goals, aspirations, and what I thought my Special Forces career would be like had changed in one step.

Now I was a wounded warrior. Whatever had happened, my life would never be the same.

Assuming I survived.

And that was still not certain.

CHAPTER 9

SEEKING SAFETY

FOB TARINKOT MEDICAL CENTER

TARINKOT, AFGHANISTAN

SEPTEMBER 12, 2010

As I was being wheeled from the helicopter to the front doors of the emergency room, several nurses rushed out to receive me. One of the standard procedures was to cut off the service member's clothes as they rushed him into the operating bay; it would be one less thing the doctors would have to do when the wounded soldier arrived. Every second counts when a life is at risk.

Little did these nurses know that I had worn my lucky Oregon Ducks T-shirt and I wasn't about to let them cut it off me without a fight. So, I fought off their attempts to run a pair of scissors through my black Duck T-shirt.

"Sir, you need to stop fighting us!" the lead nurse exclaimed. "We have to cut your clothes off, and that means your shirt too."

"This is my lucky shirt. Please don't cut it!" I was pissed.

"Have you seen your leg? How lucky of a shirt could it be? Sir, we don't have time for this. You need to go into surgery now!"

The head nurse had had enough. I heard her tell another RN,

"Cut the shirt off. We need to get him prepared for surgery. He's fading fast."

I suddenly felt too out of it to resist. Scissors tore into my black T-shirt as well as my camo pants. They were working away and moving me toward the hospital when I heard one of the nurses say, "We don't have much time. He's not going to make it."

Whether they were talking about my leg or my life, that didn't sound good. I didn't know how much blood I had lost, but it had to be a lot. I knew I was in bad shape, but not *this* bad. More pain ripped through my body, and I prayed for God to dull it. Mentally, I prepared myself for what could come, and if it was Death, then I was prepared to meet my Maker. I was surprised how calm that made me feel.

Martine, one of our team medics, had jumped on the Black Hawk to ensure I was taken care of until we reached TK, where he could pass me off to the doctors there. As I was being rushed to the operating room, he pinned a note on my uniform that read, "If you're reading this, you made it!"

There's something about living through a life-or-death situation that gives you a new outlook on life. I was learning a lot about myself and what was important, and it was all in real time. I resolved that in my agony, I wasn't about to let life beat me down. Shit, I was going to survive. That was my mind-set.

I don't remember much after that. Obviously, the docs put me under, and whatever they did to save my life, I'll never know. What I was told afterward is that they kept me in a medically induced coma and monitored my vital signs. Once I stabilized, I stayed in the ICU for a while. How long, I have no clue, but I was told that I took a turn for the worse and had to be wheeled right back into the operating bay, where my life was saved *again*.

Doctors put me into another medically induced coma to conduct further surgeries to stabilize me. When I woke up, there was a great sight awaiting me: my friends Dino and Calvin were sitting at my bedside. They had dropped by to give as much comfort as they could to a fellow Green Beret.

I was feeling so alone and unsure of what was going to happen to me that it was a real blessing to see my friends. Even though I was told that I had two close calls in the operating room, the fact that I had my wits about me was a good indication that I was going to make it. At the same time, though, I felt that I had let my team down, and now that I was out of the game, they would have to pick up my slack. Not being there for my buddies really bothered me. I wanted to be on the battlefield with my team, but instead I had gone and gotten myself blown the fuck up.

Then there was the unknown—my future. What would happen to me? What kind of life was I destined to have? What would it be like being a "wounded warrior"?

These were all very real and very scary questions entering my head at my weakest point. I certainly didn't feel like a warrior at that point. All it took was one wrong step for me to derail our mission and my future. But having two of my friends at my bedside was awesome. Seeing Dino's and Calvin's familiar faces was a breath of fresh air in a world turned upside down. God knew I was struggling, and when I needed friends more than ever, there sat Dino and Calvin.

Dino looked a little shook up. I knew what he was thinking: *I was supposed to be on that operation with Ryan. That could have been me. Maybe if I was there, this wouldn't have happened.* Instead, Dino had been needed somewhere else that day, so he wasn't part of that patrol. If he had been there, he could have stepped on that IED as easily as I did.

As with everything in Afghanistan, with death and destruction as part of the soundtrack of life, I knew I couldn't dwell on the what-ifs. If I did, it would drive me crazy. I was a fuckin' Green Beret, and I could what-if all day long and nothing would get changed. Nothing *could* get changed.

As unfair as it may seem, bad things happen to good people, just like good things happen to bad people. I had to get on with life. Every Green Beret knows that he has to face the what-ifs repeatedly in war. I could go over the possible outcomes until I was blue in the face, but the facts remained the same and couldn't be changed. Shit happens, and I got a bucket load.

Calvin was there because he was in TK getting medical supplies for his team's upcoming mission. I was the new guy in the company, and Calvin had been in Alpha Company, 2nd Battalion for a few years. He was a guy I looked up to, and I took his words as gold because he was smart and a good operator.

When Calvin said his good-byes, I had some advice: "Be careful out there." No sooner had I uttered the words than I realized that I shouldn't have reminded him to stay safe, based on the state I was in, but my words made me feel like I was stating something that mattered, like I was doing my part.

"You've got nothing to worry about." Calvin patted my shoulder. "I'll be good. When this deployment is over, I'll check up on you. We'll grab a drink."

"Sure, let's do that."

Then Calvin said one last thing to me before he walked out of the room. "Ryan, we're going to kill these motherfuckers who did this to you." There was resolve in his voice.

We never had that beer. Calvin was killed in action a couple of days later while clearing the village of Hasar. Taliban forces opened fire with a PKM—a Russian-made machine gun—and sniper fire, killing him and our Air Force combat controller, Mark.

I didn't know Calvin long, but he was there when I needed a friend the most. To this day, I will never forget what he did for me.

I was stabilized and flown to KAF. When I arrived, I went through a few more surgeries to extract more debris from my leg and continue to stabilize me for my flight to Germany. Afterward, I slobbered over myself from the pain med cocktails that I received intravenously. I'm sure I looked like a mess.

After one of those surgeries, I woke up and noticed that my colonel and sergeant major had gathered at my bedside.

"Good, he's awake," the colonel said.

I guess I was coming in and out of consciousness from all the medications I was taking.

Startled, I looked up and saw more military people filing into my room. Then a soldier walked up to my bedside, carrying a Purple Heart medal in a felt case. He stood next to the colonel.

"Attention to orders," the colonel announced. Everyone came to attention in the hospital room.

"The President of the United States of America awards the Purple Heart to Staff Sergeant Ryan Hendrickson for wounds suffered when Taliban forces attacked SSG Hendrickson's patrol with an Improvised Explosive Device." After reading through the rest of the citation, he pinned the Purple Heart to my hospital gown.

"Nurses are saying you're lucky to be here. I need you to rest now so you have the strength to recover quickly and return to the fight," the colonel said.

I had another interesting experience while laid up at the hospital on KAF. I happened to meet a Canadian Special Forces soldier who was visiting one of his guys who had been shot in the leg and lower back. He was hit on the same day as me but in a different part of the country. He was one of those injured guys the Black Hawk raced to pick up after dropping me off.

The Canadian SF guy and I had a nice soldier-to-soldier, brother-to-brother talk. The United States and Canada were allies in Afghanistan and had spilled the same blood in the same mud for years. Before this soldier left, he gave me his patch, which was the original Special Operations patch from back in World War II, when U.S. Special Forces and Canadian Special Forces started as a joint USA-Canada organization. Back then, they were known as the First Special Service Force, which were highly trained troops from both countries used to take the fight to the Germans when all other conventional troops had failed. It is now known as the U.S. Special Forces (Green Berets) and the Canadian Special Operations Forces.

A couple of days later, I was stable enough for a C-17 flight nonstop to Ramstein Air Base in Germany. With a slight jerk of my hospital bed, I was rolled out to a waiting room and readied for transport to Kandahar Air Field. I wasn't sure what lay ahead of me, but I was fairly certain I would have to undergo several more critical surgeries if I was going to keep my lower leg.

Load-in on the C-17 was very orderly. First up the back ramp were the severely wounded guys like myself. We were rolled up the ramp on gurneys and placed on cots that were hung three high and rather comfortable, but that could have been the pain meds talking. Then came the wounded guys who needed some assistance, followed by the walking wounded. Watching this all unfold from my cot was rather amusing. The organized herding of the wounded.

As soon as we were airborne, I decided to try my stand-up routine on a couple of the cute in-flight nurses.

So I'm out on patrol trying to find IEDs. My damn metal detector wasn't working, so I closed my eyes and stomped around to clear the route. Boom...found one. Mission Success.

My joke landed with a thud, but then one of the nurses smiled, which was all I was trying to do anyway. Maybe they were taking pity on me, but at least the tension in the air was cut.

Seven and a half hours of flight time passed more quickly than I thought they would. With a screech of tires and a jolted landing, I was in Germany. I'm sure the flight crew was happy— one more attempt at a joke might have resulted in an emergency landing at God knew where and a quick "See you later!"

As the loading ramp opened, I saw several buses lined up to transport us to Landstuhl Regional Medical Center, about ten kilometers south of Ramstein. After three months of breathing Afghanistan's humid, polluted air and sweating nonstop, the cool, crisp breeze of southern Germany felt like a rush. It felt damn good to be cold and not surrounded by shit-filled air particles, which seemed to land in my lungs every time I drew a deep breath in Afghanistan.

* * *

I had been to Germany many times during my military career, but this time felt different because I was fresh off the battlefields in Afghanistan. I finally felt safe when that aircraft landed, no longer in a dangerous part of the world. I could finally relax, or so I thought.

What I didn't know was that now I would have plenty of time to actually think about everything that had happened to me. I would also have time to cry over my friends who didn't make it home alive—the ones placed into coffins for the one-way flight to Dover Air Force Base in Delaware, a grim trip no one wants to take. I would have time to think about the families torn apart because of war, either because they lost a loved one or their soldier was coming home with a mangled body, never to be the same again. That was my situation as well: I knew I was never going to be the same again. As safe as I thought I was in Germany, however, my mind kept going back to the battlefield, especially when I fell asleep.

* * *

I am dead.

I'm standing on a hill, watching my family move into a valley below me.

My family is walking into a grassy field full of IEDs that's surrounded by hidden Taliban fighters.

I can see the dangers but they cannot.

I can't speak, scream, or make a move. They can't see me. All I can do is watch.

They keep walking into this field of misery, getting closer and closer to Death. They are completely unaware of the dangers ahead.

I scratch, tear, and rip at the invisible force holding me back, but as hard as I struggle and fight to get free, I can't move. All I can do is watch helplessly.

I can stop all this. I know I can save my family.

But I can't save them. I'm powerless.

One by one, they slowly advance into the field of IEDs. And one by one, their bodies are blown apart by the blast of the IEDs ripping their flesh and gutting them.

Blood and body parts fly through the air as each IED rips through their bodies, covering me with the pieces of my loved ones.

The demonized laughter of the Taliban fighters fills the air as they cut down the rest of my family with machine-gun fire.

I woke up, disoriented and sweating profusely. I was surrounded by doctors and nurses, yelling commands at each other and evaluating my situation.

What's going on? Then I saw bright red blood streaming down my arms, spattering on the white hospital sheets. What had just happened? I was bleeding everywhere. One of the nurses had a bloody nose.

This was the first of many nightmares that would visit me during my long road to recovery. The nurses told me I was tearing all the tubes out of my arms as well as ripping out my catheter. My main doctor later told me a nurse tried to restrain me, but I grabbed around her neck and started punching her.

I felt extremely embarrassed and couldn't believe I had hurt a woman. I was raised to believe that a man should never put his hands on a lady in a violent way. "Real men don't hit women," my father always said. Yet here I was—someone who'd landed some solid hits to this nurse's face, and all she was trying to do was help me.

As hours and days passed by, I was getting increasingly angry at myself. I felt like I was losing control and was on a downward spiral. I had no clue how to stop.

How could what happened in Afghanistan be affecting me in this way? I knew what I had signed up for: I was part of a Special Forces team placed into a combat zone while my country was at war. I had volunteered for a job that put me directly into harm's way. I was a Green Beret, for fuck's sake. What on God's green earth did I think would happen? I knew I ran a far higher chance of getting injured or killed than 90 percent of the rest of the U.S. military, but here I was, having nightmares and hurting a nurse who was only trying to help me. *What the fuck was wrong with me?*

I had to face the cold, hard facts. I was severely injured while doing a job in which I fully knew that I had a high chance of seeing action and being injured or killed. I had seen, firsthand, Afghan families lose a father, a mother, or young kids only to get up the next day and work the fields. They did not have the luxury of feeling sorry for themselves. Life *had* to move on for them, and they had to immediately begin rebuilding or starting over. They couldn't stay in one place for very long. For them, their daily existence was a matter of life and death.

I thought back to the time I served in Iraq in 2004 when I was in the Air Force. I met an Iraqi who was working on our base in Kirkuk, in northern Iraq. He was old and gray, and he had the scars of a person who had been through hell. I was able to talk with him one day, and he told me his story. He was in the Iraqi Army during the Iran-Iraq War for much of the 1980s. He was captured and tortured by the Iranians for two years. After the war ended in 1988 with a United Nations–brokered ceasefire, he was released back to Iraq.

Saddam Hussein, the president of Iraq, knew this Iraqi was captured by Iranian forces during the war and saw this as an act of weakness. Saddam ordered the killings of the man's father, mother, wife, and two kids as punishment for being captured and not fighting to the death. I couldn't imagine a human being acting that cruel.

Now this poor Iraqi was working to make a life for himself because, regardless of how shitty he had it, he had to press on. And here I was, lying in a hospital bed having nightmares, feeling like I got dumped on. *Who was I to feel sorry for myself?*

Shit happens to everyone. It's a part of life. But I had to figure out a way to pick myself up and move on.

One thing I had going for me was that the medical staff was extremely professional and well trained. As many times as I tried to apologize for what had happened, they would reassure me that I was not the first soldier to have a physically abusive episode and would not be the last.

"Your mind and body are going through many changes," one doctor said, "and all the medications we have you on don't help matters much. We expect events like this to happen."

I still felt ashamed for hitting a woman. As professional as these doctors and nurses were, they were not stupid. After that incident, a red warning tab was attached at the foot of my bed, which indicated that I was a violent sleeper, or something like that, and to proceed with caution.

Meanwhile, it seemed like every time I turned around, I was being wheeled back in for another surgery. One of the procedures attached a temporary X Fix, or external fixation device, on my right leg, which would keep the bones in line until I got to Brooke Army Medical Center (BAMC) at Fort Sam Houston in San Antonio, Texas. My command had decided this would be my final destination.

Somewhere along the line, I had asked to be sent to BAMC so I could be close to my friend Captain Will Lyles, who lost both his legs in an IED blast a few weeks before me. Will and I went through Special Forces training together, and we were in the same company—just on different teams. Will was on patrol in the same area as me when his team walked into a Taliban ambush. Moving about while firing at the enemy and coordinating air strikes, Will had managed to find an IED, instantly blowing his legs off. I knew what happened to Will before I left on my mission, and hearing that Will hit an IED really drilled down on me to watch out for myself—but, more important, to watch out for my team. At this point, it sure seemed like everyone in Alpha Company was getting wounded.

Meanwhile, I was fighting to keep my lower leg. Wearing an X Fix was torture. Imagine your lower leg hanging on by skin. Your tibia bone is cut in half with a four-inch gap, and your fibula, or calf bone, is nonexistent. Most of your muscle is shredded. To keep these lower-leg bones stable, you have four large metal bolts penetrating your skin and screwed into your tibia above and below the gap. The ends of the bolts stick out from the surface of your skin about three inches. Attached to the ends of the bolts is a long metal rod that fixes all the bolts in your tibia together, creating a bit of stability for transportation.

The metal bolts penetrating into my skin and screwing into my bones looked like something you'd see in a horror movie when some innocent college kid investigates a suspicious noise in the woods in the middle of the night.

But the X Fix was doing its job, even though my doctors told me that they didn't know how my lower leg was staying on. Their biggest concern was infection because if my foot, ankle, or calf started showing signs of infection, then they would have no choice: They would have to take my lower leg.

My doctors' goal was keep my lower leg attached to my body until I traveled to San Antonio, where a final decision would be made on whether I lost my lower leg or kept it. My doctors told me to hope for the best but be prepared for the worst because chances were high that they would have to amputate my lower right leg. In a strange way, I felt that if they cut off my leg, I'd be better off. What was hanging off the end of my right leg looked pretty useless to me.

After another blood transfusion and a few more surgeries, including adjustments to the X Fix on my leg, I found myself being wheeled back onto the airfield and loaded onto another C-17 for the last leg of my journey to Texas.

The treatment I received in Germany, from the doctors, nurses, and medical personnel who cared for me, all the way down to the food they served me, was top of the line. The military had come a long way since the "M*A*S*H" days of filling makeshift tents with wounded guys.

Time seemed to stand still after I was loaded on to the C-17, but just like that, we were wheels up and starting our fourteen-hour journey to San Antonio. I had no idea what lay ahead of me, but if Brooke Army Medical Center provided care half as good as the care I received in Germany, I was going to be just fine.

At least, that was what I kept telling myself.

CHAPTER 10

THE LONG ROAD BACK

BROOKE ARMY MEDICAL CENTER
FORT SAM HOUSTON, TEXAS
SEPTEMBER 2010

My eyes opened to a pair of aircraft loadmasters picking up my stretcher and slowly carrying me down the C-17's rear loading ramp. Even in the middle of the night, I could feel waves of heat rising up from the tarmac, welcoming me to Texas. I had arrived at the end of the summer and it was hot—not Afghanistan hot, but still uncomfortable.

I had made a quick stop at Walter Reed National Military Medical Center outside of Washington, DC, in Bethesda, Maryland, but that was a formality on my way to San Antonio, my final destination. As soon as my guys wheeled me off the loading ramp, a man in a crisp suit and tie intercepted me.

"Welcome to Texas," said the man, visibly tired. It was a little after midnight. "My name is Walt. Helluva wound you got there."

"You've got no idea," I grunted.

"Well, looks like you're in the right place for a leg like that. Welcome to your new home, SSG Hendrickson. Glad you made it."

With little time wasted, I was loaded into the back of an ambulance for the short drive from the airfield to BAMC. Once there, I was taken straight from the ambulance and wheeled into an operating room, where doctors and nurses were standing by to get to work.

After I woke up from my fifteenth surgery, an unexpected visitor stepped into my room, where I was resting up—my father. Somewhere between me getting blown up and getting to Germany, my dad was notified about my injuries. Seeing my father standing next to my hospital bed, a sweat-caked cowboy hat perched on his head and cow shit likely still on his boots, gave me a much-needed sense of normality and safety.

This was a major surprise. "Dad! It's good to see you."

My father gave my leg a long look, then gave me his usual tough but correct opinion. "Well, I figured if you played with fire long enough, you were going to get burnt. Looks like you stepped on a doozy. Glad you're alive, son."

From his demeanor, one would think that I had suffered little more than a scratch.

My dad didn't lean over to give me a hug, which didn't surprise me. He could be a hard guy, and I was fine with that. Handshakes were all I needed or expected from my father; anything else would have been a bit too sentimental for him—or me. His tough-guy persona had been instilled in me growing up. The only thing that mattered was that we knew we loved each other, so in my mind, it was something that didn't need to be said.

But I could tell he was moved deeply to see me. I can only imagine the thoughts flowing through his mind like a raging river while he traveled to Texas to be at my side.

Quietly, he moved over to a chair in the corner and sat down.

He was content to watch everyone coming in and out of my room for the rest of the day and throughout most of the night. For the first month of my time at BAMC, my father never left my hospital room on the seventh floor. It was like he felt a need to be there for me, observing, protecting, and taking in everything. My oldest sister, Chris, who was my half sister from Dad's first marriage, was there as well.

The Army was paying a per-diem amount per month for my dad and Chris to stay in San Antonio during the initial part of my surgeries and rehab. That was a brilliant idea because the first three months are mentally challenging for a newly wounded soldier. Who better to comfort him and get him back on the road to recovery than his family?

My doctors and health care providers were professional and down to business, but they must have all had their share of nightmarish stories. During the month of September 2010, the body count from the war in Afghanistan was high, and I was just one of many mutilated bodies they were tasked with putting back together.

It didn't take a behavioral counselor to understand that these doctors had seen more carnage than any one man or woman should ever see. One more injured soldier, one more family to comfort, one more life to see changed forever by war. This was what these medical professionals faced every day, a daunting task that they handled with genuine class, care, and professionalism.

One morning, I woke up from another medically induced coma to see a half-dozen doctors and health care providers surrounding me. I listened to their chatter, but I couldn't make heads or tails of what was going on. My dad and Chris were there, taking in the key parts I was missing—which was everything.

This outpouring of care was mind-blowing for my dad, who came home from Vietnam at a time when soldiers were literally spat upon and called "baby killers." I know the way that I was being treated made up in a small way for his lousy homecoming.

My lead doctor was Joseph Hsu, MD, an orthopedic surgeon who, upon introducing himself, was someone that I instantly knew I could get along with. Dr. Hsu—pronounced "Sue"—was a huge football fan, which I happened to be as well. His team was the LSU Tigers, and my team was the Oregon Ducks, who were undefeated and ranked number one in the BCS standings—a first in Oregon history.

I don't know if we talked more about what was going on with me or college football, but Dr. Hsu had a way of putting my mind at ease despite my world being turned upside down. The status of my right foot and leg was still uncertain. Would I lose the rest of my lower leg, or was it worth trying to keep the damn thing? Dr. Hsu never sugarcoated anything, even though at times I wished he would. I'll never forget one conversation we had:

"We have enough tissue to do a limb salvage surgery," he said. "We'll do our best to reattach your foot and lower leg, but there are no guarantees. Because your leg is in bad shape, we're giving it a 10 to 15 percent chance for success."

"And if that doesn't work—"

"We'll have to amputate. But look at the bright side. If this works, we will rewrite limb salvage medical history."

Well, that was a ray of hope. "So you think we should go ahead?"

"Yes, I do, but this will be a long, painful road. It *could* be worth it in the end. So what do you think?"

I thought for a moment. This was a big decision.

"While I still have my leg, I still have options, but the moment I have it cut off, there's no going back," I reasoned. "You've been telling me that this will be the hardest thing I've ever done but if successful, doctors will use my case to redefine limb salvage. Hell, yeah, I love a challenge. Let's do it."

I mentally played the worst-case scenario in my mind, which was that I would lose my leg and get a high-speed prosthetic limb. The best-case result, which was that I would save my leg and walk around like nothing ever happened to me, wasn't likely to happen, but it was worth a chance.

The problem with my blown-up leg was that I had lost so much muscle tissue from the blast. The bottom of my foot was blown in half, and my tibia and fibula bones had been thoroughly damaged, and chunks of my leg had been taken out during the explosion. Dr. Hsu said they would be using a lot of metal to reattach my lower leg, which at that time was something I could not fully comprehend.

Now my path was set: I was going to try to salvage my leg. This would take time and patience. Time I had plenty of; patience I did not. My life couldn't be more uncertain, and if there is one feeling a Green Beret hates, it's uncertainty. Sure, we work in the gray area sometimes, but most SF operators strive to have complete control over their lives.

Loss of control is not a good thing.

———

Living in the hospital had its ups and downs—mostly downs. As professional and caring as all my health care providers were,

I was still living in a hospital bed surrounded by wounded soldiers. Their presence reminded me that my life would never be the same.

The routine health checks made me want to hijack a wheelchair and break out of my hospital prison. Every morning at 5 a.m. I had my blood drawn, so any thoughts of sleeping in vanished. Then, at 8 a.m., the orthopedic team dropped by on their rounds to check up on me and talk about their plans for my health care. Once the decision was made to try to keep my leg, I met countless times with my orthopedic team about how that would go down and what I could expect.

Over a series of six to eight weeks, I underwent approximately fifteen different surgeries that involved everything from debridement—the removal of damaged tissue or foreign objects from a wound—to the addition of metal rods that were screwed into my bones to stabilize my damaged leg, kind of like a big birdcage around my leg. The more painful set of operations involved a series of skin grafts—taking skin from my back and my butt—to cover the exposed areas of my leg so I could begin the healing process. Each time I went under, I steeled myself for what was to come, but I was determined to do all I could to save my leg.

I learned in Special Force's Survival Course that if I was captured, small victories over the enemy were the key to keeping my sanity. Since I needed to start racking up small victories to make my time more bearable, I decided to mix things up a bit by going naked as much as possible until the nurses had all they could take.

Of course, I wasn't the first naked guy they ever saw, but my mind-set was that I really did not like wearing clothes, so I decided that I would bring a whole new meaning to the term "going commando." I'm not talking about wearing nothing under my hospital gown—I'm talking about not wearing a hospital gown at all! Of course, I would be under my sheet to spare my dad the embarrassment, but when it was time for a checkup, the sheet came off, which meant I was lying there on full display. That would break up the boredom of the day, or so I thought.

One day, while one of the nurses was checking my vitals, she stopped her examination.

"Mr. Hendrickson," she said with all earnestness, "we are trying hard to fix the thermostat in this room, but as I can see with what you have down there that it must be extremely cold in here. I will work on getting this fixed, sir!"

That was all I needed to hear. From then on, I wore a hospital gown.

Having visitors was a normal part of being a wounded guy. Some people stopped by to thank me for my service and other visitors were guys I worked with or were part of my command.

I'll never forget when my command sergeant major, whom I'll call Brian, dropped by to see me. He really set the bar high for anyone who made the effort to brighten my day. Brian happened to be from Oregon, just like me, so when he learned that we were both die-hard fans of Oregon Ducks football, we really hit it off.

One time, he walked into my hospital room and met my family, but the entire time, I noticed a big shit-eating grin on his face that said, *I know something that you don't.* After greeting my family, he walked up to my bed to get a good look at my leg while holding a plastic bag in his left hand.

"Yep, you hit an IED all right. You know what would make that leg look better?"

"No, Sergeant Major, I don't." I should have told him I made everything look good, but I wasn't as quick with the comebacks that day.

"How about an Oregon Ducks jersey signed by the entire 2010 team?"

"Are you kidding me?"

Brian reached into his bag and took out a green football jersey with the number 24 in yellow along with scribbled signatures in black Sharpie ink on the front and back.

I was stunned. I didn't know what to say for the longest time. "How the hell did you get this?" I wondered out loud. This was all I could think of after receiving such a special gift.

"You better take it before I change my mind," Brian teased. "This was hard to get, Ryan."

"No shit. Thank you."

Brian was a man of his word, and someone who put his men before himself. He understood those under his command and took the personal time to do what he could to ensure each and every man was taken care of. He was a tough leader and would crush you if you were in the wrong, but he would go to hell and back to defend any of his men.

Visiting for a couple of hours was a nice diversion from my injuries. I got to see my command team and get their perspective on what would be in my future.

One thing common among Green Berets is the willingness to do anything to get back into the fight. I was no different. Toward the end of his visit, I asked Brian the one question that had been haunting me for weeks:

"I don't know what my future holds, but I will not let this injury beat me. I fully intend on being a Green Beret and deploying again. If I can get myself healthy, will you send me back to the fight?"

Brian looked at me like I had two heads, then glanced down at my right leg. He knew what was in the heart of every Green Beret, but he had to drop some common sense on me.

"You're lucky to even be alive, Ryan. Let's figure out how to get you walking again. You've got a long road ahead of you. Relax and take it easy."

That wasn't exactly the response I was hoping for, but hell, I knew I'd be lucky to walk one day unassisted, so maybe my chances of returning to active duty as a Green Beret were a little far-fetched. All it took was one look at my blown-up leg and everyone knew this was something that just wasn't going to happen. But I wasn't giving up.

Brian had my back, but when I asked anyone in the hospital the same question, I heard something like:

It's cool you feel this way, Ryan, but you could be limping and in pain the rest of your life. Leave the fighting to the healthy young guys. You've proven yourself enough.

Before he left, my sergeant major surprised me. Brian leaned in, looked me in the eye, and made me a promise.

"Ryan, if you can get medically cleared, I will send you back to Afghanistan."

A thin smile creased my lips. In my mind, not only was I going to break new ground with salvaging my limb, but now I had a huge goal to shoot for. I knew my company was scheduled to deploy back to Afghanistan in fifteen months, so I was going to do everything in my power to be on that deployment.

———

Surprise after surprise kept coming into my hospital room.

One morning, one of the nurses asked me if I was ready to shave my beard. I had a decent one growing at the time, but I figured all good things had to come to an end. I was still in the military, and now that I was stateside, I needed to be shaved and presentable. For what, I didn't know, but it really didn't matter. I still bitched and moaned like all good soldiers do, but I followed orders.

But the timing seemed weird to me. *I must be having a visitor,* I thought. Who could be so damn important that I had to go out of my way and shave my face? *Better be the damn Pope or, better yet, Jesus.*

Turns out that neither the Pope nor Jesus dropped by my room. Instead, it was none other than Admiral Mike Mullen, the chairman of the Joint Chiefs of Staff, following up on the promise he made back at Fort Bragg.

Upon seeing him in the flesh, my first thought was, *Holy shit, the admiral followed through with what he said he was going to do. It wasn't all just talk.* This man had the leadership chops to see the troops he was sending off to war, then follow through with his promise and visit each wounded guy that came back from this deployment. That spoke volumes to his character and showed me that he actually cared about his troops—regardless of how high ranking he was, he did care.

As my dad always said, a man is only as good as his word.

A little over a month after recuperating from my series of operations, the day came when I was told that I could start using a wheelchair. That was not a ticket for me to leave the hospital, but at least I could get out of that damn bed. Hopping into a wheelchair gave me the freedom to get out of my room and wheel around the hallways. But more important, I was able to visit my buddy Will Lyles, who had both of his legs blown off by an IED. Will was still in bad shape, but we were able to talk, which raised our spirits at a time when we both really needed a lift.

I knew Will wasn't going to give up. Neither was I. Just because I had stepped on an IED didn't take away my drive or hardheadedness. My sergeant major, Brian, had given me a goal to work toward—making my first steps on my reattached leg.

Now, the fine line between "drive" and "stupidity" was very thin for me. My thinking was this: *I have all this metal holding my newly reattached leg together. Let's take this baby for a ride.*

I had wheeled myself to the seventh floor windows a few times, but today I was going to *walk* to those windows.

How bad could it be? I thought. *Worth a try.*

My dad was next to me when I told him that I was going to walk to those windows, which were no more than thirty feet away from where I was in the hallway with my wheelchair.

"You sure you want to try this? Maybe you want to get closer."

"I can make it, Dad. What's the worst that can happen?"

My father knew how headstrong I could be. "Well, I guess when you fall and bust your ass, we're already in a hospital, so give it a shot," he said.

I figured I could walk there and back before any of the nurses had a chance to yell at me. I'd had a solid twenty-eight days of rest since I was blown up, so this should be a cakewalk. Time to commence Operation Jackass.

I'm up and out of my chair. That wasn't so bad.

I'm putting my weight on my leg. Still not so bad.

Either the pain meds are really good, or this leg reattachment thing isn't as big of a deal as everyone is making it out to be.

Okay, time to take my first step.

Done. In the books. That wasn't so bad at all.

Twenty-nine more feet, and I'm at the window.

Oh, shit. I'm starting to get light-headed. I can't stop now.

I'm getting closer. But I'm getting very dizzy.

I'm pissed that it's taking so long. Now I'm getting tunnel vision.

I will make it to that fucking window.

My old high school wrestling coach always told me I was "too stupid to quit." I guess I was proving him right again.

Dad stayed a step behind me as I got closer and closer to the picture window. My vision got narrower and narrower. It felt like I was literally walking in a tiny tunnel that was getting smaller and smaller.

Still, I kept putting one foot in front of the other. I made slow but steady progress. Just as I made the window, though, it was lights out for me.

I knew I would make it to the window.

I don't think Dad caught me in time. What I do remember is

he and a couple of nurses picking me up off the floor and getting me back into my wheelchair so they could get me back in my bed. Along the way, I got a verbal ass-kicking from one of the nurses.

"What were you thinking? Are we going to have to chain you to your bed? You could have hurt yourself. Don't forget, Mr. Hendrickson, you just had a limb reattached!"

Blah, blah, blah.

But I got to that elusive window.

I grew up in a family that didn't put a lot of priority in taking pictures, mainly because my dad was a single parent. Only a handful of photos exist of me from the time I was born until I graduated from high school.

I spent my childhood in northern California and Oregon, particularly in the sleepy logging town of Lowell, Oregon, which I consider my hometown. Lowell is where I gained my confidence as a man through wrestling and football. From shoving cake down my throat at my second birthday party to being part of high-school sports teams, I would have to say that despite the cards stacked against me, I had a good childhood.

In the summer of 2010, six months after I became a Green Beret, I was deployed to Afghanistan. This would be my first deployment in the military where I would actually be on the front lines with our Afghan counterparts, clearing Improvised Explosive Devices (IEDs) and taking the fight directly to the Taliban. Also, this was my first deployment, where growing beards to better blend in with the local population was authorized.

I had many duties on my team, but my chief role while deployed was finding, removing, or detonating the number-one killer of U.S. troops—IEDs. Improvised Explosive Devices are only limited by the bomb maker's imagination, as most of the IEDs we came across were made with fertilizer; these are also known as Home Made Explosives, or HMEs. IEDs are the Taliban's weapon of choice because they can be hidden anywhere: buried in the ground, hung in trees, stashed in cooking pots, inside the carcasses of dead animals, within car trunks, next to trees—the list is endless.

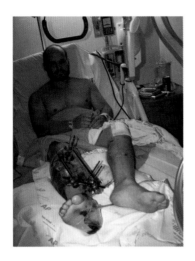

September 11, 2010, my ODA team kicked off a mission to clear Taliban forces out of the Chutu Valley along the Helmand River. During the early morning of September 12, as we approached our first village to clear, I noticed our Afghan interpreter had walked into an area that had not yet been cleared of IEDs. I moved toward the compound to rescue him when an explosion ripped through my eardrums and my world changed forever—I had stepped on an IED. Once the dust had cleared and I finally came to on the ground, I could see a lot of blood, and my right combat boot was bent at a weird ninety-degree angle. Hanging on to life, I was evacuated by helicopter from the battlefield. Once stabilized, I found myself at the Brooke Army Medical Center in San Antonio, Texas, for a long, uncertain road of recovery.

I became one of the first soldiers in a newly established Limb Salvage Program, and skilled doctors were able to successfully reattach my lower leg. Even though my right leg was hell to look at, I slowly regained my agility and ability to walk, and I was dead-set on returning to active duty and my Special Forces team. After a long rehabilitation, the Army still wanted to medically retire me. After fighting my way back and being approved to return to active duty, I rejoined my team and started deploying again. After a nine-month tour in Afghanistan, I was able to finally get to the area of the world in which 7th Special Forces Group special-izes—Central and South America. I deployed to El Salvador, Peru, and Colom-bia, where Green Berets conduct training operations with Special Operations Forces and special law enforcement groups from the host country.

After my training deployments to Central and South America, I was deployed to Afghanistan every year for up to seven months at a time from 2016 to 2019. Once again, I would find myself directly responsible for my teammates' safety while on patrol, because my job was to search for, find, and destroy IEDs. If I let my concentration wander, I or any of my fellow soldiers could lose a limb or be killed.

I served with a bunch of great guys whom I consider brothers, including (middle right, from the left) Mike, Frankie, and Brian. After a major firefight in 2016, in which I rescued several injured soldiers and recovered two bodies under withering Taliban fire, I was awarded the Silver Star, which is our nation's third-highest award for valor. My close friend Command Sergeant Major (retired) Brian Rarey was able to attend the awards ceremony at the 7th Special Forces Group compound in Florida.

In all, I have deployed five times as a Green Beret to Afghanistan, totalling over thirty-four months in combat, where I formed incredible bonds with many guys like Phil, whom I am proud to call a brother for life. No deployment would be complete unless I displayed my allegiance to my favorite NFL football team, the Seattle Seahawks. As I reflect on my military career and all of my experiences, I realize even more than ever that life can be short, unfair, unbelievably cruel, and ugly as hell. I have shed many tears thinking about my brothers who never made it home, having made the ultimate sacrifice for our great country. I will always attempt to live my life to the best of my ability while keeping their memory alive with me.

The person who has been there the most for me is my amazing wife, Dawn. She has helped me through many of my life challenges as well as a few near-death experiences. I must also acknowledge the role that my father, Larry Hendrickson, has played in my life. My dad always told me that when you come into the world, your life is a book with blank pages and it is up to you what you fill those pages with. And finally, I acknowledge my three sisters and one brother, who believe that a strong family can overcome anything life throws at you.

This (bottom right) is the only photo I have of my entire family together, taken at the wedding of my sister Chris. From the left are my nieces Lacy and Abriana, sister Wendy, sister Chris, sister Paula, niece Anisa, and nephew AJ. In the back row is my dad and my brother, Robbie.

CHAPTER 11

A SPEED BUMP IN LIFE

BROOKE ARMY MEDICAL CENTER
FORT SAM HOUSTON, TEXAS
LATE 2010

All the medication pumping through my body was taking a toll on me. One of the only drugs that dulled my pain was methadone, an opioid used to treat patients with extreme pain, and not a medication to take lightly.

The reason I needed a heavy painkiller like methadone was because I would undergo twenty-six surgeries during my rehabilitation. The doctors were doing everything they could to keep my lower leg attached to the rest of my body.

I started noticing major mood swings that I could not control. One moment I was happy and nothing could stand in my way. The next moment I couldn't stop crying, taking my anger and frustration out on my family, mainly my dad.

With two tours in Vietnam, my father knew what combat looked like. Though he'd never been shot, he had a good idea what I was going through. His patience and calm throughout my roller-coaster rehab made him a true hero in my eyes. He picked me up when I hit rock bottom, and he was a sounding board when I needed to vent. But perhaps his greatest role was not letting me travel the road of self-pity.

"Look, son," he said one time. "You got dealt a bad hand, but this is a speed bump in life, that's all. How you handle this situation and pick yourself up will determine how this affects you later. As bad as this seems right now, as dark as the times appear to be, never forget that with time, you will heal and look back on this. Please don't allow yourself to look back and feel ashamed about how you dealt with this. Take control of your life. Own this situation. Turn it into something good. Learn about yourself in a positive way, and I promise you, in the end you will be a better man."

Dad's pep talk meant the world to me. I lay in my hospital bed that night and vowed that I would *never* become a victim of life's circumstances. I would use this situation to make myself even stronger. I would face my demons, which I had held close for many years, and defeat them.

For years, I had used my difficult childhood as a crutch. After my father and my mother divorced, Dad had married two more times and always seemed to find the bad ones. I did not trust women, or really anyone for that matter, which I blamed on my past. Before I became a Green Beret, I had two failed marriages and had left a path of destruction behind me, but I found ways to rationalize my behavior. It was never my fault.

I'm this way because I grew up poor.
I'm this way because I had a shitty childhood.
I'm this way because life is not fair.

Everything was always someone or something else's fault. I did not have control of my life; life controlled me. Even though my dad had raised me right, there were some things you just had to learn on your own, the hard way. The saying "What doesn't kill you makes you stronger" seemed like the story of my life, but it didn't just happen on its own. I had to make the choice to become stronger.

That's when I determined that I would use this near-death experience to make myself a better man.

This will not beat me.

I will be the man I was raised to be.

I will take control of my life and finally be responsible for my actions.

Even with my come-to-Jesus moment, I knew life wasn't going to get any easier. As a matter of fact, the hard work was just beginning.

Throughout my more than two dozen surgeries and more medication than I care to remember, the uncertainty about whether I would keep my lower leg always hung over my head. Dr. Hsu had made it clear that the chances of my limb not responding to any number of things were still high.

Would the skin grafts take to my leg and the bottom of my foot?

Would my bones grow correctly?

Would I avoid the dreaded bone infection?

Did I have the strength and mental capability to endure the pain that I felt every day?

The pain could largely vanish after one surgery. All I had to do was tell Dr. Hsu that I was done and wanted an amputation. It would be taken care of in no time. My lower leg would be gone and most of my pain would go with it. No more skin grafts. No more enduring my doctors using the equivalent of a potato peeler to peel off my skin for skin grafts. No more metal protruding from my leg like some sort of abstract art.

All that would be over, and chances were I would heal and return to some semblance of life months or even years before this limb salvage was going to pay off. But that was too easy. That was quitting, and out of everything I had been through in life, quitting was something I just could not do.

Before I went into each surgery, I mentally prepared myself to wake up afterward and be told that my leg was gone. After each surgery, I would open my eyes and slowly look down, wondering what had happened. Each time I would see my reattached, meatloaf-looking leg still there.

Now I was in a waiting process. As week after week and month after month passed by, I started to despise my leg. The pain was constant, but something was about to rear its ugly face and hurt me deeper than even my everyday pain and struggles.

One day I was doing my normal wheelchair tour around BAMC when I was approached by a group of young, lower-enlisted soldiers.

"Do you mind if we ask you what happened?" one of them asked.

"No, I don't mind at all. I stepped on an IED in Afghanistan," I said.

Another soldier piped up. "You stepped on an IED?" he exclaimed. "Oh, wow. That must have not been that bad. You still have your leg."

That innocent comment took my breath away. I instantly broke out in a deeply enraged sweat.

Who the fuck are you to tell me it was not that bad? Do you have any clue what I've been through?

The answer was, *Of course not.* No, they didn't know the pain, suffering, and heartache I had been through and was still going through. I had nothing to say because I was fighting back tears and rage. I wheeled away in defeat and felt like I was back to square one.

Why did I care what they thought of me or what I had been through? They had never stepped in my shoes. Sure, it was an innocent comment, and they meant no harm, but once again, I felt like I had something to prove.

The IED I stepped on was over twenty pounds of explosive broken up into three cells. I got lucky because only one of the cells went off, so I ate about seven or eight pounds of the IED. What would have happened to me if all three cells detonated? I'd be a memory, a pink mist in the air. But all three cells didn't go off. Just one did, so I was alive and still had my leg, which was a great thing—a medical miracle.

So why was I so angry and hurt by those comments? Perhaps that was why I found myself again weighing my decision to keep my leg and started to question everything I thought had happened on September 12, 2010.

If the blast was as bad as I remember it, why do I still have my leg?

Were they right? How could it have been that bad if I still have my leg?

Thoughts like that entered my mind like a snake slithering through the grass looking for prey. Slowly moving, then striking at my weakness.

Would I be better off without my leg?

Who would believe that I'm one of the few people to have a limb reattached?

Is reattaching a limb like this even possible?

As these thoughts continued to take over, my pride told me a prosthetic leg would be the only way people would know how close I came to dying. But why was that important to me? Why did I care? The more I cared, the madder I got and the deeper I fell back into the "poor me, why me" shit.

Get control, Ryan. You've come too far to fall back now. Those young recruits had no clue. A reattached limb—or a prosthetic leg, for that matter—was only a passing thought to them. No one cares as much as you think they do. It's time to grow up and start to look at what you have going right for you and not what is going wrong.

Before I could get control, however, I had to look at the root of my problem. Why did I care so much about what people thought of my injury? Was it a respect thing? Did I want people to know that I had danced with the devil and was still alive? Did it really matter?

Slowly, I started adapting to my new life in rehab. With each passing day, I was gaining more confidence. My determination was stronger than ever to get back on my feet. After a couple of months living in a BAMC hospital room, I healed up to the point where I could move into the hospital's hotel-like rooms in a building next door. I was so happy! The joy I felt could be loosely compared to a prisoner being released after years of being locked up. The newfound freedom gave me a sense that I was slowly getting back to a normal life.

My dad moved in with me and slept on a cot in the front room while I took the bedroom. Not only did I have to adapt to a new life in rehab, but I had to get used to being under the same roof with my father and having him take care of me like a little kid again.

I will say this: Like the true hero my father was, he accepted his new role as my caretaker without hesitation. From emptying piss buckets to helping me through my nightmares, he was a rock when my world was threatening to fall apart.

Before I left the hospital, something amazing happened during rehab: I received a totally unexpected invitation to fly to Seattle and meet the Seattle Seahawks. I was a huge football fan and the Seahawks were my favorite NFL team, so there was no way I could turn this down.

How did this happen? While I was in Afghanistan, I was emailing with a friend who had Seahawks team connections. I asked him if he could send me a Seahawks flag so I could show off my team to the local Afghans. Hell, for all they knew, I had a tasty-looking dinner on my flag and not a Seahawk, but regardless of where I was in the world, I was going to pimp my team.

After I was wounded, though, I told my buddy that if he did get his hands on a flag, not to send it to Afghanistan since I was now in San Antonio. That was when—and my buddy swears it wasn't him—Mike and Connie, who worked in the Seahawks' PR department, reached out to me.

They invited me to visit the team and take in a game, which floored me. There was no way in hell I was not going to go, regardless of my doctors' warnings about flying and all the dangers that entailed.

I was ten weeks out from stepping on an IED and trying to

rehab a newly reattached leg, so what could go wrong? That was my mind-set. The doctors were probably worrying way too much, or maybe they weren't Seahawks fans. Either way, I figured, I'd be fine. I had no clue how my newly reattached leg would hold up to flying, the change in altitude, and the change in climate, but in the end, I thought I knew best and that was that.

Dad and I boarded our flight for Seattle. I must have looked like a zombie from a new show that fall, *The Walking Dead*, because when people saw my leg, the astonishment on their faces was priceless. I had to wear sweats with the right leg cut off at the knee, so people saw everything. Disgust, confusion, and pity seemed to line everyone's faces as I passed by. I could imagine their comments.

Oh, my God. Did you see his leg?

What do you think happened?

I couldn't blame them for saying that shit. Here I was, metal rods sticking out all over, swollen leg with skin grafts that were bright red, and pus lines running down my leg from where the rods entered my skin.

I might have been blown up, but I wasn't blind.

Knowing how astonished people were, I decided to perfect my "shark bite" story. If I had to step on an IED, I was damn sure going to use this incident to tell some crazy tales.

I got the perfect opportunity on my flight from San Antonio to Seattle for my weekend with the Seahawks. I was sitting in the aisle seat. Seated next to me were two elementary school-age kids. Across the aisle were the parents and another kid.

I leaned toward the mother in the aisle seat across from me. "Have you all been on vacation?" I asked, like I was just trying to make conversation.

Her face brightened. "Well, yes. We're flying back from our trip to Florida," the mother replied.

I acted surprised, but in my mind, I knew exactly what I wanted to say. "You were on vacation in Florida? I was too. Where were you all at?"

"Destin, Florida. The beaches have the whitest sand. We go there every year."

Just then, one of her kids piped up. "Mom, did you see his leg?"

My leg wasn't hard to miss since I was still wearing the sawed-off sweat pants. My right leg looked like fresh meatloaf.

The mother quickly hissed at her son, "That's not nice. You be polite now."

"I don't mind, ma'am. Small world. I was on vacation in Destin myself. But my vacation was cut short when I was attacked by a twelve-foot, seven-hundred-pound bull shark. Nasty creature."

You should have seen the mixture of fear, panic, and *oh shit* looks across the kids' faces. The mom, too.

"Is that what happened to your leg?" one of the boys asked.

"Yes," I replied. "He bit me pretty good. Took a big chunk out of my leg."

"Mommy!" the kids cried out in unison.

The glare the mother shot me told me that she would have to go to hell and back to get the kids to go back to Destin again.

I gave her a big smile.

You're welcome.

Upon landing at Sea-Tac, the reality of seeing the Seahawks was hitting home. Mike and Connie with the Seahawks PR department let me know that along with tickets to the NFL game between the Seahawks and the Kansas City Chiefs, I would be attending practice the day before the home game.

To top it off, I'd get to see my older half brother Robbie—also from my father's first marriage—since he lived in Seattle. I hadn't seen Robbie in years, so this was going to really be a special trip. My girlfriend of two years, Dawn Biegenwald, was also flying in from Pensacola, Florida—just a few miles from Destin, ironically—to meet up with us. Dawn, who was originally from Ohio, had never been to the West Coast. I was excited to show her around my old stomping grounds.

Just one problem. In the excitement of leaving San Antonio for a trip to the land of real trees and snow-capped mountains, I forgot to bring extra pain meds. Whoops, this was going to be a long four days. I'd have to ration my painkillers correctly to make it work, but I wouldn't live at the comfort level I was used to.

On Saturday morning, we drove to the Seahawks' practice facility. Mike introduced me to players and coaches, including head coach Pete Carroll, starting quarterback Matt Hasselbeck, and running back Marshawn Lynch. One by one, the guys came over to take pictures or sign my football while shooting the breeze with my family and me.

At one point, Coach Carroll asked me about my leg. As we were making small talk, he asked an intriguing question: "If you were talking to our team before a big game, what would you say?"

Amazed by the question, I said, "Coach, I'd say this: 'You know that I'm a soldier. You're going to war with your brothers on your left and your right. Your main priority is keeping your brothers safe, whether it's the QB during a play or your buddy on patrol, like in my world. Attention to detail and doing the small things can mean the difference between stepping on an IED or not, or making a big play or not. I could have done many things differently the day I got hit, but I can tell you that what happened to me revolved a lot around attention to detail. If I have one thing to tell you, then it would be this: Become a master of the small details. Remember, the smallest things can lead to major success or catastrophic failure. Take care of the small details, and you're going to be okay.'"

I'm sure Coach Carroll was only asking to be nice, but given the chance to say something, I took the opportunity. Coach Carroll smiled. I think he knew what I said had a lot of meaning.

As part of my trip, we'd all be guests of the Seahawks during their game against the Kansas City Chiefs. Sunday was Game Day at Qwest Field. Wheeling up to the stadium, I was excited but damn there were a lot of people everywhere.

Being in uniform, in a wheelchair, I'm sure that people put two and two together and figured I was a wounded soldier. I shook hand after hand, hearing "Thank you" after "Thank you." As much as I appreciated the concern and respect being poured out to me, the warm reception wasn't necessary. At the same time, though, I realized that America had come a long way from the manner in which many Vietnam vets like my dad had been treated. At Qwest Field that day, I could feel the love that the fans had for the military.

Then Connie asked me if I wanted to be on the field for the National Anthem. I couldn't say yes fast enough. I got goose bumps as my father pushed me to the fifty-yard line. With the National Anthem being sung, and all the pageantry and an American flag nearly as big as the football field in front of me, those minutes passed by like something out of a movie.

It was all a little too much. I needed to get off the field fast.

From behind the Seahawks' bench, fans were reaching out in the first row to shake my hand and say that they were proud of the United States and what we troops were doing over in Afghanistan and Iraq.

I was getting light-headed and dizzy. When Dad pushed me back to the end zone, one of the Seahawks offensive linemen coming out of the locker room ran up and presented me a game ball. With all the hoopla, I knew I had had enough and needed to get somewhere quiet and away from the noise, if only for a moment to collect my thoughts before the opening kickoff. My dad knew it was time as well, and he pushed me into the access tunnel. It felt good to get away from the chaos.

On Monday morning, Dad and I said our good-byes to my brother, Robbie, and girlfriend, Dawn, and flew back to San Antonio. For me, it was back to life as an injured guy. The Seahawks had really gone out of their way to take care of my family and me, but that wasn't reality. Now it was time to get back to work at BAMC.

I had a long road of rehab in front of me, and I put myself on a timeline. I knew when my company was being deployed to Afghanistan, and I wanted to go with them, but whatever happened in between was in God's hands.

Brooke Army Medical Center had a unique facility constructed for the rehabilitation of wounded and injured soldiers. Called the Center for the Intrepid (CFI), it had the best trainers in the world. I would get to work with Jonny, Ryan, Jane, Walt, Jorge, and many others. After three long months in the hospital, it was time for me put every ounce of energy I had into my come-back.

I was relocated to permanent housing with my dad and a new addition to the team: Dawn. Following her trip to Seattle to see me, she gave up her stable life in Florida to move to San Antonio and help take care of me. Dawn had worked in the medical field since graduating from college with her master's degree in occupational therapy, so she knew her way around a rehab room. The biggest thing Dawn brought with her upon her move to San Antonio was the support of a woman who loved me.

After all the excitement in Seattle, it felt good to be work-ing out again. My physical therapists made the rehab process as enjoyable as possible. All the recreational activities helped get my mind off my reality, which I was always aware of: One bad infection or loss of skin grafts, and I could still lose my leg.

You would think that I would pace myself when it came to rehab, that I would ease into getting back to one piece. I had to let a certain amount of time pass for my surgically reattached leg to adjust to being used, right? Not Ryan Hendrickson. I hit it hard, and many times I would pass out, drop weights on myself, or throw up everywhere.

Jonny, who was my lead physical therapist, had to sit me down and explain what my limits were. He knew exactly how to get me where I was trying to go—back to combat as a Green Beret, safely and effectively. Jonny, who knew how to challenge people like me, was handpicked by the Army to help rehab wounded soldiers.

I can still hear him in my head:

Push yourself, Ryan. Keep your head in the game.

Remember what you're fighting for, Ryan. Push.

Correct your form. You're creating bad habits.

Harder, faster. One more set, Ryan. You got this.

While a lot of people told me I would be lucky to stay in the military with the severe injury I had, let alone deploy again, Jonny believed in me. He knew exactly what it would take for me to break through the mental factor of rehab. As weeks turned into months in early 2011, I continued to make outstanding gains. My team's next deployment to Afghanistan was scheduled for March 2012, just eleven months away, so there was no time to waste.

I had well-meaning officers at BAMC tell me, politely, that I had a next-to-zero chance of being deployed again, let alone walking without assistance for the rest of my life. Hearing that only drove me harder. Challenge accepted. The drive to prove people wrong kept me awake at night and hungry for my next training session. I'm thankful that not everyone was a disbeliever in my efforts to overcome this insurmountable obstacle. My trainers working with me knew if anyone could come back, I was the one who could do it.

That said, I went through some of the darkest days of my life during rehab. I can't begin to explain the pain I went through during this process, but it was a pain that had me sitting in my chair and saying, "Fuck it. I'm done. Cut this leg off."

There were days when I'd stick two pain-numbing fentanyl pops in my mouth just to get through the workout. The pain at times was so bad that I didn't know if I was going to make it. The fix was easy—amputate my leg and move on with life—but I couldn't bring myself to say yes to amputation because I wasn't going to back down from a challenge.

My entire life had been a challenge. When the doctors said

there was a less than 15 percent chance of success, I knew the odds were way against me, but I had two choices: quit or get stronger. I was not going to quit, so I got stronger at a record pace.

Progress was quick—much quicker than I thought possible. The harder I worked, the faster I recovered. My physical therapists gave me the nickname "the Wolverine" because of how fast I was healing. I was grateful that my skin grafts took right away with zero complications and without infection. At one point, I could feel that those monitoring my progress were coming around. The ones who were saying that I didn't have a chance to return to active duty had changed their tune. Now they were saying that this soldier from a farm town in Oregon might actually make it.

I saw firsthand how the military really went above and beyond to take care of their wounded troops, both physically and mentally. After the Seattle trip, I attended the famous Army-Navy football game in Philadelphia with my dad, watched a college basketball game on the deck of the USS *Carl Vinson* aircraft carrier in San Diego Bay (President Barack Obama, a big basketball fan, was watching from courtside), and was able to go on a Wounded Warrior cruise in the Caribbean with other banged-up guys from Special Forces. On a separate trip, I went scuba diving with Dawn and other wounded guys at the island of Bonaire off the coast of Venezuela, courtesy of the military.

I don't know if it was because of the mistakes made with our Vietnam veterans, but one thing was for sure: No injured soldier went to San Antonio and felt alone. From the military community in Alamo City to the world-class staff at BAMC, I was taken care of 100 percent. They gave me my life back.

I'm grateful that I ended up with a first-rate doctor in Dr. Hsu, had great physical therapists like Jonny, and scores of caring health care providers who were there with me through everything—my highs, lows, and everything in between. I had two Special Operations Care advisors, Jane and Walt, who took care of everything. My counselor Jorge talked me off the ledge when I was at my darkest hour.

One of the people who had a major impact on my comeback was a prosthetist at CFI named Ryan Blanck, who had invented a new adaptive leg called an IDEO (Intrepid Dynamic Exoskeletal Orthosis) brace, which was being tested about the time I hit my IED. The IDEO brace was a second chance for severely damaged legs that in the past would have been amputated with no questions asked.

This new carbon-fiber brace basically gave me a new calf *and* foot while helping with the debilitating chronic pain of traumatic lower leg injuries. The three-piece device fit into my shoe, and the upper and lower sections were joined by a carbon support bar. The revolutionary device used a strut that ran parallel to the calf muscle, connecting a cuff at my right knee to a custom-formed plate underneath what was left of my right foot. It was like getting a new ankle and calf.

I was among the first handful of soldiers to be outfitted by Ryan with an IDEO. I felt like one of the luckiest sons of bitches on this Earth because with an IDEO attached to my right lower leg, I saw a path to active duty again.

And that was what I wanted more than anything.

CHAPTER 12

NEXT STEPS

BROOKE ARMY MEDICAL CENTER
FORT SAM HOUSTON, TEXAS
MID-2011

The Army wanted to medically retire me. After all, I was damaged goods in the eyes of many, a casualty of war.

I knew what my superiors were thinking: *Not your fault, Ryan. You did all you could and fought the good fight. Be grateful you still got a leg.*

I didn't blame them for feeling that way. My right leg was hell to look at, and while I was regaining my agility and ability to walk, I would never be a gazelle on the battlefield again.

The best I could do, if I wanted to remain in the Army, was to seek a Continuation on Active Duty (COAD) waiver. In situations like mine, the Army would sometimes find the wounded warrior some type of desk job until he could retire after twenty years in the military and receive a decent pension. This was done with guys like me because the Army had spent so much money on training—over a million dollars per Green Beret—so they wanted to get all they could out of you. The door-kicking would be left to the young, healthy guys.

As far as I was concerned, a COAD waiver was one of the ways that the Army showed guys like me that they really took care of their troops. The brass was providing a path to continue my military service and not just shit-can me because I was no longer of use to them out in the field. But after receiving a COAD approval, I'd be given a permanent "dead man's profile," meaning I was doomed to write reports and shuffle papers for the remainder of my time in the Army. My best-case scenario was that I would be assigned to Fort Bragg, where I could train the next generation of soldiers.

In practical terms, here's what getting a COAD meant to me:

- No wearing body armor
- No running
- No push-ups
- No sit-ups
- No wearing combat boots for more than eight hours a day
- No carrying weights heavier than thirty pounds if I could not tolerate it
- No deploying
- Blah, blah, blah, blah

The list was a long one.

All of this could be overridden with a 7th Special Forces Group (SFG) waiver in which they said they took full responsibility for my health and that I could return to active duty with no restrictions. Their sign-off meant they had checked me out head to toe and believed I was 100 percent ready to do everything my dead man's profile said I couldn't do. Before that could happen, however, I had to prove myself to the people I actually worked for—not some guy sitting at a desk in DC who would never meet me in person.

I found out that the 7th SFG had a program specifically for wounded guys to get back into the fight—a program called THOR III. Almost instantly after I returned to 7th SFG, I was entered into the program and started working with a team of top-notch specialists dedicated to returning wounded guys to the fight. This program was for wounded and injured guys, but I was not your normal injured guy. I was a mess, and it would take a lot of hard work to get me where I wanted to be, a challenge taken with arms wide open by the staff. I learned that if I got the good-to-go nod from 7th SFG physical therapists and strength and conditioning coaches like Paul and Dana, the command team would take their word as gold.

Now it was time for me to impress someone else with what I could do, messed-up leg or not. Getting back in fighting shape became a way of life for me. Nothing had ever been easy for me, so I viewed this as one more time when I would have to dig deep and do what I did best—kick some ass.

Working directly with Paul to strengthen myself—not just weight lifting strong but becoming all-around operator strong—was a different kind of fitness that I had not experienced before. Paul had many years of experience helping guys like me return to the fight in top physical shape.

Dana, on the other hand, was a hybrid between a physical therapist and an occupational therapist, and she was highly educated in both disciplines. If there was anything and everything wrong with you, she would find it, expose it, and put you on the right track to healing whatever the issue was.

They put me on an intense strength-training program with everything from bench presses, squats, and dead lifts to vigorous exercises with heavy ropes to develop full-body muscularity. It wasn't just strength they were after but all-around fitness. Between the series of mobility drills that took my muscles, tendons, and joints through their full range of motion to all the exercises to strengthen my core muscles, Paul beat me into fighting shape while I worked my ass off.

My fitness soared until I was almost as good as new—at least, what the height of my potential had become after the blast. Despite the limitations my lower leg gave me, I could still move well. I would never be the same man I was before, but I started outdoing guys at the gym who had no injuries, which amazed my PTs.

After a few months of working with the THOR III program, building up my body and rehabbing my sore right leg, impressing my PTs with how far I had come, my command gave me some great news: I was good to deploy. When 7th SFG said it would take full responsibility for me, my waiver was signed.

I was jacked. From the moment I got the word from Brian that if I could get healthy enough he would send me back, I had only one goal in my head—to return to combat. This was why I put in all the hard work. I didn't want to be cooped up in some cubicle, reading reports and looking at the clock, counting down the hours until I could call it a day. I wanted to be conducting missions with the guys, doing what I was trained to do—taking the fight to the enemy.

My company had already left for Afghanistan, but once I got the medical waiver signed by the 7th Group lead surgeon, I was on the next flight out in April 2012. I would be deployed to the Panjwai District in Kandahar Province in Southern Afghanistan. Known as the birthplace of the Taliban, times couldn't have been tenser in the area.

After landing in Kandahar, I was back on a team just like Brian had promised. I was determined to do everything in my power not to blow my second chance. I figured that what I had done to rehab myself made it easy for the higher-ups to say yes to me returning to war, but I wondered if the guys on my team and in my company had a different opinion.

When I stepped off the ramp of that C-17 for my second time in Afghanistan, the all-too-familiar smell of sewage, burning trash, and aircraft fuel filled my nostrils. I was accompanied by my buddy Mike Valcq, who we called Valcq because of the number of guys named Mike in the company. I had gone through a part of the Q Course with Valcq, and he was the type of guy who could get along with anyone and everyone. You would have to be a real asshole for Valcq not to like you.

Waiting there to greet me at Kandahar's Camp Brown was none other than Brian, my command sergeant major.

"See, Ryan, I told you I would get you back here," he said, patting me on the back. "You're going to have your hands full because I'm sending you back to your old team. They are in a shithole and need your help. Hope you're ready."

My company sergeant major (SGM), however, was not as happy that I was heading out to a team. Already I was seeing the different opinions that guys in my company had about my return. I was asked to drop by his office and check in with him.

"Ryan, how are you?" he asked. I could sense concern in his demeanor.

I kept everything official. "I'm great, Sergeant Major. Long flight, but doing well."

"Well, this wasn't my call. I wanted you at the company level because of your injury, but I've been directed to send you back out to your old team. You sure your leg is up for this?"

Whether my leg was ready or not, I nodded my head. "SGM, I'm good to go."

The SGM grimaced. "I sure hope so, because where you're going, lives will depend on it."

I understood where he was coming from. I wasn't quite sure how to take that conversation, but I had to respect his opinion. My SGM knew full well that eighteen months had passed since I was nearly killed in an IED strike and underwent an experimental surgery to reattach my lower leg. Now I was being sent to the most IED'd part of country. Yeah, I could see his hesitation.

Nothing got easier for me. Once my helicopter landed at my new home, Fire Base Talukan, I wasn't greeted by my team as warmly as I thought I'd be. A lot of the guys I was with in 2010 had changed out, but the core group comprising the team was still there. The same guys who saw what I had gone through and knew how bad my injuries were had questions—I could see them written all over their faces. I understood that there would be reservations, but that didn't make my return any easier.

Once I toted my stuff into the team's compound, one of the medics, Martine, who had helped save my life in 2010, walked up to me.

"Ryan, I got to say, I'm surprised you're back. Are you sure your leg can hold up to the mission out here? We are in the most dangerous part of Afghanistan, so you better be ready."

"I'm good to go, man. I was tested hard back at 7th Group's THOR III just to be able to deploy."

I didn't mind what he said. He had every right to be cautious about me being sent back to the team.

My answer satisfied him for the moment. "Then welcome back, man."

That was the nicest questioning I would receive. Some of the other guys didn't sugarcoat their feelings, but I understood their concerns about whether I'd be a liability on the team. Why was *I* sent to them, and not someone with two good legs?

They also had to be wondering if I could hold my own or would hold them back.

I didn't begrudge anyone for feeling this way. Let's be real: Not a lot of guys make it back from an IED blast. One of the hotheads of the team had to put his two cents in shortly after my arrival. I was still trying to move my bags into my hooch when he cornered me.

"You have something to prove, Ryan? Is that why you're back?"

I was thinking about the best way to respond to that when he let me have it with the other barrel.

"You think coming out here will close any doors for you? Make you feel better about yourself? Help you come to any conclusions in life? I mean, I'm glad you are alive, but I don't agree with you being out here. No offense, but you should not be out in the Panjwai. You being here could put our team in a bad situation."

Damn. Talk about a lonely feeling. After my first few days in Afghanistan, this was shaping up to be a long deployment. About half the guys were not accepting of the fact I was there. I can't say I blame any of them. I totally understood why anyone would think I had no business being out there.

Just as I was starting to feel like I had made a huge mistake, Todd, my new team sergeant, came up to me and introduced himself.

"Hi Ryan. Welcome to the team, brother. Glad you're here. We can really use your help."

Todd had no idea how much I needed that reassurance. It gave me a new perspective. I was ready to go.

After that, I saw my buddy Tommy, who had served in the company with me previously.

"Holy shit, bro. You're on this team," I said.

"Yeah, brother. What are you doing here?" he asked.

"I got sent out here by Sergeant Major."

"Good. We need your help with all the IEDs out here. We only have one 18C, so you will get your work in. The infantry dudes in the camp have been getting torn to shreds by IEDs. Having you out here is critical."

Okay, I guess I'm not going to be as much of an outcast as I thought.

Time to get to work and prove myself to the guys.

I didn't have to wait long. We immediately geared up for a mission. This would be my first test. If I failed, the tone would be set for the entire deployment. I was well aware that first impressions last the longest.

Panjwai was a hotbed for insurgents with plenty of freedom of movement because of recent events that created an international firestorm. A couple of weeks earlier, on March 11, Staff Sergeant Robert Bales had murdered seventeen civilians in a village a little less than five kilometers from where I was stationed. Newspaper accounts called it "the Panjwai Massacre." Though this was an unprecedented act by one troubled man, once the locals had zero trust in the U.S government, they saw the Taliban as a better option than getting murdered in their beds at night by U.S. soldiers.

If that wasn't enough to get everyone uptight, IEDs were everywhere, with the Taliban putting more in the ground daily. As good of an 18C operator as I thought I was, this deployment could send me home in a body bag if I wasn't careful.

To combat the increase of IEDs, we would have to take routes so difficult to navigate that even the Taliban would not dream of planting IEDs in them, or paths through farmland where crops were growing. The Taliban usually didn't plant IEDs near growing crops because of the risk they posed to farmers. Even the Taliban knew it was bad business to kill off the locals.

I thought back to my first deployment to Helmand Province when we were dealing with pot fields. Now it was the fucking grape rows because grapes were a huge cash crop for the area. Was I destined to always get the nastiest parts of this country when I deployed? How about getting shipped to a hot spot with cool weather, rolling terrain, green grass, soothing streams, and beautiful lakes? I knew that wasn't going to happen. Instead, I found myself among dozens of grape rows.

It's hard to explain what grape rows in Afghanistan look like, but I'll give it my best shot. Picture hundreds of acres of mud columns, each five or six feet tall, stretching out for thousands of meters each way, all covered in grape vines. During the spring and summer, the vines are full of leaves and grapes, reminding me of when I was back in the Helmand on a patrol through marijuana fields. During the humid summers, the foliage made it nearly impossible to breathe inside the thick leafy rows.

On this patrol, identifying your targeted compound over the height of the mud columns covered with grape leaves was incredibly difficult. If we were walking at night, I constantly checked my arrow on my GPS and hoped to catch a glimpse of a compound, so I could know that we were moving in the best direction. It was very easy to get off course.

On this particular patrol, hot, sticky air surrounded every part of my body like I was in a Swedish sauna with a snowsuit on, even though we were traveling at night. My team was divided up into two different elements: as per normal routine, I was the main 18C, on point with my guys, clearing for the second element. What lay in our way was a maze of grape rows that surrounded our targeted compounds. Even though we were likely in an IED-free zone, I wasn't about to let my guard drop one bit, especially at night.

Using night vision goggles, I continued to lead my element over numerous mud walls, en route to our first objective. Each wall seemed taller than the last. Weighed down with eighty pounds of gear and weapons, my total body weight was just shy of three hundred pounds. Each labored breath felt like I was climbing a mountain with a wet sock in my mouth.

What spooked me was that it was so dark that my night vision goggles could barely cut through the endless night. I looked down from time to time at my GPS to ensure I was somewhat headed in the right direction, then put my mine detector to the ground and moved on. Moving to an objective at night is hard on its own, but when you add navigating through a rat's maze of grape rows with only one good leg, well, that was an equation for a shitty experience.

After breaking over one of the walls, I caught a glimpse of the first compound, out of several, that we were supposed to clear. *Damn, that's a long way off.* We had a certain time that we had to be positioned near each compound before we would be given the okay by higher-ups to enter. I knew we'd better not break that time hack. I needed to kick our element into high gear because we still had a lot of ground to cover.

As my element moved on, everything was good. I knew I was clearing a path free of IEDs. Even though we were rushed, we were still making good time to the objective. At least, that was what I thought until my team sergeant, Todd, broke radio silence to ask me what the fuck was going on.

"Bro, do you know where you are? Or are you taking a fucking wine tour of the Panjwai?" Todd's voice crackled in my earpiece.

Even though it wasn't easy finding my way in the maze of grape rows, I didn't want to sound like a total incompetent ass.

"Sure, of course I know where I'm going," I replied. "I'm just trying to find the easiest path for you all."

"Easiest path? You're fucking killing me, bro. Cut the bullshit. Let's get there."

"Got it." Even though I was a little turned around, which was easy inside the grape rows, I would never tell Todd that.

Now it was time to get it in gear and lead the team to the first compound. I didn't have time to try a more circuitous route because we only had ten minutes to the deadline. Fortunately, I made a couple of good decisions, and we finally emerged just south of our first objective.

Hot and drenched in sweat, I started setting up my Afghans in preparation for the clearance of the compounds. Once we got the green light, the likelihood of finding IEDs in the compound was extremely probable. It was not a matter of if we would find an IED, but when.

As the two elements gathered up, Todd walked up to my position and placed a hand on my shoulder. *Shit, I'm about to get torn into. I know he's pissed about the route I chose and how long it took to get here.*

"Ryan, you did good, man. Next time, let's just get there. I don't need a tour guide through fucking wine country. But keep it up, brother. You're doing fine."

What? That was it? That was my ass-chewing? Todd had a way of not blowing situations out of control, and even though he was one of the most athletically gifted people I'd ever met, he was extremely humble and did not let much get to him.

Todd would prove to be a great friend, especially after the shit our team was about to endure on our nine-month deployment to the most heavily IED'd area in Afghanistan during 2012.

CHAPTER 13

INTO THE MIX

PANJWAI DISTRICT

KANDAHAR PROVINCE, AFGHANISTAN

SUMMER 2012

Just before we were about to clear the first compound, my blood pressure shot up and adrenaline blasted through my veins. I did my best to control my emotions while I concentrated on waiting for the green light from my team leader, rehearsing what I needed to do in my head. This was the real deal; I was about to face my first test since my injury.

My mind flooded with what-ifs. My biggest hope was that I was ready for what lay ahead. Just like my first mission in 2010, I was plagued by fears of letting my team down and possibly missing something that could get someone hurt or killed.

One thing was for sure: Regardless of what was going on in my head at that moment, I had to put everything aside. Whether I was ready or not didn't matter at this point. I had an important job to do, which was to continue clearing a path free of IEDs for my team. I could not fail them.

I was nervous and a bit scared. A little fear is healthy before a mission, but I needed a moment or two to gather my composure. I remembered all the talks my dad and I had, and then I had a quick talk with God. Why I waited for times like this to reach out for divine intervention was beyond me. I needed strength and peace before I stepped off, and God was the only sure answer I knew.

Suddenly it hit me like a ton of bricks:

I will not die before my time. God has a plan for me and my life. Everything has been planned for my life even before I was born. Worrying about what I can't control is useless. When it's your time to go, it's just your time to go. Nothing you can do will prevent that. How you live will dictate how you are remembered.

A feeling of peace came over me. I suddenly felt completely calm and focused. God had heard my heart, and that was all I needed. So with a clear mind, I took a deep breath, lowered my metal detector, and pushed off for the first compound.

I was stepping into the unknown.

We knew full well that IEDs were everywhere in the Panjwai, and the Taliban didn't disappoint.

We were barely underway when one of my Afghan Special Forces soldiers and I detected our first IED in a partially collapsed outside wall of the first compound. There it was, buried in the dirt and surrounded by rubble from a break in the wall that was likely caused by a previous IED blast or an RPG strike: a nice little IED. All you had to do to trip this sucker was to step on the pressure plates that connected the positive wires to the negative.

Once the circuit was completed—boom! The charge went off, and your life was changed forever.

Welcome back to Afghanistan. The Taliban had figured we would take this route because it was a shortcut into the compound.

I have to admit that finding my first IED since nearly losing my life—especially a nasty one like this—produced a whole range of emotions. My heart was racing, but I had to keep it together because my team was watching.

First, I slowly pushed the dirt away, exposing the corners of the pressure plate. I steadied my hands and searched for the arming wires. When I uncovered them, I traced the wires to a battery pack hidden behind some rocks. I disconnected the power source and clamped surgical clamps to the wire.

My surgical clamps were attached to a fifty-foot nylon cord so I could get some standoff—or safe distance—before pulling out the pressure plate. After moving the team back, I got my fifty feet of standoff, then gave the cord a hard pull. The pressure plate came flying through the air. The first step was complete, but the IED was not completely disarmed.

I then attached my cord to a plastic yellow jug buried beneath the pressure plate and returned to my fifty-foot withdraw distance. After a tug-of-war match with the jug, I was finally able to yank it out of the ground. Crap! This was a fifteen-pound IED— more than enough to kill you or blow both your legs off.

How come I didn't just safely blow the IED up? That was an option I had.

Usually when I came across an IED, I exposed a part of the pressure plate to verify that it was an actual explosive. Then I would place half a block of the plastic explosive C-4 and blow it up. But we were trying to track down the IED makers in our area. I decided to disarm the IED instead of blowing it up because of the increased pressure we were getting to collect evidence, which was key to finding the culprits.

With this first IED out of the way, I breathed a deep sigh of relief. Things had gone well, and it almost felt like I knew what I was doing. Better yet, I gave my teammates a warm and fuzzy feeling about my capabilities and showed them that I could be an asset rather than a liability on the battlefield.

Why did I deal with the IED instead of directing one of our Afghan counter-IED guys to get on it? You could call me stupid or crazy, but I wanted to get some IEDs under my belt. On some missions where we were stretched thin, I wouldn't be able to rely on my Afghans. I decided to handle this one for practice, which was an idiotic and dangerous thing to do, but any 18C worth his salt would have to feel confident handling IEDs. After disarming this sucker, I received a huge confidence boost.

I'll admit that it was a nerve-racking experience to negotiate an IED, which was why, during my off time back on the FOB, I would pick the brains of the Explosive Ordnance Disposal (EOD) specialists and have them walk me through the IED practice lanes. An EOD specialist was like gold in Afghanistan. Everyone wanted one close by, but they were hard to get because of the huge demand for their services. The more I could learn from them, the better chance I had at surviving this fucking war.

Now that I had my first IED under my belt and my confidence was high, I needed to keep my composure because the Panjwai

District had a reputation as an IED haven. Throughout my deployment, we would find many IEDs during clearance missions and destroy caches used to make more. How could an area so small—compared to Afghanistan as a whole—be so full of death?

I was in Afghan hell, and leaving here with all of my extremities would be difficult. Before each mission, guys would jokingly say good-bye to their legs, but underneath the jokes, we were all scared.

What was I thinking, coming back to this place? I had defied all odds when I basically had my right leg reattached back at BAMC. What was I searching for?

Was it my insane sense of pride in serving my country that brought me back? The special camaraderie I shared with my brothers that can be forged only in war? The thrill of battle, testing myself, that adrenaline high that can only be found in combat?

I'd say that pride in my country, battlefield bonds with brothers at war, and the thrill of combat each played a part in my decision to come back. Most of all, though, I believe I was chasing a demon that had taken control of me on September 12, 2010. I guess every man needs to face his fears and demons. Mine happened to be in the jugs of explosives buried under the earth, waiting for the unsuspecting soul—and sole—to take a wrong step.

I was back in Afghanistan to detect, exploit, and destroy what had almost beat me, to prove to myself that I was better. The Taliban might have put a speed bump in my life, but they would never divert my course. When I had left this war-ravaged country, barely hanging on to life, I'd said to myself, "I'm coming back, and there is nothing you can do to stop me."

And I made it all the way back.

IED after IED, cache after cache, every time we would go out on a mission, one thing was as certain as the sun coming up in the morning—we would run into some sort of explosive device made to kill or maim us. The Taliban were getting better at hiding these deadly devices and slowly adapting to our tactics, which kept us on our toes. Not that you would ever want to get lackadaisical anywhere in Afghanistan, but the ingenuity they would use to trick us was mind-blowing—no pun intended.

During one such mission, I realized just how many explosives were actually in our little area of operation in the Panjwai. On this particular clearance operation, we figured that we'd find the usual shit—IEDs, HME (homemade explosives), and some weapons if we were lucky. Best case: We would get in a good gun fight with these bastards and punch their direct tickets to their seventy-two virgins.

The normal hard-as-hell route we took had me exhausted before we even got to our first set of compounds. Once we arrived at our setup point, we followed normal procedure: stop, organize, and wait for the green light to go.

Once I received the nod from my team sergeant to go, I started out like every other time, slowly pushing forward with my two or three Afghans, meticulously moving my metal detector side to side a few feet in front of me, eyes darting back and forth to make sure I checked everything in my path that could be an explosive device. Slowly, purposefully, my element followed behind—stopping, taking a knee, and pulling security every time my detector would sound off with a high-pitched squeal. This happened when my search coil would pass over a foreign object under the earth, indicating some sort of metal item that could be used to complete a circuit. In the world of IEDs, a positive wire was waiting for negative wire. All these explosives needed was the weight of a human body to complete the circuit, and limbs were torn off and bodies mangled.

Stopping every time my detector went off would get me nowhere fast; there was a balance that had to be struck. I had to use my eyes and my brain each time I got a hit because a piece of trash could have been buried at that spot. Afghan villages were notoriously dirty, with debris and litter strewn about. When this trash got covered by dirt, my detector was thrown into a frenzy. That was why I also had to look for any ground signs, like disturbances in the dirt, while thinking about key locations where Americans could walk. The question I kept in the back of my mind was this: *Would I put an IED there?*

When something was out of the normal, or there was an indication of a possible IED, I would thoroughly check it out. I had to. My life—and those around me—depended upon it. This was the critical art of using ground signs to locate IEDs.

What it all boiled down to was this: When in doubt, check and recheck. Time was free, but my teammates' lives were not. Clearing a path for your brothers in arms was a thinking man's game that demanded patience. As frustrating as it must have been to slow down our advances, the team respected my approach. We were multiple missions into a deployment, and everyone still had all their limbs.

On one particular operation, the day grew hotter as we checked compound after compound for evidence that the enemy was operating there. Dehydration was a killer. All the water in the world couldn't save us from our biggest enemy—the broiling Afghan summer sun. That heat lamp in the sky had no mercy and would suck you bone-dry, but all you could do was eat that shit sandwich one bite at a time and move on. Pain and discomfort were part of a Green Beret's life—you had to love it, live it, and make it your friend, because the minute you started feeling sorry for yourself, you could miss something critical that could get you or your teammate killed.

So far, there was little evidence the Taliban had been through the area. Nothing was really off-the-charts crazy about this mission. Everything looked the same as we moved through the countryside village, which was surrounded by six-foot-tall mud walls.

Then, off in the distance, at the edge of the village, one compound stood out. Most entrances into the compounds were covered by a cloth or a rug of some type, maybe some sticks tied together with string—nothing fancy. There in the distance, however, stood a dark blue metal door that had a padlock for protection.

My senses instantly kicked into overdrive. The hair on the back of my neck stood at full attention. What was behind the blue door that was so important that it needed to be locked behind a metal door, when nothing else in the village was secured?

The dark blue door was beckoning me to come closer, almost as if it was saying, *I have a secret. If you dare, come look.*

Was it a trap? Was there a string of IEDs waiting patiently under the dirt for my arrival? Or was it a compound in the Panjwai whose owner cared about home décor and got a few tips from HGTV on satellite TV? Regardless of the reason, the blue door worked. Other guys on my team noticed it, so that door had our full attention as we moved in carefully for a closer look.

Everything in the Panjwai was dangerous, so I knew there was something up with that blue door. Slowly moving forward, the mine detector attached to my arm sweeping side to side, we pushed closer. Every little thing mattered. From that piece of trash on the ground to a torn piece of cloth on a tree branch that could be marking an IED—nothing was overlooked. Closer and closer we moved to that door, waiting for an ambush, an IED strike, or whatever it was we were walking into.

But nothing happened. No IEDs found, no ambush, nothing.

Finally, we cleared up to the blue door. Now what? Was the door booby-trapped? What was behind the door? Was the compound rigged to blow once we made entry?

I motioned for our Afghans to move forward and check it out. Just as I'd seen on many similar occasions with our Afghan counterparts, common sense went out the window. The lead Afghan pulled back, and with a running start, he jumped legs-first into the blue door.

The door buckled and opened. Several Afghan soldiers ran in with their U.S.-issued M-4 rifles raised and ready to rock. In less than a minute, the Afghan IED specialist came out in a hurry, excitedly describing the discovery of a huge cache of homemade explosives. In other words, we had stumbled upon a bomb-making factory that was supplying a lot of the IEDs used against us in the area.

Stacks of yellow jugs filled with HME were waiting to be buried in the ground, some to be used as anti-personnel IEDs. Others were ready to be put in the path of a U.S. Army vehicle convoy, powerful enough to completely destroy a nineteen-ton Stryker vehicle and everyone inside. Everything the Taliban needed to spread IEDs all over the area was nicely tucked behind this one blue door.

In the back of my mind, I wondered if this was one big joke and the Taliban were watching and waiting for the right time to wipe out the entire team—or if they were really that stupid. Who would put this enormous cache of explosives hidden in the only compound with a big blue door? Whatever the reason, I was given the order to blow up everything in place.

This was going to be one fucking big explosion. How big? I wasn't sure. But one thing was certain: The entire district would know we found this cache.

My first consideration was to ensure that the team would be far enough away from the blast to stay safe. After looking around the area, I found a location that had sufficient cover and had been already cleared for IEDs.

"You guys stay here," I said. "I'm going to place the charges and level this fucker. I'll be right back."

Then I directed three Afghans to join me in placing C-4 blocks on the cache of HME we found in the building with the blue door. The C-4 was on a five-minute time system (time fuse), which was what I would use to initiate the main C-4 explosives. Five minutes was more than enough time to fall back to a safe distance.

When the C-4 was placed and my firing system was ready to go, I took one last look around. All was clear. It was time to start the five-minute countdown. I pulled the plunger on my M81 igniter, which started the black powder burn on the M700 time fuse. I hustled to safety and gave time hacks to the team. Four minutes, three minutes, two minutes, one minute, thirty seconds... *Oh shit. Here it comes.*

Fifteen seconds... 10, 9, 8, 7, 6, 5, 4, 3, 2, 1.

As a deafening explosion assaulted my ears, I felt the ground shake. The sun disappeared. What was once a bright sunny day now turned black. It was like the hand of God snatched the sun out of the sky.

Dust covered everything in sight, then came the chunks of mud-hut walls, bricks, and rocks. I hunched as close to the ground as I could as debris rained down on me like a volcano minus the hot lava. Guys were getting hit by the larger chunks of mud compound.

Holy shit! Were we going to be wiped out by blast debris? More rubble kept falling down on us. We all hunkered down and waited for the onslaught to stop its attack on our heads. Then big chunks turned into little chunks as a light mist of sand and dirt swirled in the air. The sun peeked its face through the dust cloud, which circled overhead. Finally, after a few long moments, the air started to clear, giving us time to pick ourselves off the ground.

To my surprise, everyone was okay. There were some skin abrasions and a few bruises, but no one was hurt.

"Is everyone good?" one of the guys yelled out.

"I'm good," said one.

"Still here," said another.

"Fuckin'-A, I'm okay," chimed in a team buddy.

One by one, everyone sounded off. Everyone was good.

One of the guys wasn't happy, though. "What the *fuck*, Ryan?

Bro, you could have really fucked us up!" He was yelling at the top of his lungs as he came in my direction.

"How was I supposed to know it would be that big?" I protested.

We had to find out why the explosion mimicked a two-thousand-pound bomb strike. When we returned to the explosion site, there wasn't a whole lot of building left in a fifty-foot radius. The best we could figure was that hidden under the main cache was a dug-out cellar full of HME and other IED-making materials, which caused the blast to be twice as powerful as I thought it was going to be. Looking at where the building used to be, I could clearly see where the Taliban had dug a basement-like storage unit under the main cache and filled it with more HME jugs. Very clever.

We really hit the jackpot! All those IEDs were taken off the battlefield, which made the mission a tremendous success. I felt good that I had done my part to save many limbs and lives in the coming months.

After five months in the Panjwai, I'd been on multiple missions, most of them two- or three-day movements. Much of the time I was on my feet—always sweaty, wet, and dirty.

Before I deployed, I was told that my right leg would need to be watched very closely and that the skin grafts were to be treated like newborn baby skin. The skin graft on the bottom of my foot was extremely fragile and an area where I had to be especially careful. I couldn't beat the shit out of my legs like I used to because of the risk of skin graft breakdown. On top of that, the risk of infection was high.

I listened to what my doctors had to say, but I knew that once

I got to Afghanistan, I'd revert to the way I always went through life—balls to the wall.

Later, on a different mission, we were moving toward another group of compounds that we were ordered to clear. As we got close, we started taking small arms fire from the enemy. Instinctively, I sprinted toward the nearest area with cover, which happened to be a watery ditch. I jumped in and aimed my M-4 toward the area we were taking fire from and sent rounds at the enemy. As the firing continued, I started to smell the foulest shit odor to ever hit my senses. When the firing stopped, I took a split second to look around. To my disgust, I had landed in a sewage trench. I was knee-deep in human shit and covered in crap. The stench brought tears to my eyes and made me gag.

At that moment, all that sewer shit seeped into my boots and pant legs. I knew that wasn't going to be good for my skin grafts. Once I was sure the shooting died down and the coast was clear, I hauled myself out of that effluent mess, dry-heaving as I crawled. This was bad, man. Really bad. I probably had every variation of *E. coli* in my bloodstream now. Unfortunately, we still had to finish the mission, so changing boots and clothes wouldn't be an option for many hours.

When I got back to the base just before nightfall, I couldn't wait to rip off my boots and pants. As I looked down, I could see a few hot spots that had opened up like a rose petal on my leg. I was bleeding in spots, and I knew that wasn't a good sign.

I reached out to touch one of the crimson spots. My skin was red hot and bleeding a bit but nothing too crazy. The true test of how much trouble I was in would come from the bottom of my foot, which had been healed and rehabbed through numerous skin grafts—a painful process.

I sat down and put my right leg up to inspect the bottom of my foot.

Oh, shit. This is bad.

The skin graft on the bottom of my foot—one of four sections of skin implanted on my leg and foot—had peeled back, leaving a little flap just hanging there. Staring me right in my face was the red fleshy meat of the bottom of my foot where my skin graft used to be. Raw and exposed, there was no layer of protection from the human feces I had stepped in. The floodgates for infection were wide open, and nasty bacteria had to have seeped into my bloodstream. Even I knew this was something I couldn't tough out, I needed to let our medic know what happened.

All it took was a two-second look by our medic. "Shit, this looks bad. Ryan, we have to get you to Kandahar to get checked out. Stay off your feet, man."

I had finally met my limitations. I could go no further without risking a serious infection that could possibly take my leg. The doctors were right: I had gone against their advice to stay stateside and ride a desk, and now I was paying the price. Maybe I wasn't invincible after all.

Would I have been better off if my damn leg was lopped off in the first place? Should've, would've, could've—none of that mattered at this point. I needed to get medical attention as soon as possible. Hashing over the past wasn't going to help me now.

First thing early the next day, I was on my way with all my belongings to the main U.S. military hospital at Kandahar Air Field (KAF) for an evaluation of the damage to my foot and leg. This would be a long, lonely drive because I knew my time on the team was over. Hell, I would be lucky to even stay in-country at this point.

Was all the hard work that I did in rehab with the THOR III program and at BAMC for nothing? Was all the pain, blood, sweat, and tears I gave just to get back to this point hanging in the balance? Would I be sent home on doctors' orders or be allowed to recover and stay in Afghanistan?

The answers to those questions were crucial to my future with the Green Berets. If I had to leave the country because of my infected leg, I was sure that this would be my last combat deployment.

CHAPTER 14

HILLTOP 2000

KANDAHAR AIRFIELD

KANDAHAR, AFGHANISTAN

SEPTEMBER 2012

With a million possible outcomes floating through my head, I waited for our Group doctor to give me his verdict as well as some guidance.

"So, Ryan, you took the ol' leg for a spin, and it didn't hold up for you. With new skin grafts on a reattached leg, you just had to push the limits. Well, I got some bad and good news. First the good news. I'm going to pump you full of some meds. That way, any possible infection from the raw sewage will be put in check. Then we'll have to check on your foot and leg daily to make sure you're on the mend."

Doc paused, which could only mean one thing: He was thinking about how to deliver words I didn't want to hear.

"The bad news? You won't be returning to your team. We have to monitor your leg and foot so that we don't risk further damage. There's no need to send you back to the States, however, so you can work here at KAF until we deploy back. I know you want to go back to your team, but you can still support the fight from here."

Given these circumstances, some soldiers would want a ticket home, but I knew that, with a bum leg or not, I could still be an asset. Sure, supporting the guys out there fighting was not what I envisioned for myself, but at least I had a role to play.

Another reason I preferred to stay in-country was because my paycheck would be tax-free since I was serving in a combat zone. The downside was that instead of doing the fighting, I'd be watching the operations from some unmanned drone ISR (intelligence surveillance reconnaissance) video feed, which would make me what we in Special Forces like to call a FOBIT.

"FOBIT" is a slang term for a soldier, airman, or sailor who spends his or her entire deployment on a forward operating base, or FOB, never leaving the wire once. Only a small part of the military ever leaves the wire anyway. Without the support of the troops on base, the war fighters in the field, like the Green Berets, couldn't do their jobs. If I was going to be in a support role, then I was going to make damn sure that my guys got everything and anything they needed.

I will say this, though: It was relaxing being at KAF. The stress of nonstop missions and the unrelenting pressure in the field, along with always having to prove myself because of my leg, had taken a toll on me. I felt like I always had to go above and beyond what other guys were doing to prove that I was an asset to the team and not just a mouth-breather turning food into shit.

I had friends on the team whom I could confide in, but for the most part, everyone knew I would be leaving their team after the deployment. I was only on loan because the team needed an 18C for the deployment. After we got home, my command would decide what to do with me. Because I wouldn't be staying with this team, making those close bonds that you get when you operate with the same guys for years wasn't going to happen. Since it looked like I was heading out, I didn't know what was in my future.

I had started my career in 7th SFG when I was placed on a Special Forces Dive Team, most likely because I had been a rescue swimmer in the Navy. I had been scheduled for Special Forces Dive School in Key West, Florida, after we returned from the 2010 deployment in Afghanistan, but stepping on an IED dramatically changed those plans. Anything that revolved around badass, physically challenging military schools wasn't going to happen now that I wasn't medically qualified to attend them.

This was my new reality. Regardless of how much of a badass I thought I was, my leg just couldn't hold up to some of the physical requirements needed to pass Dive School—or any other Special Forces school I might want to attend. Life was an ever-changing beast for me. Just when I thought I had this crazy life by the horns, it bucked me off, trampled me, and left me bloody and bruised. *What now?*

I sat around KAF and thought about how after the IED blast my goal in life had been to keep my leg, which I successfully did. The next box I checked was to make a comprehensive physical recovery and earn my way to the next Afghan deployment, which, again, I accomplished. While on deployment, my goal was to ensure that my entire team came home with the limbs they left with. I accomplished that.

Now I had been sidelined again. Where was I heading? Who

was Green Beret Ryan Hendrickson? After everything I'd been through, did I just seal my fate in a sewage ditch, never to see the inside of a team room again?

Day after day, my mind was once again filled with thoughts of *What if?* What if I stepped a few inches to the right or the left and missed the IED entirely? What if I hadn't charged into uncleared territory to help that Afghan? What if I had reacted differently? What if I had stayed where I was until I was *sure* the route had been cleared? What would my life be like now?

This type of thinking kept me awake night after night. The dark seeds of uncertainty and confusion seeping into my brain felt like a cancer that was slowly taking over. I knew that most people looking at my life were thinking, *Lighten up, dude. You've done a lot for your country and you're still alive, so why are you beating yourself up? Relax, Ryan. Enjoy life. At least you've still got one.*

While that was true, thinking that way also went against the drive that was instilled into me at a young age. I was wired to never settle or use the shitty circumstances in life as an excuse not to move on. If I wasn't constantly trying to better myself, push my limits, and do new things, then I was just taking up space on earth.

I could never quit pushing. It was hardwired into my brain, so I wasn't going to sit back and let life move on. I always needed a challenge, but after sitting in a sea of uncertainty at KAF, I had no direction. Something needed to change before I was left in the dust.

Pray and you shall receive.

The answer to my loss of direction came quicker than I

thought. Living up to my nickname, Wolverine, my skin grafts closed up and were healing extremely fast. Despite that welcome development, I figured there was no way my command would send me back out to a team just a month after my skin grafts had separated from my leg. But I also knew I was in Afghanistan, where anything can happen.

I was going stir-crazy being in a support role. Sure, I was resupplying the war fighters by loading helicopters at KAF with much-needed supplies that would be transported to different Special Forces teams in the battlefield, but I also knew there were guys out there who were operating and killing bad guys and living the warrior life that I wanted.

Resupply and logistics are necessary cogs in the wheel of an army, but I wanted to be back on the front lines where the action was. After a month-and-a-half break, I felt like time was passing me by. There had to be some way to get back into the fight again.

I had made two close friends while I was at KAF—Jesse and Lynette. The two were married and, as luck would have it, they were able to deploy together, which was awesome. Jesse was an easy-going guy who loved to work out as much as I did. Lynette probably hit the gym harder than Jesse and I combined. We all worked together at the Joint Operations Center, and soon we were hanging out during free time.

Having them around meant I could vent and talk out my frustrations without dealing with the typical macho, big-dick mentality. They listened and heard me out when I needed to bitch—and I did the same for them. We talked about everything, from any issues we were having to what we wanted to do when we got back to the States, and everything in between. Our friendship helped me keep my mind off things, but not getting back in the action was eating me alive. Just when I thought the war was passing me by, Jesse told me about a mission that was going down in a few weeks.

He said there was an operation in the works to climb Hilltop 2000, a steep mountain overlooking a key valley. The goal was to get our command element—comprised of the CSM (command sergeant major), battalion commander, and other supporting personnel—to this hilltop overlooking a valley that multiple units, including both Army Special Forces and Navy SEALs, were directed to clear.

The intent was to give our battalion commander and the command element a bird's-eye view of the battlefield and all the moving parts, in real time, from the lookout point. Basically, though, it was a really good reason for the command staff to get on a mission before we left Afghanistan.

Even better, Brian was the CSM on this mission. I would never forget that he left my hospital bed in San Antonio with a promise that I could return to Afghanistan if I was cleared. If I could get on this mission, we would be heading out together, and I could prove to him that he made the right decision.

The next time I saw Jesse, I told him, "I have to get on that mission. I don't care if I have to pack everyone's gear up the mountain, I want to be on that fucking mission."

I pleaded my case whenever I interacted with someone from the command team. Each time I worked a different angle of why they needed me on the mission, but I got shot down every time.

"Ryan, we need you here for the logistics, supporting the teams."

"Ryan, what if your leg gives out again?"

"Ryan, have you seen the jagged rock ledge they'll be climbing? Looks nasty."

Jesse described Hilltop 2000 as a steep trek up a mountainside with a three-thousand-foot elevation gain in a little over two kilometers. This wouldn't be a nice Saturday morning hike but a lung-bursting climb that would test even the fittest, he said.

Looking at the list of twelve people on the mission, I noticed a mixture of Green Berets and support personnel. The list included specialties from communications to joint terminal attack controller (JTAC), but one job was missing. There was no 18C or EOD (Explosive Ordnance Disposal) specialist manifested for the mission. Didn't they need someone clearing the route of IEDs? Of course they did, so I had an in. I knew I would have to make my pitch the right way.

Jesse was on board. Shit, he *wanted* me clearing the way because without a 18C on the roster, who would be on point? They needed someone to clear, but time was ticking down with that one major position to fill. I'm sure there weren't too many volunteers. Let's face it: No one likes to fuck with IEDs.

I found Matt, the first sergeant organizing the mission.

"Who's clearing the route?" I asked. When I heard what our first sergeant had to say, I would have been less surprised if Bigfoot walked up to me and handed me a case of beer.

"Looks like I'll be clearing the route because we don't have anyone else who can do it. Can you give me a few tips about using a mine detector?"

Matt knew me well and knew I was an 18C. I smiled. He had no one else to clear IEDs and wanted a tutorial on the mine detector. Just when I thought the cards were against me, an opportunity had fallen in my lap.

"First Sergeant, you know I'm an 18C, right? I've cleared a lot of IEDs and routes in this country." I said that to be a wiseass, but I tried not to act excited, even though I'm sure that it showed.

Matt looked at me. "That's right. You're an 18 Charlie. What are you doing in two weeks?"

Here was my chance to escape desk duty and loading supplies.

"I don't think I have too much going on," I casually replied. Actually, my heart was pounding out of my chest. I had a real chance to get on this mission.

"Who do you work for?" Matt asked.

I told him the name of my boss and gave him a little background on how he was always micromanaging me and probably wouldn't give me up without a fight because that would mean he would have to do the grunt work instead of me. He lacked all the qualities that make a great leader but somehow managed to find himself in that position.

"That's your boss? I know him. He's a piece of shit," Matt said. "I'll just tell him you're going and there's nothing he can do about it. Don't forget—I'm the first sergeant. Do me a favor and make sure you train someone up on what you're doing so you can be gone for five days. We don't want the resupply train to fall apart."

How in the hell did this come together for me? Forty-five days earlier, I had skin grafts hanging off my foot; now I was going on an important mission with my command team. It was amazing how things worked out. If I was still at FOB Talukan with my old team, I never would have had this opportunity. In a twisted way, my issues with my skin graft set me up for a crucial opportunity to prove myself.

Working out and staying in shape had always been a big part of my life, but three thousand feet of elevation gain in about 2K was going to be extremely difficult, even for a guy with two good legs. My attitude was that the only way I didn't make it to the top was if I were dead. If I stepped on another IED, I would grab my limbs and crawl to the summit—nothing was going to stop me. That was the shit I filled Jesse's and Lynette's ears with while we were in the gym.

In a way, this was my chance to prove what I was made of and show the brass that I was still an asset to the team and to 7th Special Forces Group. What better than to have the decision-makers in my battalion scaling Hilltop 2000 next to me?

Time to kick some ass.

Each of us was loaded down with ninety pounds of body armor, weapons, ammo, water, food, and communication equipment as we made our way to the flight line at KAF. We would be jumping on Black Hawks and flying for a little under an hour to a drop-off zone in no-man's-land. This valley area was classified as "the Belly Button."

The Belly Button was surrounded by multiple mountains including Hilltop 2000, the steepest and highest. This ring of foothills and mountaintops created a bowl—hence its name. According to intelligence, the Taliban had placed a lot of IEDs throughout the Belly Button because this valley was frequently used by Taliban forces to move drugs and weapons.

By taking Hilltop 2000, we'd have the high ground, but to get there, we would have to climb every step of the way. The helicopters would drop us off just outside of the Belly Button so that we would be far enough away from the villages to not compromise our position.

As the rotor blades spun up on the UH-60 Black Hawks, I could feel my anticipation rise. My heart beat fast with excitement. Not only was I getting out on another mission, but I was part of a high-profile one. It wasn't every day that you had a command sergeant major, a battalion commander, a battalion first sergeant, and other high-ranking personnel along on a mission.

This operation would be watched by every ISR aircraft available, supplying real-time movements to the Joint Operations Center at KAF. Since the top leadership in my battalion was climbing Hilltop 2000, every general at KAF would be watching it unfold.

"Load up!"

The command was given, and it was time to go. The moon decided to stay indoors that night, making it pitch-black outside. We would be climbing up a hellishly steep incline that was as dark as being in a room with no windows and all the lights turned off.

Slowly, the helicopters taxied one by one. Suddenly the engines let out a high-pitched scream and we lifted off. We were on our way.

The pilots flew low over the terrain, banking left and right and moving up and down as the land unfolded in front of their night vision devices. I sat nearest to the side door, which was kept open, so I could see that we were flying low. I thought it would only take one lucky shot for some shithead to ruin our day. Next to me was a door gunner who tilted his machine gun left and right out the door, looking for possible threats. His thumbs were ready to spray holy hell down on anyone dumb enough to take a shot at us.

As I sat back watching the terrain fly by under my NVGs, I was thinking through the various threats that we could possibly face on infil. Taking small arms fire or stepping on IEDs was always a threat in Afghanistan. If we took fire upon landing, we would need to exit the helicopter quickly so the bird could get elevation and engage the threat. The most dangerous part of helicopter operations was always the landings and takeoffs, when the aircraft was the most vulnerable.

I also mentally reviewed the plan for encountering IEDs once we stepped off the Black Hawks. We had rehearsed repeatedly the motions of dismounting the birds, sweeping the area for IEDs, getting some distance from the helicopter, and laying prone with weapons out, ready to rock. When the Black Hawks took off, everyone would pause while still pulling security, looking and listening for anything that could be a threat.

This would be the time when stepping on an IED was most likely. The Taliban knew that in areas where they operated a lot, we would eventually send troops to hit them. Because of this awareness, they planted IEDs in the areas that the Americans would most likely land with a helicopter or arrive by vehicle.

Working through all the situations in my mind made the time fly by as we sped toward the LZ. I could war-game all I wanted, but the fact was no one knew what we would encounter when we landed. When I finished running through my mental checklist, I was ready to land this bird, get on the ground, and start moving.

"Ten minutes," I heard one of the pilots say into my headpiece. The countdown started. When I heard "Five minutes," I could feel the adrenaline surging through my veins. At "One minute," I was ready to go.

I saw the ground approaching fast. Game time. The Black Hawk came to a hover, then set its wheels down. I had my weapon, rucksack, and mine detector in hand when I flung myself off the bird as quickly as I could.

Getting a little distance away from the helo, I hit the ground and got prone with my weapon ready to go, pulling security for the rest of the guys getting off. Within seconds, everyone dismounted the helicopter, and with a violent blast of wind and debris from the rotor blades, the two Black Hawks lifted off and were airborne. Just seconds before it had sounded like I was standing in the middle of a tornado, but now it was quiet. The noise of helicopters flying into the night quickly faded and was replaced by absolute silence.

As my ears started to adjust, I heard the faint sound of dogs barking, as if to warn the Taliban that the Americans were here. All my senses were in overdrive. What was I seeing, hearing, and smelling? This was Afghanistan, so everything was out of the ordinary for an American, but was there anything out there that was a direct threat to us?

After a good three to five minutes lying prone and getting our bearings, the silence was broken. Over the radio, Brian said, "Okay, we waited long enough. Let's get going." I stood up and took my position in the front. My mine detector was out, my night vision goggles were focused, and we were on our way.

The helicopters had landed about five hundred meters from the base of where we were to start our ascent of Hilltop 2000. It was dark, but daylight would be coming soon, so we needed to be well on our way up this rock fortress before the sun came up. No one wanted to be caught out in the open. We had pushed off twenty-four hours before the main clearance element would start their mission in the Belly Button. Except for our air assets above, we were all alone.

Under my NVGs, I looked up and spotted the summit of the Hilltop. *How in the hell are we going to make it to the top of that?* Climbing this sucker seemed to be an impossible task, but this was the chance to impress my command that I had been waiting for.

Step after step, though, I could feel the elevation getting steeper. Before long I started breathing hard. This was going to be a long day. I was slightly relieved when I spotted a goat trail heading up the hill. The path was mostly rock, so this would be our way up. The Taliban were very good at hiding IEDs, but I had yet to see one buried in solid rock.

As I labored to keep pressing up the mountain—while searching for IEDs—I recalled how our forefathers in the First Special Service Force made a name for themselves during World War II when they defeated a heavily fortified German position in the Italian mountains at a place called Monte la Difensa. Their mission was to climb up an almost vertical escarpment because it was the best way to approach the entrenched Germans without being noticed.

In doing this, the First Special Service Force—made up of American and Canadian operators—hoped to catch the Germans off guard, assault their positions, and take the mountain defenses, which had the entire U.S. Fifth Army at a standstill. After five days of intense fighting with heavy casualties, the First Special Service Forces were able to clear the "gatepost" dominating the Mignano Gap, allowing the Fifth Army a route through the Liri Valley and on to Rome in December 1943.

Our hilltop was nowhere near the herculean task that had been handed to the First Special Service Forces, but it still sucked. During one of our breaks, I jokingly thought, *Why do Special Forces guys like to climb so much?* Regardless of how much my body screamed at me, I was happy to be right where I was, slowly but surely making my way to the top. I was handed this chance to prove myself, and I was kicking this hill in the ass.

The movement was exhausting and seemed impossible at times, but I had no choice. Since we were in enemy-held territory, giving up was not an option—or so I thought. We were halfway up the hill when the first rays of daylight peeked over the horizon, giving me a spectacular view of the valley below. Despite this land being such a shithole, Mother Nature was still able to shed some beauty on it.

We had made a lot of ground and were far enough up the mountain that I thought the Taliban would have to deploy billy goats to track us down. After another break, though, we were picking up our gear to get moving when I heard someone say, "I can't go anymore."

What? This had to be a joke. We were in enemy territory, and besides, no one quits on a mission. And if you quit, where are you going to go? There was no reset button here, no pause on the game we were playing. This was real war, and people die.

I looked back to see who had said he was done. I saw one

of our SOT-A attachments—who I will leave unnamed—sitting with his head in his hands, rucksack and weapon on the ground. I moved to his position to find out what was going on.

"Bro, what's up?" I asked.

"I can't go any farther. My ruck is too heavy. I didn't know it would be this steep of a climb."

"Dude, you can't quit here. We all have heavy equipment, and we have to make it to the top."

"I can't. My legs are done."

Shit, this was not good. Just then our Battalion commander came over.

"What's the issue?" he asked.

"Sir, I can't go anymore. My legs gave out."

"Okay, we will cross load your equipment and carry it up. Can you at least carry your body armor and weapon?"

"Yes, sir, I think I can."

Holy shit. You think you can? This guy just showed how weak he was to the Battalion commander. Not a good move on his part. I understand being so smoked that you don't think you can take another step, but your mind quits way before your body is exhausted. During training, I would feed off other people's weakness and willingness to quit so easily. In a crazy way, it made me feel all that much stronger. But this was combat. The weak should have been weeded out already.

We learned what our bodies were capable of in Special Forces training, but this guy was not a Green Beret. He was part of the signals intelligence–electronic warfare support element for Special Forces A-teams. I'd worked in the past with strong SOT-A guys who held their own in the field, but this guy was not one of them. I couldn't expect that he knew how to push past his mental barriers, but this also gave me a chance to show the team what I could do: I was still going strong with only one good leg. If I had to lug some of his shit to the top of the mountain to show the command element what I was capable of doing, then that is what I'd do.

"I'll carry some of his equipment," I said.

Legs don't fail me now, I thought. Jesse and a couple of other guys pitched in as well.

I could see the top as we continued to climb in the morning sunshine. I was starting to regret carrying some of this guy's equipment, but I picked up an energy boost when I realized how close we were to the summit.

I had no clue why this particular mountain was called Hilltop 2000, but we were about to make it to the top after more than ten hours of exhausting climbing. Throughout our climb, we had to cross load not just one but *two* support guys' equipment. The second guy did not quit, but he cramped up so bad that we had no choice but to carry his gear. Like we always say in the Army, hydrate or die. Jesse, Brian, a few other SF guys, and I divided up his equipment and made it happen.

Finally, we reached the summit. I wanted to throw all my gear down and give my body some time to recover from the shock I had put it through, but getting to the top was only the start of the mission. Now it was time to get to work. With my body tightening up in muscles I didn't even know I had, I knew I was running on empty. I needed to replenish my body quickly and get to work on setting up our observation post (OP).

OP was a military way of describing a position high above

the battlefield where our command element could watch what happened below. This OP was in a perfect position to look down on an area that would be crawling with U.S Special Operations troops in less than twenty-four hours. Security positions were set, communications equipment was checked, and we established our battle rhythm. Now, a little downtime—which meant grabbing some chow.

Military Meals Ready to Eat (MREs) can be pretty decent chow, especially if you can heat them up, but even cold, this would be the best food I would eat in years. My body was screaming for replenishment, and it would come in the form of a self-contained individual field ration used by the military for troops in training or deployed environments. While MREs weren't the greatest eats, they were way better than what the guys got fed in the Vietnam War and earlier.

When I got off my feet, though, I could feel my right leg swelling. I was not moving, which meant the blood was not moving. I didn't dare take off my IDEO brace and compression sleeve. I figured the minute I took off my brace I would lose the stability I had, thanks to two titanium rods. The compression sleeve kept my leg tight and compacted, but also gave me the added benefit of not being able to see if any damage had been done to my skin grafts. I figured that what I didn't know wouldn't hurt me.

Playing the game and looking like I was ready to go at the drop of a dime was my way of showing my command that I could hold my own. In reality, though, my leg was screaming at me after I stopped to take a break. The pain became so intense that I wasn't sure if I had broken bones in my foot or my ankle, but as long as I kept my IDEO brace on, I thought I was good. I knew sometime during the next three days that I would have to take it off to clean my skin grafts, but until that happened, I just hoped for the best.

The day passed, and now it was our first night up at the OP. I had a little time to lay my head down before my guard shift—a much-needed two-hour nap. Waking me up with a slight shake, Jesse let me know it was my turn for guard duty. It was still dark, but the sun would be rising soon as morning crept in. I crawled out from under my thin weatherproof blanket, dreading the moment I put weight on my leg. I had removed my IEDO brace, but I had kept my compression sleeve on throughout the night and wasn't sure how my leg would fare after two hours of sleep.

I stood up, favoring my left leg while slowly putting weight on my right. So far everything was good to go. Yes, my leg hurt, and yes, it had been put to the test the day prior, but to my surprise, the pain was not as severe as I anticipated it to be. When I put some weight on my right leg and walked around a bit, I expected a sharp, stabbing pain that would bring me to my knees, but that didn't happen. I was shocked.

During guard shift, I took a brief moment to check over my leg and foot. I took off my compression sleeve, not sure what I would be looking at. Would I see the same raw hamburger mess that my leg looked like just two months prior? Under red-lens light, I slowly inspected my leg. Inch after inch, I felt for hot spots and liquid seeping from my skin grafts. Nothing. Each time I did a swipe of my leg, my hand came back dry. How was that possible—not a single hot spot on my leg? I was amazed and greatly relieved.

As the sun peeked over the horizon, I knew that the mission

would begin within a few hours. I had never witnessed a battle from this vantage point before. Reports of many Taliban fighters and hundreds of IEDs made me uncertain of what exactly would unfold today. Our job was to keep a close eye on the valley below, watching for any threats that would put our guys in danger as they cleared the area.

The valley was quiet—too quiet. Did the Taliban know we were coming and flee? Did they hear our helicopters land the previous night, go into hiding, and fade into the civilian population? Every now and then, we would see villagers moving about, doing their daily routine, but nothing was a threat. How could this be?

In the midafternoon, I spotted dust clouds on the horizon. Our air assets relayed that it was the different Special Operations elements moving into the valley. The mission was kicking off. As the dust clouds drew closer to the Belly Button, though, we still saw no movement. No one was running in fear of the approaching Americans, and no one was running to fighting positions to engage the incoming troops. Nothing was out of the ordinary.

Did the Taliban have a major counterattack planned and were still hiding in tunnels, waiting for the Americans to get close before springing their assault? All we could do was wait, watch, and report anything suspicious.

The first U.S. element entered the valley and stopped short of the initial set of compounds they were to clear. Within a few minutes the next element was in place as well.

Minutes passed. Still nothing—no shots, no explosions, nothing. Things stayed that way for a while. As the day dragged on, I could hear a few blasts from U.S. troops blowing up a small cache of IED-making material, but in the end the Belly Button would turn out to be a dry hole. The Taliban must have caught wind of the mission and fled days or weeks before, leaving only traces of evidence that they'd ever been in the area. We stayed another night to observe any movements after the mission in the valley, but nothing changed.

The day arrived for us to pack up and head down the mountain. Before we departed the summit, we snapped a few pictures of the group with an American flag that I kept folded in my body armor. The flag was stained with mud, dust, and sweat from all the missions I had taken it on since 2010.

We left in the afternoon with plenty of sunshine for the steepest part of the climb down, but late enough that it would be dark before we hit the valley floor. The helicopters couldn't pick us up until after dark, and we didn't want to be exposed in the valley during the day. All other elements had left the Belly Button, so we were on our own again.

By all measures, it had been a successful mission. We were sure the valley had been cleared of the Taliban. But we would find out that going *down* the mountain could be harder than climbing up. The loose rock and steep incline made the trek to the valley floor treacherous. Some of the guys slipped and fell, tearing their uniforms and boots.

Each step down the mountain was a gamble. I didn't want to be the guy who stepped on a loose pile of rocks and fell on my ass and took out a bunch of other guys like a bowling ball knocking down a set of pins. While I concentrated on not slipping and sliding, I heard the same guy who quit on the way up bitch and moan every step of the way down.

"Who picked this fuckin' route?" he asked. "I can't wait until we get off this shithole mountain. Why the fuck did we even have to climb it in the first place? No one was even here."

I had had enough of his whining. I stopped and headed straight for him, then grabbed him by the front of his body armor.

"Dude, you're making a fool of yourself in front of the commander and sergeant major. Is this really the way you want them to remember you? You don't think we all are hurting? You know what the difference is?"

"No," he replied.

"We don't have any option but to keep moving. Crying won't change that. Force yourself to keep your emotions inside. Use the pain and discomfort to make you stronger. Man the fuck up. You have no fucking choice but to make it down the mountain. Last thing, dude: Embrace the suck!"

I'm not sure if I got through to him, but the whining stopped.

We made it down faster than we thought we would, but walking down a steep grade for five hours worked different muscles in my legs and back, which left me just as exhausted as the climb up. Once we were on level ground, it took me a little bit to get my balance back. We had made good time, but that also meant we would have to wait three hours for our ride home. The first thing we did was set up a security perimeter and let the wait begin.

After darkness swallowed up the light of day, we conducted one last inventory of everything we brought to the mission to ensure that we left nothing behind. All good.

When I heard the faint sound of the helicopters coming in, my heart quickened. Soon we would be going back to the safety of the base.

Louder and louder, the familiar *whopp whopp* of the rotor blades from the helicopter drew closer. The distinct sound was comforting—the sound of freedom. When the helicopters swooped in overhead, the wind turbulence blew dust, dirt, and debris violently as we hunkered down and waited for the wheels to touch down.

We loaded up quickly and lifted off from the ground. As our chopper rose into the Afghan darkness, I took one more glance at Hilltop 2000, this time dimly lit by a small sliver of moonlight.

I will never forget that place. I proved myself on that physically demanding mission. Hilltop 2000 likely saved my Special Forces career.

CHAPTER 15

AREA OF RESPONSIBILITY

7TH SPECIAL FORCES GROUP

EGLIN AIR FORCE BASE

FLORIDA PANHANDLE

FALL 2012

The rest of my 2012 tour in Afghanistan was uneventful, which was a good thing. After returning to our base at Eglin, we had a few weeks to reintegrate, then took a small break for leave.

While back in Florida, I learned about our next assignment: my new team, 7216, was slated to go to El Salvador.

El Salvador?

Even though I had been deployed twice to Afghanistan, 7th Special Forces Group's main Area of Responsibility (AOR) was Central America and South America. This may sound confusing, but all Special Forces Groups in the Army, whether it was 1st Group, 3rd Group, 5th Group, 7th Group, or 10th Group, sent guys to Afghanistan and Iraq for combat rotations. In addition, each Group was responsible for deploying troops for missions in their respective areas of the world, and ours happened to be

Central and South America. This meant I had to be prepared for a deployment south of our border.

I was ready for any challenge after stepping on an IED and earning my way back to the battlefield. I had only been to Afghanistan as a member of Special Forces, so in a way I had yet to actually experience the part of the world where 7th Group specialized. Each 7th Group operator was fluent or highly conversant in Spanish and trained tirelessly in preparation for each team's deployments down south to conduct Joint Combined Exchange Training (JCET) programs.

Basically, 7th Group ODAs conducted JCETs in Central and South America as an opportunity for us and for the Special Operations Forces of the country where we were deployed to work, train, and learn from each other, which also helped us maintain strong relationships in the region. Through our training and mentorship, we ensured that our allies in 7th Group's AOR sustained a capable Special Operations Force to combat mutual enemies.

Traveling to El Salvador would be a new part of the world for me. Cabo San Lucas, at the southern tip of Baja California, was the farthest south I had been before this, so I was excited to go.

El Salvador is a Central American country bordered by Guatemala to the north, Honduras to the east, and Nicaragua to the south. The country was plagued by gang violence. The brutal MS-13 criminal gang has its talons dug deep into the country, causing instability throughout the major cities and in the countryside. They took advantage of a populace that was still trying to recover from a civil war that had lasted from 1980 to 1992, killing around seventy-five thousand people. The violence between left-wing guerrillas and the military-led government paved the way for the rise of street gangs in El Sal, mainly MS-13.

Our team house was located at one of the El Salvadorian military bases in Ilopango, a city of one hundred thousand that happened to be right in the heart of MS-13 territory. Some nights I could hear gunshots and tires squealing—signs that different gangs were fighting for turf on the gritty streets surrounding the military base and throughout the city.

Although U.S. forces were never a direct target, one would question why we lived so close to the front lines of a gang war. Not that I minded; life went on for me regardless of the fierce crime and grinding poverty riddling the country. Despite the troubled streets, I ended up having a great time and was able to experience the El Salvadorian culture firsthand and improve my Spanish during my two short back-to-back deployments.

On my first deployment, I traveled with a different team in our company to fill the void of the 18C they were missing. Then I returned to the States and went right back to El Sal with my team—7216.

Our group was not sending ODA teams to different Central and South American countries just to sit around and look good. Actually, a deployment down south was quite the opposite of a vacation. There was important work and training to do, so getting out to see the sights and experience the country while we were there was a small bonus for the job we were doing. Everything, however, took a back seat to training in-country military and police units that the U.S. government was investing time and money in.

A prime example was during my first trip to El Salvador when our team was tasked with training El Sal's counter-gang and drug units, mainly the Comando Especial Anti-Terrorista

(Special Counter-Terrorism Command). Afghanistan and Iraq were always front-page news back in the States, but the media never reported on how U.S. Special Forces were fighting a "hidden" war on drugs south of our border. Central and South American countries were historically known for the production and distribution of addictive street drugs throughout the world but mainly in the United States. To stem the pipeline, the U.S. government decided to bring Special Forces into the equation to help combat this epidemic dating back to the 1970s. This was where 7th SFG would shine.

The drug and gang situation was out of control at the time, so the El Sal government had its hands full conducting military and police operations nonstop. Because of this, the training we provided came in handy for our counterparts. One of the best parts of training and advising these units was that, at times, we would get to help.

Once I was approached by an El Salvadorian first sergeant, who was our direct link to the guys we were training. He pointed out a Ford F-250 that had been sitting in front of our team house for a few weeks. The Ford truck had been confiscated from drug runners. As a matter of course, if weapons or vehicles were seized from drug cartels or gangs during a raid or bust, they would be taken to the base or moved to a disposal yard.

"You got enough demolition to blow the truck up?" the first sergeant asked.

"Damn, you mean this nice truck? Why?" I responded.

"It was used by drug cartels, and I've been given orders to destroy it."

Sounded like a good enough reason to me. "Say no more. We'll get rid of it for you."

We drove the truck to the firing range—hell, it was in good enough shape that I would have driven it back home—and said our last prayers for the F-250, which I knew was minutes away from destruction. The truck would be scrap metal by the time Tyler, my 18C counterpart and close friend, and I were finished with it.

We placed charge after charge of C-4 on different parts in and around the vehicle to get the biggest bang for our buck. Once everyone was clear, we initiated the charge and witnessed a tremendous explosion, watching this Ford F-250 disintegrate into little pieces of metal, just like in the movies. By the time we were finished, all that was left of the truck could fit in a trash can.

These were times when I really loved my job.

Not everything on a down-south deployment was as much fun as blowing up a nice F-250 caught in a drug bust, but I certainly found every moment to be extremely rewarding. After training hard with our counterparts, we took advantage of our free time to experience the local culture. From the excellent food—the pork, cheese, and bean pupusas were my favorite—to the friendly people and the sights, smells, and sounds around us, there never seemed to be enough off days to take it all in. Two highlights were visiting the capital city of San Salvador and a Mayan ruin in the countryside.

About halfway through my second trip to El Salvador, during the summer, our team decided to go on a trip. We had been training hard with our counterparts, and we needed to relax and unwind. The guys thought we should do something simple like sightseeing in the countryside, visiting some other ruins, heading to the beach, or hitting the city—anything to relax.

The plan proposed to the team by our team sergeant was a relaxing hike up a small volcano nearby that overlooked Lake Ilopango, a freshwater lake occupying a crater formed by a volcanic eruption in the sixth century. I was told that Lake Ilopango was El Salvador's version of Crater Lake in southern Oregon, so I was up for a hike to a mountaintop overlooking an emerald-blue lake that was roughly a third bigger than Crater Lake.

Without doing any research on how hard or long the hike would be, we all agreed that our team sergeant had a great idea. The views had to be amazing, and besides, how hard could the hike really be when it was supposed to be short and scenic?

After fifteen minutes on the trail, sweat streaming out of every pore on my body, I realized this was going to be anything but easy. Thick clouds of mosquitos and flies circled my head, waiting for the opportunity to dive-bomb into my mouth. I was breathing so hard that I was sucking for every gasp of air I could get.

The gnats made it their personal mission to dig their way into my eyes as I watched every step I took on the jagged rock path that made its way up the volcano. *Nice relaxing hike, my ass.* I was dying. Step after step, I could feel gallons of water draining from my pores.

The locals who passed us on the trail—which shows you what good shape they were in—looked at us *Americanos* with curiosity and amazement. We must have been quite the show—a bunch of rugged guys soaked in sweat, sucking for air and cussing every step of the way as they effortlessly passed us. *We better be able to see heaven when we reach the top of this shitty hike*, I thought.

I didn't see anything celestial, but I wasn't disappointed with the incredible view from the top of the volcano. Looking beyond the lake to what seemed to be the entirety of El Sal, I could see the lush jungle blanketing the landscape, giving way to smaller cities dotted around the capital.

In the distance, no matter which direction I looked, I could see other volcanos towering high into the sky with a skirt of jungle canopy surrounding their bases—thick, lush, and green. Below us was Lake Ilopango, where we had conducted water training with our El Sal partner force earlier in the deployment. This bird's-eye view of the country was well worth the death march up the mountain.

After returning from El Salvador, our team had some much-needed downtime in Florida. Being in my own bed again was nice. Even though the Army does its best to keep soldiers at home with their families, Special Forces is a different beast. In an average year, when you add up time spent on the road for various schools, training, and deployments, I would say the normal SF soldier is gone seven to eight months a year, if not more. It's hard to have a family or keep a relationship going under those circumstances—though not impossible.

I was still dating Dawn, whom I had met in September 2008 while going through Airborne. We were making the most of our time when I was home, but often I felt like I was just passing through.

Just about the time I got comfortable in my own bed, I was back at it again, heading somewhere halfway around the globe. It wasn't a bad life, but I knew that always being gone could run a relationship through the wringer.

That said, whenever I felt I was getting into a day-to-day routine at home, I got bored and was ready to deploy again. One thing all my travels around the world did was make it impossible for me to sit long in one place. I needed adventure and excitement, and there was nothing better than being part of a Special Forces team.

My next trip—this one to Colombia—came at a perfect time because I was going stir-crazy. Nothing better to shake things up than to go on a one-month training trip to Colombia. This time, the tables would be turned: We wouldn't be training forces in a South American country—the Colombian Special Forces soldiers would be training us.

Over three weeks, we were going to learn how to survive in the rain forest. I had traipsed around a bit in the jungles of Southeast Asia and El Salvador, but nothing too crazy. I mean, let's get real: The jungle is beautiful, but who in his right mind would try to live in one?

I was aware that in the jungle, big, bulky Americans like myself suffered greatly. Maybe in the days of Vietnam our Special Forces forefathers could slither around the jungle, leaving behind no trace, but times had clearly changed. This time around, I was extremely happy the Colombians were on our side. I would not want to fight in this shit. The arid Afghan deserts and mountains were fine with me.

When we arrived in Colombia, I found the country to be beautiful, and like most parts of Central and South America, the nation was rich in culture. From the food and people to the overall atmosphere, I fell in love with the place. I was also impressed by the diversity in the terrain. It seemed like one moment we were in the capital city of Bogotá with cool temperatures, crisp air, and a modern-city vibe, and the next moment we were in the jungle, sweating our asses off and drawing in air thick with humidity. Not only that, there were parts of the country where one could run into tribesmen who had never seen a white person before.

Colombia was another country in the region crippled from years of civil war—fifty, to be exact—resulting in more than 215,000 casualties. Every 7th SFG guy knew about the Marxist insurgency led by the Revolutionary Armed Forces of Colombia, or FARC, because 7th Special Forces had been involved in Colombia for years helping to stabilize the country, and with good results. I was getting my chance to finally experience this part of the world and be a part of the great relationship that our two Special Forces communities shared.

As beautiful as Colombia was, I soon figured out that everything living in the jungle was—in my American opinion—out to kill me. From leaning on the wrong tree and being swarmed by wasplike ants, to car-length snakes slithering around the jungle floor, it seemed like everything that could kill, eat, or hurt you lived in the Colombian jungle.

At least that was what I thought after we traveled across the country en route to our training site in one of Colombia's most verdant pockets. As I looked around, I really wondered just what the Colombians' definition of "survival" was. Were we going out in the jungle for a few days to camp a bit, talk through some training, and then relax and enjoy each other's company? Surely they weren't going to run us through days of jungle hell like we were starring in an episode of *Naked and Afraid*!

Arriving at the training site, we linked up with our Colombian counterparts who would be training us for the next ten days. With shit-eating grins on their faces, they welcomed us. I could tell right away that they had something in store and it wasn't going to be pleasant. We were in their backyard, and they knew it.

They were the experts on how to survive in the jungle, and looking around at my guys, I was sure that most of us wouldn't last one night on our own. But that was why we were there, right? We all wanted to become experts on jungle survival, yet expertise is not taught in ten days. A week and a half would be long enough to make our lives so uncomfortable, miserable, and overall shitty that we would crawl back to the United States, praying that our time in a Colombian jungle was all a bad dream.

With little more to go on than hearing them say, *We'll teach you everything you need to know,* we set out for the depths of the jungle, destination unknown. Good or bad, this would be a once-in-a-lifetime experience. No need to pay thousands of dollars for some eco-vacation or star in one of those *Survivor* shows. The U.S. military was paying us to come here and get our asses kicked by the Colombian jungle and learn a few things. Win, lose, or draw, this would be something I would remember forever, and it'd give me plenty of opportunities to tell stories over a few beers at some VFW outfit one day.

After a few days of classes on what to eat, what not to eat, what to touch, what not to touch, and the ever-frightening *Here are all the animals in the jungle that are trying to kill you,* we set off. The first obstacle was more than two miles of river that we had to navigate.

Now, one might think that, as Special Forces, we set off in

high-speed boats or jumped in a few kayaks to get us down-stream. This was not the case. Before we left, we were told that we could only use what we had on our bodies or in our rucksacks.

Our rucksacks were filled with all the stuff we would need. When packing, one of the Colombians strongly recommended we use waterproof bags to seal everything inside our rucks to try to keep our stuff dry. Well, yeah, that made sense: We were in the middle of a rain forest. So that's what we did.

But then we learned that wasn't the real reason we had to wrap up all our gear in waterproof bags. We were told that the way we would get down the river would be by compressing our rucks as much as possible and then using them as flotation devices. Perhaps they didn't want to tell us that part until the very last moment because they didn't want a bunch of wussy Americans backing out at the last minute, but that was never going to happen. We were in it till the end.

Still, I had some things to think about before we pushed off. When I got into the river, my torso on top of my rucksack and legs dangling under the surface, I prayed that I would stay afloat and that any man-eating creatures in the water wouldn't want to take a bite out of me. Just to make sure we Americans had a clear picture of what was in the river, a Colombian Special Forces soldier dragged a five-foot alligator out of the water as we were getting ready to set out.

"He's a baby." The Colombian soldier added that the bigger ones liked to stay in the middle of the river to hunt prey.

Perfect, I thought. *An IED in Afghanistan can't kill me, but a damn Colombian alligator is going to make me his snack.*

When we got the go signal, I grabbed my ruck and headed off the ramp and into the river. As we let the current take us downstream, we linked arms and nervously joked about what creepy crawler was lurking just under us, waiting for the perfect time to strike. It was a blessing the water was murky and brown. We couldn't see the shadows of whatever lay below our legs, which played with our minds.

After two miles of floating, we saw our arrival point and exited the river like a bolt of lightning. We felt like we had tempted fate long enough and were glad that we were not a midday river-monster snack.

With our Colombian instructors in the lead, we headed deeper into the jungle as quietly as we could. Watching and observing the environment around us, we attempted to step like they stepped, move like they moved, and soak up every technique we saw. I was amazed to observe the Colombians progress through the jungle like they were walking on water, flowing over every obstacle. Stealthy in every manner, they were masters of the jungle.

We Americans were the complete opposite. Stronger and bulkier, we were crashing through tree limbs, flattening stalks of bamboo, tramping through thick ground cover—and cussing up a storm. We left enormous trails and stomped-down vegetation behind us. If enemy scouts or trackers were on our tails, they would have easily spotted our position and swore that we were using elephants to infil the area. We weren't graceful, that's for sure.

The other thing was that the enemy could have heard us coming from miles away. The only thing working in our favor was that we sounded like ten thousand government soldiers thrashing through the jungle, so maybe any enemies would have turned and run away in fear. I guess years of fighting in desert terrain hadn't done us any favors when it came to moving about the jungle.

When we arrived and began setting up camp, the second part of training started. Before we left, it was made clear to us that the rules on food were simple: we couldn't bring anything with us. That meant we would have to catch something to eat or scavenge the jungle for something edible. Our instructors knew full well that we would starve unless they helped us, so they brought along a live goat, one chicken, one iguana lizard, and a ten-foot boa constrictor. The plan was to kill, cook, and eat one of these animals each day.

The goat and the chicken were no problem. I had eaten snake and lizard while in Cambodia, but I had a hard time stomaching the taste. I hated snakes more than any other animal in the animal kingdom, so let's just say I wasn't looking forward to that type of dinner on day three or day four.

After a long first day of training, we were all dead tired from floating downriver for more than two miles and smashing through several miles of dense jungle terrain. Now we were preparing our first meal—chicken. I guess our hosts wanted to start us off easy. Poultry, rabbits, and other small game are easy to kill, skin, and cook, so this chicken would be an uncomplicated dinner. The iguana and boa constrictor were in separate burlap sacks tightly secured at the top to prevent them from getting out. The goat was tied to a tree in the middle of camp so we could watch it and make sure no other wild animals snuck in and ate it during the night.

After dinner, we talked over our experiences with our instructors, who invited questions. There weren't many because we were too tired and beat down. Everyone was interested in getting some rest, so we found trees to string our hammocks across, each with the built-in mosquito netting. One by one, we had our hammocks up and guys were passing out for the night. That was when I looked out of the corner of my eye and saw our Colombian counterparts laying mats out on the ground.

"You're sleeping on the ground?" I asked. "What about snakes and whatever else moves around here at night?"

The lead instructor shot me a look that said *Don't worry—we got this.*

Then a few of the Colombians unzipped and started pissing around their sleeping mats. The lead instructor told me human urine deters 99 percent of the animals in the jungle. That wasn't a good enough percentage for me. I was staying off the ground, although I did piss on the ground around my hammock before climbing in and zipping up the mosquito net.

Bushed beyond belief, I fell asleep right away.

The feeling that something was crawling all over my body woke me up from a dead sleep in the middle of the night.

Fishing around to find my headlamp, I used my free hand to brush away whatever was crawling on me. Finally, I found my headlamp and turned the light on. What I saw next was like something out of a horror movie. The mosquito netting that I had zipped up prior to falling asleep was completely covered in the most prehistoric-looking insects I had ever seen, all trying to crawl their way through the netting to feast on my body.

What I felt crawling on me was the little legs of those gnarly bugs through the netting holes. Turns out I had made a jungle-rookie mistake. I did not tie off my mosquito netting at the top, so it was sagging down one inch or so from my body. Making matters worse, my bladder was about to explode so I had no choice but to get out of the safety of my hammock and face these demon bugs on their turf. After kicking and shaking the mosquito net until most of the bugs were off, I made a break for it. Quickly, I pissed around my hammock one more time, then tied the netting off. In the minute or two that it took to do this, I got bitten no less than twenty to thirty times by mosquitos looking for a midnight snack.

Finally, back in the safety of my hammock with the mosquito netting zipped up, I tried to sleep again. I could not get out of my head the images of these insects hovering over me, trying to figure out how they could get a bite of the big white guy. Every ten minutes or so, I would turn my light on just to make sure my netting was holding up, so there went any quality sleep. In my mind, I kept telling myself: *Go to sleep, Ryan. You're a damn Green Beret for goodness' sake. You're supposed to love this shit.*

During the night, with my headlamp on, I looked over at our Colombian instructors. They were fast asleep, not a single bug bothering them—and they had no mosquito netting. What was their secret?

I finally dozed off but was startled awake by the sounds of our Colombian instructors moving about, cautiously looking for something. It was still dark. In fact, it was 3 a.m. So what could be so damn important it couldn't wait for sunrise?

I peeked my head up. "What's going on?" I asked in Spanish. I didn't think the answer would be good. When was I going to learn to keep my big mouth shut and quit asking questions? Seeing Colombians cautiously looking around the camp at three in the morning had trouble written all over it.

"The snake got out of its sack, and we can't find it," one of them said.

"You're joking, right?" Was this another trick they were playing on the jungle-virgin Americans?

Turned out it was no joke. The boa constrictor had gotten out of its sack and made its way into the iguana's sack. That was where the boa had eaten the iguana, and following that dinner, the ten-foot snake was slithering around our camp—or somewhere. Besides the blatant fact that a big-ass snake was out roaming free, the boa constrictor had just eaten the iguana and escaped. This was two days of food for us. All this happened on the first night, and we still had four more nights to go. What was next? A tyrannosaurus rex from *Jurassic Park* smashing its way through camp?

After getting through the first night of chaos, I felt like I was adapting to my new environment. The next four days of training taught me a lot about survival in the jungle. I learned how to build makeshift shelters and create a water filtration system using a log, leaves, and sand. I learned what plants could be used as natural insect repellent and how to trap jungle animals. We soaked up everything our instructors could throw at us.

My favorite lesson was how to track animals *and* humans. We went through the most minute details, from inspecting a broken twig on a branch to finding areas where leaves had been overturned. Everything in the jungle environment mattered. We studied footprints to determine the direction of travel, examining the angle of the footprint and which part of the footprint left a deeper indentation. We were shown details as small as the signs that someone had brushed up against a tree or how an interruption in an ant trail could signal that someone had been in the area recently. They also presented their ideas about jungle warfare and survival, including tactics they used in their fight against FARC, the guerrilla movement in Colombia. Now I had a taste of what it was like to survive in the jungle and felt like I had a fighting chance if I found myself in that situation.

Our Colombian instructors put their hearts and souls into giving us the best training possible. They were extremely professional and willing to share their jungle expertise, which was unmatched. They gave us an experience we would never forget. Once again, I had something memorable to write on the pages in the book of my life.

After four days in the jungle, our training was complete, and I had a whole new set of skills in my toolbox. I hoped that I would never have to fight in the jungle, but if I did, I was a lot more prepared. Our instructors had done their job. This training also gave me a whole new level of respect for our Vietnam veterans, many of whom slogged their way through jungles without a tenth of the equipment or knowledge that we had. Jungle warfare was no joke.

I came away from the experience in Colombia knowing one thing: Unless Uncle Sam dragged me there kicking and screaming, I would never volunteer to fight in the jungle.

CHAPTER 16

ON TO PERU

LIMA, PERU

JULY 2014

I returned from Colombia to the same old song and dance—train and gear up for the next deployment. I had been to El Salvador and Colombia with pit stops in Honduras and Panama, so I was getting used to the routine. Each trip wasn't too long but was enough to get an idea of the area and local culture, and have some fun.

Next up was a four-month deployment to Peru. Not only was I excited because it was another notch on my in-country belt, but Peru was also a bucket-list place for me, a prime destination that all 7th SFG guys wanted.

Because ODA 7216 was such a tight team, the trip would be even more rewarding. My good buddy Mike Valcq and I had been together since we went through parts of the Q Course side by side in 2008, and then we were deployed together to Afghanistan in 2012. Tyler and Frankie were my junior 18Cs; Derrick, Dave, and three other Mikes made up the rest of the team.

Sure, we were good friends, but most of all we were brothers.

As for the 18C Engineer section, Frankie and I became even closer during our three months in Peru. Frankie was a city kid from Miami and I was a farm boy from Oregon, which meant that we didn't exactly have a lot in common, but our personalities clicked. Tyler was like me when I was younger—a bit reckless, loyal to a fault, and ready to kick ass when the mission started. As a team, we did everything together: working hard, training hard, and playing even harder.

Training with the Peruvian forces was rewarding. They wanted to learn what we knew, and we were more than willing to teach them. Peru had basically the same backstory as much of South America did. The Peruvian government was still fighting a never-ending war against Communist-led guerrillas known as the Shining Path, or Sendero Luminoso.

Sendero Luminoso launched its insurgency movement in 1980. Like most conflicts in the region, this one waxed and waned over the years. When we arrived, this so-called guerrilla war wasn't as hot as it once had been.

One of the reasons we were there was because Peru was the number-one producer of cocaine in the world. Of course, the United States had a major interest in helping the Peruvian government deal with what was left of the Sendero Luminoso guerrillas, but more important, we were there to assist with Peru's war on drugs.

We had a couple different locations around the capital city of Lima where we trained with the Peruvian Special Forces. Lima, a massive city of nearly 10 million, was the center point for everything. Our team house was located in the middle of downtown Lima, which was too much hustle and bustle for me.

I preferred staying out in the countryside, which I got to do periodically.

We conducted training on land navigation, live-fire maneuvers, and demolition at Villa Rica, a small village that was an all-day drive up into the mountains. I loved the little town because there wasn't traffic or many people, but Villa Rica still had plenty to do—sampling the local restaurants, shops, and the like. It was in Villa Rica that I experienced and enjoyed the Peruvian culture, not just city life.

It was almost funny how few restrictions we had for training. We could use about as much explosive as we wanted to, shoot whatever team weapons we felt like, and we had plenty of room to roam when it came to land navigation.

One day, Valcq and I found ourselves trekking through the jungle following our Peruvian counterparts. The plan was to spend two nights in the rain forest and observe how they moved and conducted operations. Then it started raining—hard—which made the training experience all the better.

A driving rainstorm didn't slow anyone down, although Valcq and I got our arms and faces torn to shreds by sharp thorns and thistles when we busted through the dense jungle vegetation. Then there were steep embankments we had to scale, three hundred feet straight up in some places, but they had turned into slick mud banks. We'd grasp vines that covered most of the hillsides on our way up, only to lose our footing and slide all the way back down the hill to where we started. Covered in mud from head to toe, we looked like creatures out of a horror movie.

Crossing raging rivers in chest-high water sucked as well, but in a crazy sort of way, I had a blast. The water was swift, but it washed the caked-on mud off. For me, this was Colombian jungle training all over again.

When we stopped to set up camp the first night, Valcq revealed to everyone that it was my birthday. As far as I was concerned, it was just another birthday away from home, but our Peruvian hosts wanted me to feel special. Late in the evening, Valcq and I were scarfing down our packaged MREs under a rain poncho when I saw a small flame coming my way in the dark night. The Peruvian guys had taken a cookie from one of the MREs, put a candle on top, and presented me with one of the most special birthday cakes ever while singing a hushed "Happy Birthday"—in English. As crazy as it sounds, it was one of the best birthdays I ever had.

We trained hard in Villa Rica, but we made sure we had time for fun. On one occasion, we found waterfalls that were perfect for rappelling training. The cliffs of the waterfall were twenty-five to thirty feet high and dropped down to a twelve- to sixteen-feet-deep natural pool.

Surrounded by lush green foliage, the waterfalls looked like something you'd see on the Travel Channel. After rappelling the falls, all it took was for one guy to say, "I bet you won't jump that," and the game was on.

After a bit of recon, we found a narrow area where we could land safely—as long we missed all the rocks sticking out from the cliffs on our way down and landed in the deep part at the base of the waterfall. Back home, most people would say, *That looks too dangerous. Maybe we should find something safer to do.* That would have been the smart thing to say, but none of us really cared if it was safe or not. But I should have remembered that my fear of heights would be an issue.

I watched guy after guy jump off the ledge and into the falls. I melted into the background and tried to sneak back down the trail, but my reputation for being chickenshit about heights made me an easy target.

"Get your ass up there and jump, Ryan," one of the guys said, and that was all it took for the other dudes to egg me on. I was known for hating heights, so they got me there. Since I couldn't get away or hide from the team, I had no choice but to jump.

I took my time climbing to the top, thinking about how I was going to do this. This time, there would be no static line and no parachute. I'd have to jump and land in the right place—the deep pool at the base of the waterfall. Otherwise, I'd be in a world of hurt.

I made baby steps and walked out onto a narrow rock ledge. At the edge I looked down and did my best to put on a show of confidence.

Holy shit! I thought the guys said it was thirty feet down, not three thousand!

I was back at Jump School all over again, wondering how the hell I kept getting myself into this type of situation. None of that mattered, though. I needed to suck it up and jump.

I looked at the landing spot and positioned my body just right... then I pushed out into the open and down I went. Arms flailing like a baby bird stepping out of the nest for its first flight, it seemed like it took forever to reach the water. *SLAP!* I hit the water a million miles an hour with zero grace. The crash landing took the wind out of me because I landed on my back first—and that hurt!

As I kicked for the surface, I was sure my team would be

swimming out to make sure I was okay. Instead, they were laughing their asses off and making fun of me.

"Bro, are you good, man? You ate shit. But that was awesome," said one.

"Yeah, I'm good," I said, "but that sucked." My back was as red as a lobster shell.

"Cool. We're all jumping again, and so are you. Let's go."

Sometimes peer pressure is a bitch.

***

Trekking through the jungle, jumping off waterfalls, rappelling down mud walls, or conducting weapons training were all great, but nothing compared to good old-fashioned demolition training. Explosives are a Special Forces Engineer's bread and butter and best friend. There is something about working with demolitions that is completely addicting. Maybe it's knowing the power that's within these explosives, or maybe it's having the power to use them. Either way, I love handling C-4 and all the other "bang"—our slang term for demo explosives—that we used.

It seemed like every SF guy I knew wanted to have his picture taken while a large explosion was set off in the background. The sacred team photo that every Special Forces ODA wanted was when everyone was all geared up, looking ready for battle, while a large fireball explodes into the air behind them.

Tyler, Frankie, and I were no different, so whenever there was going to be a pretty big explosion, we knew that cool-guy photos needed to be taken. It was a must because of the way Hollywood action heroes always seem to walk away without looking back at a huge explosion going off behind them. That's why we had a saying on 7216: "Cool guys never turn around for explosions."

We were coming to the end of our time at Villa Rica, so a few souvenir pictures were necessary. How about a shot with a little explosive flavor? Frankie, Tyler, and I put our heads together and came up with a brilliant idea. We decided to rig explosive simulators, which had the same explosive power as a few quarter-sticks of TNT, around the bases of a couple trees. We positioned several GoPro cameras at the right spots to record everything, and then we'd turn and walk away as the explosion went off in the background, which we three would be too cool to turn around for.

We weren't going to wire the trees with a lot of explosives, and we were certainly going to make sure that we would be far enough away so as not to get injured, but with enough demo so that our video clips from our GoPro cameras would be amazing, just like the movies. We could see it now: Three heroes walking into the sunset as multiple explosions were set off behind them. We had the perfect plan. What could go wrong?

We rigged the trees up and set all the cameras at the perfect angles to capture the greatest never-turn-around-for-an-explosion moment in the history of cool-guy shots. Being the professionals that we were, we even did a few dry runs to make sure the cameras caught every angle. When we were satisfied that everything was set up just the way we'd drawn it up, it was time for the epic moment—the moment that would define our careers in Special Forces. We would be the cool guys who didn't turn around for the explosions.

Getting in line with the cameras rolling, we stepped off as the countdown started. Five, four, three, two, one—*BOOM!*

We felt a bit of the overpressure from the blast but nothing too bad. *Keep walking. Don't turn around. Cool guys never do.*

When we thought we had enough video capturing the moment, we stopped to congratulate ourselves, high fives all around. Just then

I heard a sound that was similar to what I heard in Afghanistan—a *zip* flying past my face.

I turned my head to see Tyler start sprinting up the road, tearing his shirt off. *What the fuck is going on?*

The next instant I felt something—like a nail being driven into my back. *What was that?*

"Run, Ryan!" Frankie said as he sprinted by me.

Then I felt another sharp pain in my back as I started sprinting up the road after Tyler. *What the hell is going on?*

Tyler made it back to where the rest of the team was watching the show. He started stripping off his clothes and then rolled around in the grass, trying to get whatever was on his back off of him.

Meanwhile, I stopped and took my shirt off to inspect the damage. One of the guys said, "Dude, you got two large welts on your back."

Come to find out we had been chased by an angry swarm of Peruvian wasps that had a large nest up in the tree. The wasps were pissed off and looking to get whoever blew up their home. It never occurred to us to look around for a wasp nest, and we were paying for it now.

I guess there is always a price to pay for being a cool guy.

Whether we were in Peru, Colombia, Afghanistan, or any other country throughout the world, winning the hearts and minds of the locals was always one of our primary missions. We had different ways to help out the local population, and one of them was through medical and dental checks. Basically, we would go out to an area that didn't have any doctors or nurses, or the means or money to see a medical professional. The medics on our team would provide treatment, and we would hand out toys to the children who wandered up to see what was going on.

On one occasion, we were in the jungle giving medical and dental help to villagers. Valcq, Frankie, and I were playing soccer with some of the children when an older man and woman approached with pails of milky-looking liquid. They stopped, and the old man dipped half a coconut into the milky substance and tried to give us a cupful.

"Frankie, what is that stuff?" I asked. It didn't look appetizing.

"Bro, I have no clue. He's calling it Chichi or Masato. I don't know what that means."

Just then, one of our Peruvian commandos came by. He quickly sized up the situation and told us that the drink was a local custom and it would be disrespectful if we didn't take a coconut cupful.

Well, shit. I didn't want to be disrespectful. Neither did Valcq or Frankie.

"But what is it?" I asked. I wanted to have at least an idea of what I was getting myself into.

"Just drink it. It won't hurt you," the commando replied.

Okay, when in Rome, I guess.

The gray-haired man handed me a coconut shell filled halfway with the milky drink. I leaned forward and smelled. So did Valcq and Frankie. It didn't smell that bad. It actually smelled like nothing, so it couldn't be that bad, right? By that time, we had gained the attention of a bunch of soldiers who gathered around to watch what would happen to us. The guys were trying not to laugh, which was really making me second-guess what I was about to do.

Screw it. I tilted the coconut shell back and took a long drink.

The concoction didn't taste bad. But what the hell was it? After Valcq and Frankie finished their drinks, everyone started laughing and patting us on the back.

"What's so funny?" I asked.

One of the commandos explained that the drink they called Chichi or Masato was a Peruvian spit liquor drink.

A spit liquor drink? That didn't sound good. When I asked for an explanation, one of the Peruvians explained that the locals in the rainforest chewed yucca roots and then spit the roots into a jar for fermentation.

I was stunned. No words could describe my thoughts right then. We had drunk fermented spit from how many villagers who helped in making this batch? I had no clue, but it had to be a lot.

The old man held out a second glass, half-filled with fermented spit. I reluctantly accepted it and finished it. I had already done one, so what was two?

The drink actually had a kick to it, thanks to the fermentation. I was feeling good. Maybe it was all in my head. I had no idea how they turned chewed-up yucca roots into liquor, but I have to say that their local drink left me feeling good and relaxed.

I try not to think that I really drank spit, but I did, and participating in this local custom gave me another experience that I could add to my list, which was getting longer and longer.

During most trips down south, I tried to pack in at least one once-in-a-lifetime trip or experience, and I'm not talking about drinking fermented spit. My attitude was, *Hell, if the military is paying for it, then why not?*

Toward the middle of our deployment, we, as a team, decided to go on a four-day motorcycle trip to Machu Picchu, the iconic, sprawling Incan city ruins from the fifteenth century that had become one of the most sought-out places to visit in the world. We had to get approval from our command before we could go, which took some doing, but in the end the trip was a go.

The first part of the journey was to fly from Lima to Cusco, a city of 350,000 in southeastern Peru, which was known as the gateway to Machu Picchu. At 11,152 feet up, Cusco hit us with altitude all at once.

Just walking up the stairs to my hotel room had me putting my hands on my knees and sucking for breath. I guess that was to be expected after flying into the ninth-highest city in the world.

That night Frankie and I went out to grab a beer and see what Cusco nightlife had to offer. Add in the elevation, multiply by a few beers, and I was feeling the effects. Turned out to be an early night for me.

The next morning, bright and early, we picked up our rental 250 cc Enduro motorbikes for our ride to Machu Picchu. I had owned a motorcycle when I lived in Idaho but sold it before I went to Korea, so it had been more than a few years since I'd ridden one.

Getting back in the swing of things was easy except for one issue—the traffic in Peru, or, to be more precise, the *I don't give a shit* attitude of the local drivers. They would pass on blind corners, drive on both sides of the road, nearly push vehicles off cliffs so they could pass—just about anything went. The rule of the road was easy: Whoever had the bigger vehicle owned the road. Accordingly, we gave them a wide berth on our 250 cc motorcycles and eventually made our way to Machu Picchu without issue but with plenty of scares.

We arrived in the village of Santa Teresa at the base of Machu Picchu, where we could catch a train to Aguas Calientes. We planned to spend the night in Aguas Calientes before trekking to the ancient ruins. Bad luck—we just missed the last train of the day.

We didn't have a whole lot of options, but the best one was walking over five miles up to Aguas Calientes, in the dark, with the only for-sure path being the railroad tracks. Even though I had my IDEO brace on, my leg had swelled from being on a motorbike all day. I knew that this would not be an easy walk for me, but I was happy to have the opportunity to see this great historic sight known around the world. My leg would just have to deal with it.

Valcq and I hiked together while the rest of the group charged out ahead, but we were in no hurry. We would stop every now and then to listen for the last train of the day making its return trip back to the base station for the night. Knowing my luck, I could see myself getting hit head-on by a train and that would be that.

With the little bit of moonlight being drowned out by the dense jungle canopy, we spent over four hours tripping and falling our way up to Aguas Calientes, but we made it.

Bruised and bloody, the first thing we did was to find a little liquor shop so that we could buy a twelve-pack of ice-cold Cusqueña beer.

Once we got that important task out of the way and popped

the lids of a few cervezas, we cleaned up at our hostel and hit the brightly lit streets of Aguas Calientes for dinner and a little nightlife. Knowing full well we would spend all of the following day walking up and down Machu Picchu, I knew I couldn't stay out long. I needed to get to bed and let my leg recover. I was in a lot of pain, so I hoped that a few beers and a handful of meds would take the edge off.

When I woke up, my leg was stiff and sore not only from the hike in, but also from the elevation change. I couldn't care less because I would be visiting one of the Seven Wonders of the Modern World. I had been to two others—The Great Wall of China and Chichen Itza in Mexico—as well as one that should have been on that list, the Angkor Wat in Cambodia. Now Machu Picchu was in my sights.

We started our hike up the mountain and eventually reached the information center at the base of Machu Picchu. Linking up with our tour guide, we set off exploring every nook and cranny that the site had to offer. Picture after picture, I snapped away, but my camera could not come close to capturing the true beauty and spectacle of the site.

That day on the mountain, time stood still. Trying to absorb all the breathtaking sights with my band of brothers—very few things, if any, would top this in my life. Machu Picchu was a true bucket-list event that I had just crossed off.

It was only a matter of time before I would be back in Afghanistan or somewhere in the world just as deadly. I just hoped that the next time I was deployed to a dangerous part of the globe, I'd come home in one piece.

CHAPTER 17

BACK TO THE FRONT

7TH SPECIAL FORCES GROUP

EGLIN AIR FORCE BASE

EARLY 2016

In 2016, I was slated to deploy to Guatemala when my plans changed—or were changed for me—shortly after the New Year. It started when another company in my battalion was heading to Afghanistan and needed a few soldiers who had certain qualifications that Frankie and I met. We were bumped off the Guatemala deployment with 7216 and told to go to Afghanistan with Bravo Company. Our destination: Kabul city in northern Afghanistan, home to Camp Duskin.

Another trip to Afghanistan—one of the world's hottest spots for nearly fifteen years—was fine with me. My previous tours had been during the summer in the sweltering southern half of Afghanistan, so if I was going there, I was ready to experience the cooler environment of northern Afghanistan this time around. I actually looked forward to getting a change of scenery in this treacherous, forbidding country.

I left for Afghanistan in early January. I figured this would be a noneventful deployment. Since the Taliban historically didn't fight in wintertime and usually spent the cold months in Pakistan, I assumed this would be a nice relaxing trip: I'd collect some combat pay and be done with it. I felt confident that my job with Bravo Company wouldn't see much action.

Instead, I was informed that I was being brought over to fulfill more of an intelligence role. My days would be spent collecting intel, writing up reports, and kicking information up the command chain, where hopefully the intelligence would be put to good use. This meant my six-month tour would be spent riding a desk, punching a keyboard, and emailing a bunch of analytical reports that might or might not be acted upon—in other words, no big deal. The way I saw things shaping up in Afghanistan, I might as well pull some light office duty and get jacked in the gym.

In fact, the winter of '16 would be one of the warmest in years. Instead of hunkering down in Pakistan to plan and train for the next fighting season, the Taliban decided to stick around Afghanistan and play ball.

Well, that's just my luck, I thought. *I'm here to do a six-month desk job, and now the Taliban are sticking around to fight.* I didn't want to miss out on all the excitement while rocking an office chair back at Camp Duskin.

Then, in early February, a little more than a month after I arrived, I was approached by my operations sergeant.

"A new mission just got dropped into our laps. You want a piece of the action?" he asked.

I couldn't say yes fast enough. My newfound buddies on the

team felt the same way. We were stoked to leave the confines of Camp Duskin and head out to Baghlan Province in search of some bad guys. The date of the roll-up: February 10, 2016.

Baghlan Province was a known safe haven for Taliban insurgents, who used the area to launch attacks on Kabul city and nearby Kunduz city, Afghanistan's sixth-largest city with a population of more than 250,000. The notable thing about Kunduz city was its strategic location. Part of Kunduz Province, it bordered the country of Tajikistan, which meant whoever controlled that area controlled the border. Whoever controlled the border could filter money and guns into Afghanistan unopposed.

We knew the Taliban would put up a fierce fight to maintain their hold on parts of Kunduz Province, and U.S. Special Forces needed to crush them where they were dug in. That's where Baghlan Province, which occupied most of the land between Kabul city to the south and Kunduz city to the north, came into play. The Taliban were using controlled areas in Baghlan Province to form, plan, arm up, and launch attacks against these major population centers. Our job would be to disrupt the Taliban's activities, which in Army terms meant killing as many enemy fighters as we could.

The news that our mission was built around the element of surprise got me excited. The way things were mapped out, we would infil Baghlan Province's largest city, Pul-e Khumri, under the cover of darkness and link up with our Afghan counterparts. After that, we would stage out from a local Afghan base. Even though we were excited to get going, we knew it would take a few days to get all the moving parts in order.

When the mission got the green light, my team would use nighttime darkness as our ally. Because the mission depended on stealth as one of our main weapons, the goal was to reach the front lines safely, quickly, and, most of all, undetected. After positioning ourselves, we would disguise our "village clearance" operation as just another foolish attack by Afghan forces, which the Taliban would think they could easily repel. This would be our opportunity to do some serious damage to the enemy.

The way we drew things up, the Taliban would see the Afghan commandos heading into the village and fire at them, knowing for certain that the Afghan soldiers would turn and run away like they had many times before. Once a bunch of Taliban assholes started shooting, however, that would be all we needed to call in close air support assets overhead, which would give the Taliban a healthy taste of American firepower. The insurgents would know in a New York minute that the Americans were in the fight, and that would change the battlefield in a hurry.

On paper, everything read well. We would start with the village of Niazullah and go from there. We all knew what we would be doing and the role each one of us was expected to play. Clearance operations was something I had a lot of experience with.

Once again, I would find myself at the front with my select few Afghans, leading a patrol, clearing IEDs, and giving us a safe passage until we reached our objective. The way we planned things out and rehearsed, Frankie and I would clear different routes for the two elements and meet up at the southernmost point of the main village, where our teams would combine and begin to clear Niazullah of IEDs, weapons caches, and the Taliban. If unopposed, we'd complete our mission quickly and be back for lunch. We didn't mean this literally, of course, but our attitude was to get this job done and get out of there.

Like everything else in this country, though, I knew that

once that first round flies past your head, every perfect plan goes to shit.

Over a ten-day period, we prepared for launching from our base in Pul-e Khumri for our mission to clear Niazullah.

We were told in a pre-mission briefing that a large hill named OP Burns overlooked Niazullah. Located at the end of a major ridgeline that separated Pul-e Khumri from the Taliban-held villages on the east side of the ridgeline, OP Burns was a line of demarcation. We knew that we would have an overall view of the battlefield from the top of OP Burns. The Afghan National Army had an outpost at the summit, so it would be relatively safe for us to drive up. The Afghan government and the Taliban had reached an unwritten deal about OP Burns over the years: *You stay on your side of the ridgeline, and we'll stay on ours.*

Or: *Don't fuck with us, and we won't fuck with you.*

Fair enough, if you're in the business of making deals with the enemy.

That understanding lasted until the Afghan government started pushing into Taliban-held territories during the 2015 fighting season. Whenever the Afghan army would tread into a hostile area, however, they'd get their asses kicked and retreat with tails tucked between their legs.

The Afghan army had no chance because the Taliban had been handed a tactical gift: a few years to build bunkers, dig tunnels, and prepare trenches for the inevitable attack by government troops. See, the Taliban weren't entirely stupid. They knew their unwritten deal wouldn't last and there would come a day when they would be drawn into a fight. So, with time on their side, they prepared, and they prepared well.

Again and again during 2015, Afghan forces were unsuccessful in taking villages like Niazullah, so the 911 call went out to U.S. forces for help. The Afghans knew if the United States came to the fight, they would also get our airpower—and that was the best way to defeat a well-dug-in enemy.

When we arrived at the Afghan base on top of OP Burns, I noticed that the Afghans had their D30s (artillery pieces) staged on top of the hill, which allowed them the opportunity to rain down artillery rounds day and night on the valley below. The Afghan army knew that most civilians had fled because of the fighting, so one could presume anything moving in the area was bad.

When I saw for myself how much firepower was being put on the enemy's head, I wondered, *How in the hell can anything survive?* And yet, any time the Afghans made an excursion into Taliban-held territory, they got their asses whipped.

Since I had a front row seat from OP Burns and witnessed the brutal beatdown the Afghan soldiers were taking, I knew that any clearance operation would be a nasty mission.

Finally, after all the moving parts and pieces were put in place, it was our turn to go. We were tired of sitting around, and ready to fight. The usual hurry-up-and-wait took longer than expected, but it was time. Clearing at night was necessary to catch the enemy off guard. Walking around in the open during the day was a Taliban sniper's wet dream—seeing a bunch of Americans clearing right into his crosshairs. Since the Taliban didn't have advanced night vision capabilities (that we knew of), conducting at least the first part of the "push" into the village of Niazullah at nighttime was important.

With a crack of static over the radio, the call came out that the mission was a go. We loaded up our vehicles and started our movement to the valley below and toward the front lines. Under the cover of darkness, we traveled in Humvees, which were common for the Afghan army to drive, so as not to tip off the Taliban that U.S. forces, especially Green Berets, were in the area. In the Taliban's eyes, U.S. forces were different from the Green Berets. They were scared shitless when they heard the Bearded Ones were nearby.

Our plan to disguise the mission was working, to the best of our knowledge. Hopefully, when the Taliban engaged us, they'd think they were only firing at Afghan forces, but before they knew it, *BOOM!* We would drop so much firepower on them that they would have their first-class tickets to eternity punched in seconds.

Sounded good, and looked good on paper. Now it was time to see if the Taliban would bite.

Driving at night while looking through NVGs wasn't easy. First, I had zero depth perception. Second, just like every road in Afghanistan, the dirt route was six inches too narrow for American military vehicles. Third, steering a vehicle while using NVGs and barely seeing the road meant it was impossible to spot IEDs. Driving under those conditions maxed out my nerves, and we hadn't even started clearing yet. This was going to be a long night.

Slowly, our convoy made its way down the moonlit dusty road

to the Afghan army's final position. When we arrived, we knew this was the Wild West—Taliban-held territory.

With a screech of brakes bringing our fully loaded Humvees to a stop, we arrived at the last friendly position in the valley. Our Afghan commandos were ready and waiting. Quickly, we briefed them on our plan, formed up, and started our movement by foot to the village of Niazullah. It was shortly after midnight.

Almost immediately, we could hear gunfire coming from the village and spotted tracer rounds punching holes in the darkness. We didn't know who was firing at what. The best bet was that Afghan soldiers in overwatch positions were shooting at ghosts or shadows. We moved on.

I remained at the front of the formation with four Afghan mine-clearance soldiers assisting me: Jawaid, Abe, Bismullah, and Kahan. At 2 a.m., we had about five hours to clear a route with our mine detectors to the first village compound, which was located more than a kilometer away. If I were taking a nice leisurely stroll down a country dirt road in Oregon, it wouldn't be that far a distance, but when you factor in IEDs, not being able to see much in the dark, and an entire village of shitheads waiting to kill you, I was certain it would take a long time to get there.

I knew from my recon that this village was heavily IED'd. Slowly, I pushed my element forward: Jawaid in the lead, followed by Abe, then me and Bismullah and Kahan split to the sides in a triangle pattern.

As our mine detectors swept left to right over the path, we listened for anything that would send the devices into a chirping frenzy. I had my guys spaced out so we could cover the largest amount of ground.

We all knew how dangerous this part of the mission was. Few Afghans volunteered to clear IEDs, and the ones who did usually didn't last long. Unfortunately, many of the IED-clearing Afghans I had met during my past deployments were dead. As I slowly moved forward, I thought of this sobering reality. This was a war where more lives were lost to what you couldn't see *under* the ground than to gunfire *above* the ground.

Inch after inch, foot by foot, we cleared the path while looking for anything out of the ordinary—a rag tied in a tree, rocks lined up to create a marking, or any ground disturbance. Everything in this area was a potential IED.

Because I had been attached to a different team in Bravo Company prior to this deployment, I didn't have a good grip on the different personalities that made up the team. I didn't have the years of getting to know these guys and how they thought, how they trained, and how they reacted when the shooting started, like I did with my regular team.

I looked at the path and my surroundings, intensely searching for anything out of the ordinary that could indicate an IED, listening for any chirp from my mine detector as it swept left to right over the path. I was locked in total concentration when my radio squelched in my headset.

"Ryan, what's taking so long?"

It was my team sergeant. Apparently, he wasn't pleased with how slow and methodical our IED clearance was going that night. "You need to hurry the fuck up so we can get to our first compound," he said. "We're running behind, man. Push those guys."

Easy for you to say, I thought. "I can only move as fast as the

IED situation up here lets me," I replied. "I promise you we'll get there—with all our limbs. But I'm not going to rush my guys."

In the back of my mind, I was thinking, *If you want to speed this along, then bring your ass to the front and give it a shot. It's easy to say "Hurry up" from the back.*

I don't know who gave him a timeline to die, but I knew that hustling to this compound would put every guy's life at risk, so I ignored his call to push faster. I wasn't about to let any of my guys go down, including him, because I missed something.

As the clearance mission continued, we eventually reached our first major obstacle: The main path into the first compound cut right through the middle of an orchard.

The Taliban loved to hide tunnel entrances, weapon caches, and other nasty surprises in orchards just outside a compound, all protected by IEDs and booby traps. Orchards were a favorite hiding spot because the Taliban thought that green, leafy trees made it hard for our ISR aircraft to see what they were hiding underneath the foliage. Unlike farm fields, which were out in the open and had to be worked and tilled every harvest, orchards were low-maintenance areas where it was easy to hide caches under trees or install a web of tunnel systems. Because orchards were commonly used for these purposes, it was in the Taliban's best interest to booby-trap and IED them to protect what they had inside a compound.

This was strategic information I had committed to memory from previous tours in Afghanistan. I hadn't forgotten that I had to always pay special attention to orchards leading in or near any shithead village, something any good 18C learned right away or faced the deadly consequences. And to the surprise of absolutely no one, the orchard outside Niazullah was reported to be heavily mined with IEDs and contained tunnel entrances to God knows where.

At the edge of the orchard, I took a quick moment to group my guys together and make sure we were ready to push through. I gripped Abe by the shoulder. He spoke English and was a translator on the team.

"Listen up, man," I said as quietly as I could. "You know just as well as I do that this orchard could be rigged with a shitload of IEDs. Bro, take no chances at all. If we get into a fight or pinned down, tell the guys to fall back the way we came in because we know at least that will be clear. Do not, for any reason, go anywhere that has not been cleared yet. If one of us gets hit in there, it will be hard to get him out, so keep your eyes open and don't get killed. Got that? Okay, let the boys know."

If clearing an orchard was dangerous work during the day, a nighttime sweep was much riskier. We continued to proceed cautiously, with the rest of the patrol behind us, until Jawaid, Bismullah, Kahan, Abe, and I had cleared a good foothold in the orchard. Now the guys behind us could move up and provide security while we cleared the next portion. We would repeat this until the entire orchard was cleared and we were inside the first compound.

My body was on full alert and my senses were on overdrive as I continued the task at hand. A cold but gentle February predawn wind gave me chills as it blew lightly past my skin, adding to my sensory overload. As my mine detector swept the ground, everything was quiet except for the dead leaves getting tossed around by a slight breeze, possibly hiding what ground signs I needed to find those IEDs.

On the left side of the main path was a two-foot-wide irrigation ditch that paralleled the direction we were heading. Rows of trees on either side meant that we also had to be on the lookout for IEDs with trip wires stretched from one tree trunk to another, as well as pressure-plate IEDs buried under the ground.

As Jawaid and Abe pushed deeper into the orchard, I followed close behind with Bismullah and Kahan off to the sides. The main patrol backed us up from about twenty meters away, providing security and watching our every step as we moved forward. Frankie, with the second element, had already cleared a two-story compound that overlooked the orchard and our first target compound.

From there, Frankie and the other members of his element set up an overwatch position that had eyes on any enemy threats coming from a distance. We felt confident that we weren't walking into an ambush because twenty minutes before my group entered the orchard, Frankie's overwatch position gave us a good five-minute fireworks show with all the weapons systems they had, firing into the orchard in hopes that the enemy would return the favor.

The response was the sound of crickets. Either the Taliban held their fire or knew better than to shoot back because that would bring death from the sky.

Slowly, after clearing a good twenty-five meters into the orchard, I called for the first few guys from the main patrol to move closer and set up security along the ditch. Up to now everything was calm and quiet. The only thing I heard were faint chirps from my mine detector as it passed over tiny fragments of metallic trash.

I could see our first target compound, which was about one

hundred meters up the path, still a long distance to clear. The path started to narrow, and rows of dormant fruit trees swallowed up the open ground as we patrolled deeper into the orchard. I reminded myself to concentrate on any significant details that were almost impossible to see under night vision.

POP!

What the fuck was that?

We all hit the ground, unsure of the loud snap we'd just heard.

Was it a gunshot?

Snipers in the area?

We waited for a shitstorm of bullets to rain down on us, but nothing happened. Then I noticed that Jawaid and I were tangled in some type of line—almost like fishing line. *Holy shit!* We had hit a trip wire IED that didn't explode.

How did I miss that?

As Jawaid carefully investigated the trip wire against his chest—without any quick movements—I determined that the Taliban had tied the wire that ran from a set of explosives hidden in the mud wall all the way to a tree on the opposite side of the path. The wire had been tied at chest level, not at the usual ankle height, a clever move on the Taliban's part. They knew we would be using our detectors to clear, which meant we would be looking down at the dirt—and walk right into a chest-level trip wire.

Why didn't the IED go off? The best explanation I could come up with was that when the overwatch element laid waste for five minutes—firing everything they had into the orchard—fragmentation from one of the mortars had hit the IED and disabled it. Luck was on our side.

I blew a heavy sigh of relief from the close call. Once again, God saved my ass—it wasn't my time yet.

After untangling myself, I helped Jawaid to his feet and cut away what was left of the trip wire tangled up in his body armor. With a sense of urgency that comes from cheating death, we returned to clearing the path. I was still a little shaken and disappointed that I had missed that wire, but hell, it was dark and we were under night vision. It was hard to see my hands in front of me let alone to spot a thin trip wire in the darkness.

Man, this was nerve-racking.

***

We had cleared another fifteen meters of path when I saw movement in an open field near the first compound.

I turned to Abe. "What the fuck was that?"

And that was when all hell broke out.

Before Abe could respond, the night was lit up by a barrage of gunfire coming from the compound's outer wall. First, it was a *zip-zip-zip*, followed by the *crack* of 7.62-caliber rounds flying past our heads. These rounds, which ripped holes in the darkness, looked like a laser light show with the tracers streaking across the night sky. Next came an explosion from an RPG being fired at us. Then more automatic fire. We had walked directly into an ambush!

Shit! With my heart beating out of my chest, I hit the ground and started returning fire.

The Taliban had set up a complex ambush—and the trip wire IED was supposed to start the whole thing off. One of their PKM machine guns let out a burst of fire twenty meters from our position—a distance so close that it was almost like I could grab the flame coming out the end of the barrel.

Jawaid, Abe, and Bismullah jumped into the ditch, while

Kahan darted back and took cover behind a tree. I hit the deck and lay as flat as I could in the middle of the dirt path. Bullets kicked up rock and gravel fragments around me, stinging my skin. When bullet rounds hit the ground around me, splintering fragments sprayed everywhere. I could tell some fragments struck my body armor's protective plate.

I engaged the flames, figuring that where there were flames, there was a gun; and where there was an AK-47, there was a fighter.

"Ryan, your strobe light!" my buddy Zac yelled over the radio. "They have NVGs. They can see your IR strobe!"

Our interpreter, Dost, was monitoring Taliban radio traffic and heard them saying they had an American cut off from the main group. They could see my strobe light, which I wore so aircraft could see that I was the most forward-friendly element on the battlefield. But the leader of the ambush could also see my strobe and was directing fighters to fire on my position.

Once I heard that, I tore the strobe off my helmet and threw it in the direction of the PKM machine-gun fire.

"You see my strobe flash now?" I yelled over the radio.

"Yeah, we see the flashes," Zac replied back. "That's close to where that fucking PKM locked on to us."

Even though there was a tremendous amount of lead raining down on me, I poked my head up several times for a good shot, knowing it was the risk I had to take to return fire. Not only did the Taliban have at least one PKM machine-gun nest set up, but they also had a fighter firing the RPG, along with probably another dozen insurgents with AK-47s giving us all they had. This was the most firepower ever directed at me and my guys at one time. Compared to my other firefights in Afghanistan, this was the worst by far. We were pinned down but not helpless.

By keeping fire on their position, I knew it would be more difficult for the enemy to get an accurate shot off at me. Another RPG flew over our heads and exploded when it struck a mud wall of a different compound behind us. His second rocket-propelled grenade did the exact same thing; it seemed he hadn't corrected from his first misfire. I noticed that each time he stepped out from behind a wall to fire his RPG, he stood in the same place.

The third time he came out, he took more time than the previous two tries, attempting to get a better shot off at us. It was like he was daring me to light up his ass. I knew I had him. I locked in with a clear shot and let go a ten- to fifteen-round burst out from my M-4. I watched him drop. His body lay still on the ground. It felt good to kill him, but I couldn't relish the moment too long. We were still pinned down.

Our main element, which was about twenty-five to thirty meters behind our position, put as much firepower on the enemy as they could, hoping to keep their heads down long enough for U.S. aircraft to start dropping bombs. I knew, from the many fights I'd been in before in this country, that a call for air support had been made within seconds of their attack.

In the meantime, Frankie's position let it loose, but the Taliban were well protected behind mud walls. Unless they stepped out into the open—like the guy with the RPG launcher—there wasn't much we could do without an air strike. At the same time, I was aware—given how close we were to the enemy—that being killed by friendly fire was a real worry.

Yet as our situation deteriorated by the second, I knew that without bombs on target, Jawaid, Abe, Bismullah, Kahan, and I would all die. This was about to turn into a body recovery mission, and it would be our bodies they would be taking home.

Within a couple of minutes, the decision was made for us when our Air Force JTAC called in a five-hundred-pound bomb just twenty meters from my position. This was considered a Danger Close strike, but one that would give us a fighting chance of making it out of the orchard alive.

The call went out over the radio, and then I heard the Air Force JTAC's voice in my earpiece. "Ryan, we're dropping close to you, man. Keep your fucking head down."

After receiving the radio transmission, I relayed the info to Abe, who told the others to get as low as they could. There wasn't enough room in the ditch, so I grabbed Kahan and pushed him into the trench while I stayed on the footpath. I ordered them to hunker down and prepare for the blast. Since we weren't firing back at the enemy, the volume of fire on our position picked up.

I knew that in the next few moments I could die—either from a Taliban bullet or U.S. ordnance. *Please God, let this bomb hit the right target, or this will be our last stand.*

Overhead, I could hear the rocket motors of an F-16 ripping through the sky. As the fighter jet came inbound, I received one last warning over the radio: *Bombs away, man. Stay low.*

I lay as flat as I could on the path, holding my hands over my head and planting my face in the dirt. Then I slightly tilted my head and opened my mouth to give the overpressure or shock wave a place to exit. All I could do was wait for the blast.

When the bomb hit, the overpressure from the explosion sent grass, dirt, gravel, dust, and tree branches flying in our direction. I waited for the big chunks of the mud compound to land on me as well as bits of earth and other debris. Thankfully, I was spared from hunks of mud wall hitting me, which would have broken my back. Instead, I was covered with dirt, leaves, and branches, but the concussive force was so great that I felt like my skeleton had just walked out of my body, turned, slapped me in the face, and reentered my body. As I tried to stand up, I kept falling. I almost felt like I was drunk.

In all my time in Afghanistan, I had yet to experience a concussive explosion of that magnitude. It took a good minute to regain my senses. Just as I was figuring out what happened, I heard my guys screaming over the radio.

Ryan, are you good?

Ryan, answer your fucking radio if you're alive.

Their voices sounded like someone was yelling down a long tunnel, trying to get my attention.

I got my bearings. "Fuck that was big, but I'm good, man," I answered. I couldn't believe what had just happened. "How big of a bomb was that?"

"Five hundred pounds, brother. You just ate a big one, man."

And I'm still alive?

I thought I had come away without a scratch until I felt warm liquid coming out of my ears from the monstrous blast. *Damn, that was close.*

There was no time to worry about an ear drip because I had no idea if the enemy was still moving around or all tapped out.

I took a moment to shake the cobwebs out of my head. Then I checked on my guys to ensure they were good. After everyone was accounted for—uninjured—I had my guys fall back to the closest position, which was twenty meters behind us.

Once we were back with our main element, our JTAC called

in another air strike, which would ensure that if anyone was still moving in the compound, they were sure to be dead. Within a matter of minutes, a second bomb went off, setting off another fireball explosion within the village compound.

This was our chance to move. I gathered up my clearance team and pushed forward into the compound. My head was fuzzy and my ears were still ringing, but we had a job to do. I had no idea what was waiting for us, but I silently prayed the air strikes killed the fighters. I thought those five-hundred-pound bombs better have wasted them because at that moment I doubted I could have shot straight if I tried. The cobwebs hadn't cleared yet.

Entering the compound, ready for anything, we found debris everywhere. The bombs had destroyed a sizable portion of the structure, so finding bodies wasn't easy. The stench of burned flesh lingered in the air, reminding me of when I took part in the body recovery on the USS *Cole* after the terrorist attack in October 2000. As I tried not to use my sense of smell, we moved cautiously, gathering all the evidence that we could. We still had an entire village to clear, so we couldn't waste all day in this one compound.

We found a few Taliban bodies, which were checked for intelligence. As we picked our way through the compound, I witnessed the hatred that our Afghan commandos had for the Taliban. Even though the enemy fighters were dead, the commandos kept kicking and spitting on the bodies.

Getting control of the situation was a must. We kept the Afghan commandos away from the bodies so we could thoroughly check each one for intel. Even though this was the enemy, we had to make sure the rules of engagement were followed.

After clearing the first compound, the sun was starting to

show its colors over the horizon. The sky was beautiful that morning. Red, pink, green, and yellow sun rays blanketed the battleground as our soldiers walked between them. Maybe this was God's way of saying that he was right by my side and I was to have no fear. At that moment, a verse from Psalm 23 in the King James Bible came to mind:

Yea, though I walk through the valley of the shadow of death, I will fear no evil: for thou art with me; thy rod and thy staff they comfort me.

This Bible verse took on a whole new meaning to me after that day. With the daylight came huge relief: IEDs would be a lot easier to find.

My four-man team pushed forward again, twenty meters in front of the main element as we moved deeper into the village. I preferred more guns and support close to us, but I understood why we had to maintain this amount of distance. If any of the clearance guys hit an IED, we would limit the number of other guys cut down by frag or caught up in an ambush.

All of that made sense, but there was still one little problem. Make that a big problem. The guys in the front were *almost always* the first to draw contact from the enemy, and a four- or five-man team were often sitting ducks.

Think about the situation we were in. If we did our job right and found the IEDs, we were good to go, but more important, others were not killed or injured. But if we didn't do our job right, then lives were lost and blood was shed.

On the other hand, if the assault element was more than twenty meters behind us, that didn't give them much time to react and save our asses. It was a lonely feeling being in the front, but in the end, being on point was my job and there really was no place I'd rather have been than here, leading the way.

Those of us in the U.S. military would have expected that by 2016, Afghan soldiers would be pulling security for the IED clearance element, with the Americans trailing and advising our counterparts. By now, one would think that the Afghans would be eager to rid their land of the Taliban.

You know, it's your country, so fight for it.

It's funny how fast that notion was forgotten once bullets were fired and everything went to shit.

After the first ambush, the Afghans dropped even farther behind while my team cleared IEDs. That wasn't going to work.

I approached the Afghan commander and reminded him of the plan for his guys to pull security just behind us while we cleared IEDs. His response caused my jaw to drop.

"I'm not pushing my guys forward because there are too many IEDs," he said with a wave of the hand. "The route must be cleared first."

"How the fuck do I clear the route if I have no security?" I asked.

"You have guns," he replied, as if that solved everything.

"So do you," I said sternly. "You know the risk and you know that war is dangerous, so what's the fucking problem? If I'm up here in the front, your men should be, too."

If I was in command, I would have packed up right then and left, but it wasn't my call. All we were doing was talking in circles and wasting time. We needed to return to the task at hand: pushing further into the village of Niazullah.

Once again, my element led the way into the next village compound. We met no further resistance from the Taliban, which left us free to clear the entire village of IEDs and sweep for intelligence. Just being in Niazullah was denying the enemy terrain and sending a clear message that we were here to fight.

As we moved past damaged mud-hut buildings, we saw that the village bore the scars of days of relentless artillery shelling by the Afghan army from the top of OP Burns. I saw homes ripped to shreds, collapsed buildings, and trees cut in half from fragmentation. There were no signs of life.

During the rest of our clearance, I encountered more than twenty IEDs. I personally blew up fifteen before I ran out of C-4 explosives. We marked the rest. Abe, Bismullah, and Jawaid handled another thirty IEDs. I bypassed many IEDs because we didn't have the time or the explosives to blow them up. Once marked, we could easily move around the danger areas without risk to the patrol. Overall, we located more than fifty IEDs, four 107 mm rockets, multiple booby traps, and a complex bunker-and-tunnel system. This particular part of the village lived up to its reputation as a hotbed for Taliban fighters.

The Taliban had reinforced bunkers spread throughout the village, many connecting with tunnels. This was the main reason why days of constant artillery fire from the Afghan army had little effect on these guys. Every time the Afghan army would send troops to clear the village, the Taliban would move undetected to their bunkers. So the Afghan army kept getting their asses kicked because the enemy could be in several different places in a matter of minutes.

This discovery of the tunnel system brought up a chilling question, however: Were the Taliban still in the vicinity, hiding in tunnels that we had yet to discover? Were they out there watching and waiting for us, using the tunnels to move around?

At every tunnel entrance we found, we would throw a frag grenade down the hatch to make sure there were no stragglers. Everything indicated the Taliban had packed up and left.

All this made sense to me. From my past trips to Afghanistan, I knew the Taliban might stick around and fight for a bit, but once we started dropping bombs, they would sprint for the exit door to fight another day and let the IEDs do their work.

In the middle of the afternoon, we were making our way down a small dirt road that ran through the village. The mission was wrapping up, and we could head back to the safe side of the ridgeline while the Afghans stayed behind to cement control of the village.

The Afghan commander, however, did not see things this way, which blew my mind. The Americans had brought the firepower and technical experience to clear a village that had been held by the Taliban for the last three years, but to keep this ground, the Afghans had to stay behind to protect what we had fought for.

I guess this Afghan commander hadn't studied military history or war tactics at whatever place in Afghanistan he received his training.

To hold ground and not give it back to the enemy, you must deter the enemy from wanting to return. That was Warfare 101—leaving a well-equipped fighting force behind to protect what you had fought for, a tactic dating back to the early days of battle. Common sense to me, but this guy couldn't get the point.

Upon hearing word that the Americans were pulling back, the Afghan commander took this as a sign that he and his men could vacate as well. Once again, our team leader attempted to explain the need for Afghan soldiers to remain in the village to hold the ground we had gained, but the Afghan commander wanted nothing to do with that.

"The Americans should stay, not my Afghan soldiers," he said through an interpreter. "You're better equipped to fight the Taliban than we are."

"If this was Texas, I would agree, but we're in Afghanistan, your country. I'm here to help you, not to win your battles," my team leader said.

We all knew the Americans were not staying behind, but that concept escaped this Afghan commander. No amount of reasoning could convince him otherwise, but my team wasn't about to get sucked into an argument about something so simple and commonsense on the battlefield.

We were getting nowhere quickly. Suddenly, one of the Afghan commandos approached me and pulled me to the side, along with our interpreter Dost.

"There are fifteen to twenty men moving our way," he said.

I was immediately concerned. "Are they bad guys or villagers coming back to check on things?"

I received a shrug. He didn't know.

I approached our team sergeant and relayed the information, but he didn't take me seriously at first. He was engulfed with trying to coordinate an element of Afghans to stay behind and hold the area.

Seconds later, the Afghan commando tugged on my shirtsleeve to get my attention again.

"The men are still heading this way. We need to do something because I don't think these are villagers from the area," he said.

I went back to my team sergeant and was more direct. "We need to get out of here. We have fighting-age males moving in our direction. I'm grabbing my guys and getting into position to move out."

The team sergeant nodded. "Fuck this," he said. "I'm done negotiating with these guys. Let's move out."

He had barely finished his sentence when the first shot whizzed by my head with the all-too-familiar *zip*, followed by a *crack*.

We were immediately in a fight for our lives.

CHAPTER 18

NO ONE GETS LEFT BEHIND

NIAZULLAH VILLAGE

BAGHLAN PROVINCE

FEBRUARY 22, 2016

*Z**ip. Crack.*
   Zip. Crack.
Crack, crack, crack.

Rounds were coming in all around us from automatic machine-gun fire. A series of RPG explosions took us by total surprise.

Everything turned to chaos in an instant. Everything was happening so fast that it was impossible for the human brain to comprehend it.

Instinctively, I knew I was sprinting for cover, but for a split second, I felt frozen in the pandemonium of everything happening around me while my brain scrambled to make sense of the attack's ferocity.

In the midst of the turmoil, events appeared around me like a war movie playing out in slow motion. When a *crack* of a 7.62 round kicked up dirt between my legs, all the fear, adrenaline, excitement, and overall terror hit me like a ton of bricks, and I was back in the moment. Now I was moving quickly, screaming instructions, and returning fire at an enemy I could not see.

Rounds sprayed everywhere, hitting compound walls like a garden hose watering down a dusty road. Just then, I heard Abe grunt as if he was hurt, but for some reason, it didn't occur to me that he could have been hit. I darted toward a ditch that paralleled the dirt road running through the village. After diving for cover, I peered out cautiously, but I couldn't see any of my guys or where we were taking fire from.

The bullets started hitting faster and faster around me. Limbs from trees fell as the hot lead ripped through them. The dust kicking up from the bullets was so intense that it looked like a cluster of horses was running down a dirt road on a dry summer day. A lot of firepower was coming in our direction, and there was no way to know how many fighters we were up against or where they were.

Over the radio, I heard reports of fighters to our east, then to the north—but then we took fire from the west. Were we surrounded on three sides?

Looking around, I saw a few of our guys bandaging up two wounded Afghan commandos just down the ditch from me. Across the road, another three commandos were cut off and under heavy fire.

Bullets were tilling up dirt all around me as we tried to stay as low as possible. Then I noticed that three commandos in the ditch ten meters from my position had drawn the attention of a Taliban machine-gun crew that had zeroed in on them.

I waved for the three Afghans to move to my position, which would give them more cover, but they were too scared to move. I knew that if they didn't get their asses in gear and start moving, they were going to die. I don't know what possessed me, but I climbed out from my ditch and sprinted to their position, praying to God that my adaptive leg would hold up.

I reached the first commando and grabbed the very first thing that I could get a hold of—his hair. I yanked him up and pulled him back to my ditch, hoping the other two would follow. They did. As we ran, dust kicked up as more rounds impacted around us. I slid into the ditch like I was legging out a triple, then reached back and dragged three scared-shitless commandos down with me.

We had company in this part of the ditch. Frankie was providing aid to another wounded Afghan.

"Frankie, you okay, man?"

"I'm good, brother. How about you?"

"Yeah, I'm okay. You see Abe or anyone else?"

"Not yet, man."

I moved closer to a small mud wall that paralleled the ditch. This wall provided decent protection from enemy fire and allowed me to look down the dirt road, where I saw an Afghan soldier lying motionless. I brought up my rifle scope to get a better look.

"Frankie, I think that's Bismullah in the middle of the road."

"Bro, I think he's dead."

My heart jumped straight to my throat. One of our guys was killed.

Fuck, where's the rest of my team? Frankie and I were the only two Americans in that ditch.

I scanned back down the road where Bismullah lay. I knew Abe was next to him before the ambush kicked off, but I could only see Bismullah. I hoped Abe wasn't hit, too.

What I could determine was that we had two wounded Afghan commandos and Bismullah lying in the middle of the road. I figured Bismullah was dead, but until I had my hands on him, I couldn't be 100 percent sure.

I knew I needed to get to him, but the amount of live fire coming in was too heavy. The radio crackled again, and then I heard a heart-stopping message in my headset loud and clear: "Eagles down, Eagles down."

The phrase "Eagles down" was code for Americans wounded or killed. This fight had just taken the worst turn possible. There were Americans wounded or killed somewhere on the battlefield, but I didn't know where.

We needed some air support—in a hurry.

Why haven't we started dropping bombs yet? We're going to get mowed down if we don't get some air support soon.

What I didn't know was that the Taliban were using the tunnel system to move around the battlefield, which made it impossible for us to get our eyes on them, and explained why fire was coming in from three sides. Confusing the situation even more was the fact our Afghan partner forces had spread out, so our aircraft could not tell the good guys from the bad guys.

"Bro, this shit is bad," I said to Frankie.

No sooner did the words leave my lips than I heard the one sound that gives every Green Beret chills: an explosion from a mortar round, which landed thirty meters from us and shook the earth.

I hit the ground and turned toward Frankie. "Shit!" I yelled. "They got a mortar tube up. We need to move before we get hit."

Gunfire is one thing. If the enemy is close enough to shoot you, then you're close enough to kill him. Mortars are a different story. They can be two or three kilometers away and engage you with deadly fire, and by the time you figure out where they're coming from, it's too late.

Another explosion hit the compound to the left of us—too close for comfort. Yep, that was our "Q"—time to make a move.

Frankie and I engaged Taliban targets as much as possible, trying to keep their heads down with return fire, which would give us a little time to pick up our wounded Afghans and move back.

Crack.

A round hit directly into the wall above my head.

Crack.

Another round too close for comfort.

Crack.

And another one. Then two more rounds hit the mud wall in front of us. A sniper had our position dialed in. Every time we stuck our heads up, he sent rounds our way. To make matters worse, the Taliban were dropping mortars closer and closer to our position.

One of the Afghan commandos beside us spoke a little English. He pointed to his radio and said he heard the Taliban had our position and were trying to capture us.

Capture. Hearing that word struck fear in my heart.

I nudged Frankie again. "The Taliban are trying to flank us and cut us off from the rest of our guys so they can take us. It's time to move, brother!" I shouted.

First things first: How do we avoid getting shot by this sniper? I saw a protected area near a compound a couple of hundred meters from us, where I recognized several Americans, including our medic, Joe.

"Frankie, I see Joe. Let's move to him."

Frankie and I gathered everyone up and made sure our wounded guys were good to move, then we cleared out. The only way to safely move to Joe's position was staying as low as possible in the ditch so the sniper couldn't get a fix on our heads. That was the chance we had to take; otherwise, there was a real possibility we could fall prey to a sniper's round or mortars.

After a long, back-breaking, hunched-over movement, we finally made it to the compound, a distance of about 200 meters from where we were pinned down. We hooked up with the rest of our ODA along with other Afghan commandos.

Joe was working on the wounded guys, and the scene looked bad. All the blood, moans, cries for help, and the state of shock could be seen on the commandos' faces. We knew we were in a real shit storm.

So far, we had one dead Afghan commando, two wounded Afghans, and three wounded Americans. We were missing five Afghans, including Abe and Bismullah.

Inside the safety of the compound, we set up our Casualty Collection Point, or CCP. The CCP was a secure location, far enough away from enemy fire, where our medics could stabilize the wounded guys.

I looked around for Jawaid and Kahan. Jawaid was sitting up against the wall, trying to catch his breath. Grabbing Dost, our interpreter, I asked him if he knew where Abe was.

Jawaid shook his head. "No, I haven't seen Abe."

Just then I saw Frankie, Kahan, and two Afghan commandos carrying Bismullah from the road to the CCP.

"Bismullah is still alive, but he can't feel his legs," Frankie said.

"Thank God, we got Bis, but where's Abe?" I asked.

A puzzled look came over Frankie. "No one has seen Abe since the firing started. Bro, he's still out there."

Just outside the compound wall on the east side of our CCP was a white two-story building. This building was made of lumber, not mud like most of the compounds in the village. We were told this building was a school before the Taliban took control of the village.

Crack, crack.

Once again, a Taliban sniper was putting rounds directly on us, this time from the second story of the white two-story building just east from us not more than 150 meters. We fired back at whatever window, small cutout, or empty space we could see, sending hundreds of bullets out, hoping one would be lucky and kill this asshole. No such luck. Sniper fire kept coming in.

Now that we had most of our friendly forces back in one location, the aircraft could start engaging targets. Up first was the white two-story former school building.

After forty-five minutes of intense fighting, we finally dropped our first bomb. As the F-15 jet screamed across the sky—and extremely close to our position—the first bomb dropped. The white building was reduced to wooden debris in a nanosecond, instantly killing the sniper inside.

Next, we called for air support against other compounds giving us fire. Explosion after explosion caused the ground to shake, followed by a dust cloud mushrooming into the blue sky, blanketing the village with rubble. We thought there was no way anyone could survive a blast of such power, but the Taliban proved us wrong and continued putting our heads down with nonstop fire.

How are they able to move around and avoid the strikes? I wondered.

The answer was simple: the tunnel system.

After the air strikes ceased, we received a report that the Taliban were trying to flank our CCP. We didn't want to risk holding ground and taking more casualties. We needed a better CCP—one with an open field where we could start landing Medevac helicopters to pick up the wounded and dead. At that point, we had two wounded Afghans, three wounded Americans, and now two dead Afghan commandos.

Three hundred meters to the right of the compound was another mud-hut compound with tall walls for protection and a large open field big enough for helicopters to land in. This was going to have to work because we needed to get going. We picked up and quickly moved to our new location and started calling "dust off," which was our radio call sign for medical evacuation helicopters.

Once we got set up at the new location, I did a head count of our guys. My entire team was accounted for except for Abe. I ran around until I found Frankie, who was providing aid to Bismullah.

Bismullah had been shot three times in the back and couldn't feel anything below his waist, but he was alive. I walked over and held his hand, telling him he would be okay, even though I knew that wasn't true. Being a paraplegic in Afghanistan was a death sentence in its own right. The country was too far behind the times to properly care for Bismullah's type of injuries.

I calmly asked him if he knew where Abe was.

"Abe was next to me when the fighting started," he said, "and then he jumped into the ditch near the footbridge at the last compound we cleared."

Okay, now I had a starting point. But we couldn't move down or go near that area of the village. The enemy was too well dug in. Every time we poked our heads up near the road, we got lit up by the Taliban. Somehow, I had to get to Abe. I was not leaving him behind.

We moved Bismullah to an awaiting helicopter and went back to get the rest of the wounded Afghans. Our new CCP ran parallel to the road on the south side of the village. We thought Abe was in a ditch next to this same road but on the north side.

The footbridge that Bismullah had mentioned was three hundred meters away—a long distance when the Taliban had eyes on the entire road and could shoot anything that moved. Frankie and I decided we were going to find Abe anyway. At that same time, I had an Afghan commando pointing to the footbridge, saying another commando was there with Abe. That meant two wounded guys now, which also meant I would need more help.

Our Air Force JTAC said he had a plan to keep the Taliban's heads down while we sprinted for the footbridge.

"I'll call in the Apaches to fly in front of your movement and shoot the shit out of everything ahead of you guys," he said.

I liked the way that sounded. Adding attack helicopters to the mix would make it easier to dodge enemy fire as we ran. I already had a good taste of lead coming my way that day, and I didn't want a second bite. We had to be careful because the Taliban had almost shot down one of our helicopters earlier when the helo tried to pick up the wounded. But I also knew without air support, the rescue mission would fail.

At the same time as we were putting together our two-minute game plan, the team sergeant stopped us.

"We can't risk you going down there to get those guys," he stated. "Too much enemy fire."

"Well, we're not leaving them behind," I said.

My team sergeant wasn't happy with my answer but he knew what we had to do.

I spoke up again. "If we leave without them, we could have a mutiny on our hands with the Afghans. We have to go. No one gets left behind!"

The team sergeant looked at us, knowing this was something that must happen. "Okay, we'll go," he said.

This was going to be an American-led recovery operation. Why the Afghan commandos wouldn't go recover their own guys was beyond me. If an American had been left behind, we would go to hell and back to get our brothers out, dead or alive.

The JTAC interrupted the discussion, stating the Apaches were inbound to do a gun run on enemy positions. We needed to use this cover as our chance to move.

"Here they come. Everyone ready?" the JTAC asked.

It was go time. The sounds of the large-caliber bullets echoed off the compound walls as the Apaches opened fire, blanketing the area with 30 mm rounds. Frankie, our JTAC, our team sergeant, and I sprinted down the road toward the area where we assumed Abe and the missing commando were. As we ran like hell in the direction of the footbridge, we took on small-arms fire but nothing compared to what it could have been if those Apaches weren't helping us.

The closer I got to the footbridge, though, the more I prepared myself for what I might see. Leading up to the bridge, the terrain shifted upward slightly, making it hard to see what was in the ditch. I was almost to the footbridge when I looked down.

There, floating lifeless in the water at the bottom of the ditch, was Abe. His body was sprawled out with a blood-soaked bandage around his pelvic area. Abe had attempted to stop the bleeding himself, but I knew that pelvic wounds were almost impossible to treat without proper medical help.

Abe had bled out so much that the muddy water in the ditch had turned bright red. My friend was dead, and I could not save him. A Taliban sniper had perfectly placed three rounds into his pelvis.

"Oh, Abe. They finally got you."

Abe and Bismullah were best friends who'd grown up together in Khost Province. Both linked up with U.S. forces around 2002 and had worked with U.S. Special Operations units as Afghan advisors ever since then. They volunteered to be a part of IED-clearing units, which is the most dangerous job in Afghanistan.

Every Afghan who volunteered to clear IEDs did so for different reasons. Some chose this life because they had lost family members to IEDs. Others did it for the money, but Abe and Bismullah were different. They wanted in because they wanted to work closely with U.S. Special Forces. Everyone knew that where Special Forces went, so did the action. And we quickly learned that Abe and Bismullah were action junkies.

Listening to Abe's stories was like reading a Tom Clancy novel. The stories were full of danger and shit that all men would love to do to their enemies but that most only read about in books. Abe and Bismullah had lived lives of making bad people go away, but on this fateful day, Abe's story ended.

As I got to his body in the ditch, Frankie was providing

covering fire while the team sergeant and I attempted to pull Abe out. Lifting a lifeless body out of a six-foot muddy ditch was especially difficult. Adding to the difficulties was the fact that Abe's body was covered in blood, which had made him extremely slippery to hold on to. We couldn't get a good grip on him and struggled to carry his body to dry ground.

I became more and more drenched in Abe's blood and even got some of his blood in my mouth—a taste that's forever etched in my mind. Finally, after giving it everything we had, we freed Abe from his watery grave, but the smells, the tastes, and everything about that moment still haunt me to this day.

After moving Abe's body to the road, we needed something to carry him on. My buddy Brian happened to be running toward us, carrying the ladder that we had used to climb the mud-hut walls earlier in the mission.

The ladder would work as a stretcher. We quickly put Abe's body on the ladder and hustled him back to the CCP. Now that we had Abe, we needed to recover the other missing commando that we knew was with Abe at the footbridge when the fighting started. Just a few feet down the ditch, I saw our Air Force JTAC and two Afghan commandos bringing the dead commando's body to the road.

It was time to move.

That wasn't easy, because Abe's lifeless body hung halfway off the ladder as we got going. We had to stop to reposition his body, a task necessary after every few steps because his body slipped off repeatedly. As we entered the CCP, we were still struggling to keep Abe's body on the ladder. Several other Afghan commandos stood there, watching us wrestle with his body.

"Don't just stand there! Fucking help us!" I screamed at the commandos.

Everything in my being wanted to tell these Afghan soldiers that four Americans just risked their lives to recover Abe's and another commando's body while they sought cover. The least they could do was help us get them to the helicopter.

But they stood there like statues as we continued on to the landing zone to wait for the helicopter. I was helping carry Abe on the makeshift gurney. When I saw the helicopter hovering overhead, it finally hit me. My buddy was really dead. My heart sank.

When the helicopter touched down, I helped load Abe onto the last flight he would ever take. I reached out and grabbed his lifeless hand as the helicopter lifted off from the ground to take him away.

Yes, Abe was gone, but we had recovered his body so that his family could give him a proper burial, a true warrior's funeral. If the Taliban had recovered his body, they would have desecrated it. Instead, we did right by him. As American fighting men and women, we have one belief we will fight and die for:

No one gets left behind.

The sun was getting hotter as we gathered all our equipment, got a final head count, and moved out of Niazullah village. Afghan reinforcements had arrived, so we could leave. Despite the Afghans' bitches and gripes that we were leaving, it didn't matter. We were not staying there.

All of us were completely exhausted, physically and mentally. The amount of death and close calls had taken a toll—even on the strongest. Everyone was in shock, especially the Afghan commandos.

This would have been a perfect time for the Taliban to hit us again, but thankfully they didn't, perhaps because we hit them hard that day. Our air strikes had pounded them relentlessly, so I'm sure that as bad as we were hurting, they were worse off.

We walked back to the point where we had left our vehicles. Even though we tried to keep some semblance of security, we must have looked like the walking dead.

I couldn't stop thinking about everything we had been through and the guys we had lost, but I reminded myself that there was no time for that. We were still in enemy territory, so I needed to pull it together. Back at the Humvees, we completed a 100 percent inventory. Once everything was accounted for, and the Afghan commandos finally came to terms with the fact that they would have to hold the village without Americans holding their hands, we loaded up and drove back to our base on the other side of the ridgeline.

Arriving back at our camp was like a scene out of *M*A*S*H*. As we walked into our main building, we found the hallway soaked in blood. I could hear medical operations happening in the background as doctors attached to our team tried their best to stabilize the wounded American and Afghan soldiers.

Two body bags lay at the end of the hallway, in a corner. One of them was Abe, who had run toward enemy fire when the fighting broke out, allowing us the opportunity to get to cover. Now he was dead, a true hero.

The passage from John 15:13 came to mind: "Greater love has no one than this: to lay down one's life for one's friends." This Scripture has stayed etched in my mind ever since then because of Abe.

The emotions were starting to take a toll on me. I could see the pain in everyone's faces. We all knew Abe. He was part of our Special Forces family. When you work with, live with, and spend most of your time with someone, it's hard when he dies.

Frankie, Brian, and I tried to comfort Jawaid, Kahan, and the other Afghans, in shock and visibly mourning. After a while, I needed to get away myself. My breaking point came when my major came up to me with tears in his eyes and gave me a hug.

"Ryan, we thought we lost you out there," he said. "I'm sorry Abe was killed, man. You did your best. I know you did."

I thanked the major, but it was my job to bring my guys back alive, and I'd failed Abe. Bismullah might die next.

The thought was overwhelming. When I started to choke up, I decided to walk out to our Humvee, which was out of sight. I sat in the driver's seat, put my head in my hands, and just cried.

The emotional toll of everything that day came out at that moment, and I was able to decompress. I was wiping away tears when the team sergeant walked up. To my surprise, he reached for me and gave me a hug.

"Ryan, if it wasn't for you today, a lot of guys would have died. You're a hero, brother."

That was hard to hear because I wasn't able to bring Abe home alive, but it was true. Frankie and I had cleared paths that allowed our team to move freely without one IED strike. We did this in the most IED'd village I had ever been to in Afghanistan. The only casualties were from bullets. Still, that didn't lessen the pain. I sat in the truck for another few minutes until I could pull myself together, regain my composure, and take a deep breath.

A few days after the mission, my major approached me and said he was putting me in for the Silver Star, which is our nation's third-highest award in combat. As honored as that made me feel, I still could not escape the fact I had not brought all my guys back alive. Combat is a rush we all look for as soldiers, but the realities of war are far more difficult to handle.

The rest of my deployment was relatively quiet, definitely not as eventful as this mission in Baghlan. Once I returned to the United States in late June 2016, I was awarded the Silver Star at a ceremony at the 7th Special Forces Group compound in Florida.

A few weeks later, I traveled to Canada to receive the First Special Service Force's Major General Robert T. Frederick Award, which is given to only one U.S. Special Forces soldier and one Canadian Special Operations Soldier each year. I guess it was the combination of what I did in Afghanistan in 2016, along with everything I had been through after I avoided death on September 12, 2010, that resulted in me being presented with this award.

Receiving the Frederick Award was one of the biggest honors of my life. The First Special Service Force men who fought and died during World War II for our great nation are the reason I can live in a free country today.

These are the same ideals I hold near to my heart each time I deploy to Afghanistan. All humans should have the right to live in peace, free of terror and repression. Upon getting this award, I could only hope I did my part and made these men proud.

There's not a day that goes by when I don't remember the sacrifices of so many and see the faces of my friends who did not make it home from the battlefield. Bismullah survived his wounds, but he was paralyzed from the waist down. Five commandos and Abe were killed during the operation, bringing the total number of Afghans killed in action to six, with ten Afghan commandos wounded.

Every Green Beret survived, but three have the scars of a hard-fought battle forever etched into their bodies. Though Afghan soldiers recovered one of the bodies of their dead companions, American soldiers recovered the other four dead Afghans because of our belief that no matter who you are or where you are from, everyone should be brought home alive or dead.

Though I will always have these memories, I will never let them control me. My friends who died on the battlefield would not want that.

Life can be short, unfair, unbelievably cruel, and ugly as all get out. I have shed tears thinking about the many brothers I knew who were taken well before their time.

Grieving is natural, but I believe it should be temporary. I choose to control my thoughts and actions and try my best not to become a victim of negative circumstances. I choose to set the rules for my life and not let the memories of the past haunt me and dictate my future.

The reality is that nobody gets out of here alive—we will all die one day. This is something we can't control. Because death is inevitable, the moment you fully understand and embrace this is the moment you are truly free.

CHAPTER 19

COMING HOME

MILTON, FLORIDA

SPRING 2019

When our 2016 tour of duty was over in July, our team boarded a C-17 at Bagram Airfield and flew west until we landed at Eglin Air Force Base near Pensacola, Florida, following a fuel stop at Ramstein Air Base in Germany.

This reentry was different from my previous tour in Afghanistan, in 2012, when we spent two weeks in Germany while our aircraft was worked on for mechanical issues. Kicking back and sampling the local beer gave us time to process what we'd been through after living in a war zone for nine months.

After this 2016 deployment, though, there was no time to decompress. We basically hopped from the dangers of Afghanistan to tranquil Florida within twenty-four hours—the quickest I ever returned home. I still had Afghanistan dirt underneath my fingernails.

I didn't realize that I had suffered a traumatic brain injury (TBI) during the firefight where the five-hundred-pound bomb had landed just seventeen meters from my position. The explosion had felt like it crushed my inside, ruptured my eardrum, and jiggled my brain pretty good. Even though I had felt out of sorts and had headaches for weeks, it took me almost two months after the February incident before I went and saw Joe, my medic, who sent me to BAF to get checked out. I was told that I'd be okay but needed time to fully recover from the TBI.

So that was where my head was at, so to speak, when I landed in Florida—a place where people's biggest concerns were SEC football and where they'd go out for their next meal. I was on edge, and it didn't take much to set me off. I remember moving through one of the aisles of our local Publix. I was pushing a bunch of groceries in my cart when a guy in front of me blocked my way. He was standing in the middle of the aisle and reading the ingredients listed on every box on the shelf.

"Are you going to move?" I asked him.

The guy glared at me, but he didn't budge.

"If you don't get your fucking cart out of my way, I'm going to fucking move you myself," I seethed.

That didn't go over well. It was a miracle we didn't get into a major altercation—or that I didn't break the guy's jaw.

I started drinking more, too. When my work week was over on Friday, I liked to hit Happy Hour with Frankie and have a couple of beers, but it was taking us four or five pitchers to unwind. Binge drinking on weekends became the norm for me, including the consumption of a lot of beer at home. I could easily clear twelve to fifteen Miller Lites in an evening.

My breaking point hit when I was sitting at a table inside a crowded bar with Frankie and Joey, one of my other teammates who I've been with for years, working on my third or fourth pitcher. I heard a dude one table over talking to his friends. It was almost like my ears were amplified. I could hear all the stupid shit he was saying, which annoyed me. He seemed to be whining about some problem he had at work.

You think you got problems? You have no fucking clue.

Then a guy walked behind my chair and bumped into me.

"Hey, man. Watch where the fuck you're going," I snapped.

The guy stopped in his tracks and spun on his heels. "What did you say?" he demanded.

I rose out of my chair. "I said watch the fuck where you're going."

He had five friends with him, which didn't matter to me. I was more than willing to fight all of them. The commotion caught the bouncers' attention after Frankie, Joey, and I squared off with the group, ready to start the beatdown. The bouncers jumped into the middle of the fray, separating us and demanding we leave, which really threw gas on the fire. I slammed my fist on the table and stormed out, but not before giving the front door a swift kick that nearly tore it off the hinges.

We were followed by the six guys out to the parking lot. Not a problem for us—we were ready to pick up where we left off. Just as I started to reach out and grab the first guy, a few friends from work sprinted over to break things up.

"Ryan, you okay, man? What the fuck is going on?" asked one of my buddies.

"I'm good, but these guys are not going to be in a few seconds."

Six against three were bad odds, especially since we didn't know who might pull a razor-sharp knife, a loaded gun, or a baseball bat. No matter. Frankie, Joey, and I were ready for a good fight.

Just when things were getting really tense, one of the guys from base talked some sense into me.

"Ryan, you don't want to do this, man," he said. "You just got home. This will sink your career for sure."

I looked over at Frankie and Joey, who were also realizing this was a bad move for us.

"Guys, I'm good," I said. "I think I need to get the fuck out of here. Shit is happening too fast right now."

As I left the area, I heard one of the guys from our base say to me, "Dude, you need to talk to someone."

Even though I had no business being behind the wheel, I thought long and hard about what was happening to me as I drove home. I was accelerating on the anger scale rather quickly, and that wasn't good for me or for anyone else. *You need to get yourself under control. You've got some real anger issues.*

But it took another incident for me to admit that I needed help. I was driving along Nichols Lake Road with Dawn, my girlfriend. Some idiot cut me off and yelled at me through the passenger's-side window, which really shot up my blood pressure. I gunned the engine and chased after him like we were in a *Fast and Furious* movie. He noticed me in his rearview mirror and sped up. I matched him and had stayed on his tail for a good mile or so when he swerved into a neighborhood.

The entire time Dawn was screaming at me, "What are you doing? Stop! Are you crazy?" She was scared, but I didn't care.

I wouldn't let this guy go. He had to pay for cutting me off. He was an asshole driver and deserved a lesson in pain.

"Stop the car! Stop the car! Stop the car!" Dawn yelled.

I drove like I was in a tunnel. I could hear her, but what she was saying wasn't relevant. My mind was focused on the piece of shit who flew by me and cut me off for no good reason.

Inside a warren of residential streets, the dude suddenly turned into a driveway and ran into a house. I slid into the curb and put my truck in park. I was about to run after him when—

—Dawn grabbed my arm. "What are you doing?" she asked. "Are you going to chase him down? Beat him up? And then what? We've got guns in the house. What makes you think he doesn't have them? This is stupid! What's going on with you right now?"

She had a point. I let out a huge breath of air, which dialed back the adrenaline surging through my body. "Fuck this," I mumbled as I got back into the truck.

I eased away from the curb and turned toward home. For the next ten minutes, neither of us said a word. My mind was locked on this thought: *You need to get your temper under control.*

Dammit, I was a Green Beret. That meant I was a professional, and flipping the switch between civilian life and being in a war zone was the professional thing to do. Yet here I was, acting like a bully if someone did something I didn't like.

I took some active measures over the next few days and weeks. I opened up to Mike Valcq, Tyler, and Frankie about some of my struggles. It turned out I wasn't alone. After sharing my innermost thoughts with Frankie, he said he was going through the same issues as me. *Finally! Someone gets it!*

Mike Valcq, who'd been on my team going on five years but had left before the 2016 deployment, said something that really made me think.

"What would have happened if you went into that guy's house and beat the crap out of him for cutting you off?" he asked. "Your career would be over. You'd be done. You'd get arrested, and they'd take your Special Forces tab away, and you're no longer a Green Beret. Over what? Because some idiot in America cut you off?"

He had me there. My next step, I decided, was to see a chaplain. I met with our base chaplain several times, but one piece of advice he gave me made all the difference in the world. After listening to my story, he suggested that I write down everything that happened to me. He urged me to reach back into my past and write about everything that had had a big effect on me throughout my life. Get it all on paper, he said—the good, the bad, and the ugly.

When I told Dawn what the chaplain said, she agreed with him and encouraged me to start writing. She knew that I had a lot of issues. I could tell how concerned she was about my drinking because she told me, but I also had enough presence of mind to know that drinking placed me on a very slippery slope. I knew from the way I was raised that once you start sliding downhill, it's hard to pull yourself out before you hit rock bottom.

But Dawn said something else that gave me pause—she said if I didn't get my temper under control quickly, then I was going to kill somebody, or someone was going to kill me. And that scared her.

Dawn was such a rock to me. We had been together for eight years, yet despite the long periods of separation, she was there for me. I needed to be there for her.

Though nothing happened overnight, I slowly got my shit under control. My anger issues, at times, were still an open question, but I started to focus on what triggered me, which helped me ratchet my aggression way down.

Life returned to what I assumed was normal as I geared up for my next deployment to Afghanistan.

We had nine or ten months stateside before we deployed to Afghanistan in the summer of 2017. This time we were sent to Camp Stevenson, which is in northern Afghanistan. Our base of operation was Kunduz Province and Kunduz city, the strategic metropolis near the Tajikistan border and a Taliban haven for drug running and resupplying their soldiers with weapons and matériel for making IEDs.

I spent most of my time in Mazar-i-Sharif, Balkh Province, with the B team, which is the support team for the company. This is where the more senior guys are sent to better assist the teams. Normally, this would mean a quiet tour for me, but we had three different teams short of 18 Charlies, so I went on missions with them nonstop—probably fifteen different missions all over Kunduz Province.

It seemed on this deployment, however, that mass casualties were a common occurrence every time we went on mission. I must have helped out with a dozen mass-casualty events involving Afghan soldiers who had been shot, hit with IEDs, or taken shrapnel from a nearby explosion. Because we were pushing the Afghans farther in front of us, that also meant they were the first to encounter IEDs. Many lost limbs in explosions or were wounded by hostile fire from the Taliban. That was when my team and I would be called in to stabilize them, load them on helicopters, and get them flown to the nearest military trauma center.

The Taliban, in some locations in Kunduz, were daisy-chaining their IEDs, meaning multiple explosive devices were wired to a single detonator. If one Afghan soldier stepped on an IED, several explosions went off and often maimed several Afghan soldiers severely—meaning the instant loss of two or three limbs—or killed them. These mass-casualty events were bloody and gruesome, with a great deal of suffering, but they were situations that we had all trained for.

When I had some extra time back at Camp Stevenson—and to take my mind off of everything—I continued writing down things that had happened to me over the years, something I had started in Florida. I wrote about my childhood and who my father was and how I didn't have a mom growing up. I wrote about stepping on an IED in 2010 and my determination to keep my leg and return to active duty. I wrote about how I rescued wounded soldiers and recovering bodies in a 2016 firefight, ensuring that no one got left behind.

These writings became the basis of the book you are now reading, but initially I wrote solely for my own benefit. I always thought it would be cool if my kids or my grandkids would go through an old trunk after I was gone and find a manuscript from Grandpa Hendrickson. They'd start reading pages and think to themselves, *Wow.*

When the 2017 tour was over, my reentry went a lot better, thanks to the lessons I had learned the previous year. I came to the realization that people just didn't understand what I had been through. It wasn't their fault, and I shouldn't have made it their fault. I had to realize that I was a professional soldier, and that required me to understand that people will never know what soldiers go through. Keeping this thought in mind helped me avoid situations that set me off. Basically, I was being an adult.

Another big help was taking a few trips with Dawn, including a hiking expedition to the Great Smoky Mountains. We stayed in a cabin near Gatlinburg, Tennessee, and grew closer hiking all over and enjoying our time together. These trips were much needed; by being away from everything, we could just focus on each other.

One evening, back in Milton, we drove to a nearby Applebee's and parked. I was just about to get out of the car when Dawn said she had something to say to me.

"Do you realize that if you die or something happens to you in Afghanistan that the military won't tell me? It will have to be your dad or your sisters who tell me. I've invested all this time and effort into our relationship, I've stuck by your side, but if something happens to you, the military doesn't care about me because I'm just a girlfriend."

She was right. According to the military, I was single. If we were married, she would be entitled to benefits as a military widow, but if I died while I was still single, she would get nothing, not even a phone call from the army to inform her of what happened.

We had talked about marriage in the past, but she said she wasn't interested in getting hitched. A few years later when the subject came up again, I said I wasn't ready yet. Our common saying was *We're fine the way we are.*

I think Dawn felt that way because she had a good career going as an occupational therapist, and I liked my space and the military camaraderie. We had both gotten used to me being gone, often for nine months a year, when I was deployed in Afghanistan or training in a foreign country or a different state. No matter what location the military took me to, near or far, gone is gone.

I looked over to her from the driver's seat. "Well, we should get married then."

A look of surprise came over her. "Are you serious? You're not joking with me, are you?"

"I'm not messing with you at all."

"Okay, let's get married then."

"Good. Let's do it. And now I'm hungry, so let's go into Applebee's and get something to eat."

I know—an Applebee's parking lot. I'm not the most romantic guy in the world or the type to get on bended knee at some special place and ask for her hand in marriage. What Dawn said about getting married made sense. I knew I loved her and she loved me. So why not tie the knot?

This conversation happened sometime in November 2017. But we didn't set a date. We left that hanging out there…and resumed our normal lives, which, for me, meant pre-mission training. When the topic of marriage came up again, we agreed that we didn't want anything extravagant. Dawn doesn't like people focusing on her, and I've never been a big wedding guy. We talked about having a small, intimate ceremony at our house or a buddy's place with only a few close family and friends in attendance. We just didn't want to make a big deal out of it.

Truth be told, many of our friends thought we were married already since we'd been together nine years. We didn't want the attention or to spend the money on a fancy wedding.

Over a couple of beers with some of the guys on the team—Frankie, Tyler, Ferny (another teammate and longtime friend from 7216) and Mike Valcq—I mentioned that Dawn and I were thinking of getting married. They all thought that was a great idea, but it was more of a "It's about time, Ryan." I also heard "Shit or get off the pot" more than once.

Valcq had a question: "Who's going to be your minister?"

"I don't know," I replied. "Maybe the base chaplain or someone like that."

That's when Mike's face turned into a big smile.

"What are you smiling at?" I asked.

"I have a crazy idea, but hear me out. I can get ordained online and marry you guys legally in the state of Florida."

"What? You're kidding me."

"No, I'm serious. It's easy, man. It would be an honor."

This was sure to be the craziest hitching ever.

So now we had a preacher. Well, Mike wasn't a preacher, but he was my buddy from Afghanistan and the Q Course, and we had been teammates for years. He even volunteered to do the wedding in the backyard of his place. The last thing to work out was a date that would work for Dawn's mom. We settled on Saturday, February 17, 2018.

We wanted a casual wedding, and a casual wedding was what we got. We catered some food and invited some of our friends over to Valcq's house, and that was about it. He had a great entertainment area in the backyard that included a swimming pool, a barbecue pit, and an outdoor bar.

The festivities started in the late afternoon. Around 7 p.m., after the sun had gone down, it was time to exchange vows. Valcq took a spot in the backyard, and Dawn and I stood in front of him. I had a Miller Lite in my right hand, and Dawn wore a nice dress, but it wasn't a wedding gown.

Valcq raced through the vows, and before we knew it, we were pronounced husband and wife. We were legally Mr. and Mrs. Ryan Hendrickson. That felt good.

We spent the evening celebrating, laughing, and making memories with our small group of friends. It felt great to get that ceremony behind us. Now if something happened to me, Dawn was protected.

Unfortunately, you have to think about those things in my line of work.

I had another important decision to make: whether or not I was going to retire from the military and go on to the next chapter in my life.

My next deployment was coming up in August 2018, but as I well knew, I'd hit my twenty-year retirement mark in September 2018, which meant I couldn't go on this deployment unless I sought an extension waiver.

I spent a lot of nights tossing and turning in bed, trying to figure out what to do.

I wanted to go back to Afghanistan one more time. I know that sounds crazy, but I was chasing ghosts from the 2016 tour. Since the 2017 tour didn't live up to what happened in '16, I wanted one last trip to cap off my military career. I wanted that one last big firefight, that last "hoo-rah" to go out on.

Dawn saw how much this meant to me, so I had her support. I requested an extension, which got approved. I was cleared for a seven-month deployment starting in August 2018 and ending in March 2019.

In a few words, my last deployment to Afghanistan was boring and cold. Now, boring has tons of upside for coming back with all your limbs intact. Sure, we got in some good fights and killed our share of Taliban, but the team dynamic wasn't as close as it had been in the past. We had some new guys rotate in, and the cohesion wasn't there like it had been before. I could see that I had done my time and should retire.

The cold part was the worst. Early in 2019, I did two of the hardest missions of my life. On one of the missions slated for Wardak Province in central Afghanistan, we had objectives that placed us in the mountains. In the dead of winter, with a temperature of minus four degrees Fahrenheit, my team and I were aboard a CH-47 Chinook helicopter that took us into snow country.

Once I stepped off the bird, I sunk to my knees in snow. I looked in the direction of our targeted compound and saw on my GPS that it was more than two kilometers away, uphill. Trudging through two feet of snow with a hundred pounds of gear, I knew this would be the hardest infil I'd ever done. The miserable temperatures were so cold that I ended up getting frostbite on one of my toes, and all the water sources we carried froze. The second mission was about the same, even though it was a lot warmer at three degrees Fahrenheit. Both missions were conducted in bone-chattering cold and deep snow.

The other mission to Farah Province in western Afghanistan put us in a sandstorm that shredded my sinuses. The Taliban fought us on that mission, but it wasn't like before. The void from 2016 was still there, and I finally realized that it would never be filled. It also became apparent to me that there was a new generation of Special Operators coming through, and it was my time to move on. It wasn't that I couldn't adjust, but the "old days" that I leaned on were over. I made up my mind that I was going to retire when our deployment was over.

When I returned to Florida in March 2019, Dawn and I

discussed what we wanted the rest of our lives to look like. Maybe a family is in our future. We shall see.

I told Dawn the story about when I was in high school and my dad shared the tale of the two old men: One man regretted his life because he hadn't done anything noteworthy, and the other man was happy because he'd done it all and had no regrets.

"I have no regrets," I told her.

There isn't much in life that I haven't done—except to have a family, of course. But I've gotten to fill the blank pages my dad talked about with some unbelievable adventures in some incredible places around the world. I've definitely made my mistakes, but that has made me who I am today.

There is one thing still gnawing at me, though, and it's Afghanistan. I do want to see the Afghan campaign all the way through.

That's why I might go back, as a civilian contractor.

I have a feeling that I haven't found my last IED.

ACKNOWLEDGMENTS

After my 2016 deployment, I saw how issues that had festered over the years, mainly from my severe leg injury in 2010, were coming to light. Between my thoughts and my dreams, I seemed to always have Afghanistan on my mind to the point where I had problems concentrating on anything else.

I tried talking out some of my feelings and concerns with friends, family, and even a counselor, but in the end, it was all just dead air that was quickly forgotten. When I sat down with our 7th Special Forces Group chaplain and heard his recommendation to put down my feelings, emotions, and concerns on paper, I didn't think too much of his suggestion at the time, mainly because I didn't view myself as much of a writer.

Something propelled me to give it a shot anyway. During my 2017 Afghan deployment, I opened up my laptop one night and typed out thoughts regarding some of the issues plaguing my mind. One page led to two, then three, then four, and many more pages as my feelings and descriptions about what I had been through spilled out of my mind and onto my keyboard.

The entire time I was writing, however, I wanted to keep everything under wraps, mostly because of my insecurities as a writer. Even though I did not set out to write a book at first, oftentimes I wondered: *Why would anyone care about my story?* or *Are people really interested in reading another war story about Afghanistan?*

As my book started to take form, I asked several close friends their opinions about my military career and what I had been through. The overwhelming response from many was this: Ryan, you need to tell your story. Their reinsurances pushed me forward. While there were times when I wanted to give up, their positive reinforcement and encouragement kept my fingers going.

The next thing I knew, I was spending my nights when I was not on a mission just typing away, which felt good. After five or so months of writing and rewriting, I wanted to get an opinion on how I was doing, so I turned to one guy whom I could trust to give me his honest assessment: Frankie Hernandez.

Frankie read through everything and told me that I had a strong story that could reach a lot of people. I deeply respected and honored Frankie's opinion, but I was still insecure and wanted a few more viewpoints.

I asked Tyler Gieck and Zac R, whom I also deeply trusted, to take a look at what I had written and give me their opinions. Tyler and Zac came back with the same message: I had a story that could reach a lot of people in a positive way.

After that confidence boost, I contacted a top-notch author who'd written many successful books and was herself a U.S. Navy veteran—Lynn Vincent. I thought that she could help me with my book and make it better. Lynn said she couldn't help me because she was in the midst of writing *Indianapolis: The True Story of the Worst Sea Disaster in U.S. Naval History*, but she put me in touch with Mike Yorkey, a veteran author.

Mike offered to look at what I'd written, so I sent him my manuscript. He loved my story and wanted to help me, so we formed a powerful team. After a lot of work over many months, we not only have a book, but we have a testimony that Mike and I believe will speak to many.

There's another thing you should know about Mike: He took on this project as a gamble, without ever knowing if *Tip of the Spear* would see the light of publishing day. I had no money to get him started, but for two years, Mike and I emailed chapters back and forth as he pushed me to improve the manuscript. His work ethic and dedication inspired me. He's authored or co-authored more than a hundred books, including *The Shot Caller,* with Latino gangbanger Casey Diaz; and *After the Cheering Stops,* with ex-NFL wife Cyndy Feasel.

Another person who took a risk was my literary agent, Greg Johnson of WordServe Literary, who saw the potential in *The Tip of the Spear* from day one and has a heart for military books. I can't thank Greg enough for his invaluable advice that comes from many years of experiences and contacts. I also want to thank Kate Hartson and Sean McGowan at Center Street, an imprint of Hachette Book Group, for their hard work, as well as my super editor, Jaime Coyne.

I also have to say that my book would not be where it is today if it wasn't for the dedication and determination of Angela and Jessica Nicosia. Angela and Jessica are sisters who make it their life's goal to personally help and support the veterans community. From the book review by the Department of Defense, the multiple legal documents that I needed to sign and the assurance that all my "t"s were crossed and "i"s were dotted legally, these two ladies took so much pressure off me. Not only do these sisters fight for benefits for hundreds of veterans, but Angela has battled breast cancer; and even though she continues to deal with health issues linked to the cancer treatment, she puts others' well-being ahead of her own. I will forever be grateful for these two ladies and consider them family.

The person who has been there the most for me, the one who witnessed my ups and extreme downs, not knowing if I was alive or not during my tours to Afghanistan, is my amazing wife, Dawn. With the greatest thankfulness to God, I acknowledge her indispensable contribution to my life. Dawn has been a driving force, helping me through many of my life changes and a few near-death experiences, along with staying strong when times got hard. She has done so willingly and without complaint, and I know she loves me just as much as I love her. I really mean it when I tell others that Dawn completes my life.

Along with Dawn, I need to acknowledge the support I received from my family, beginning with my dad, Larry Hendrickson, who kept encouraging me and would always put my worries, fears, and unknowns into perspective—something only a dad can do. My sisters, Wendy, Paula, Chris, and my brother, Robbie, all kept my drive alive through our many heart-filled conversations and through the love our family has for each other. Both Chris and Paula read my book in the early stages and further echoed the fact that I should keep writing, which gave me encouragement along the way.

During my 2018 Afghan deployment, as Mike Yorkey and I were putting the finishing touches on my book, I was having a lot of doubts. I was in Afghanistan, after all, which provides an ample amount of time to think through all the negatives and "what-if"s, playing tricks and planting seeds of doubt, but two individuals on that deployment helped me in ways they had no clue: Phil Melendez and Matt R.

Phil and I are friends who've known each other since 2012, but this was the first time we were on a team together. Throughout our seven-month deployment, Phil and I would talk for hours over life, religion, and politics, and at times I would express my concerns with the book. Phil and I often shared deep, philosophical conversations, which I enjoyed and learned from. One time he said, "Ryan, you have a story, man. Why wouldn't you want to let people enjoy it?" I was all ears.

Matt, on the other hand, would try to guilt me into staying the course. One conversation I remember having with Matt went something like this:

"Bro, I'm not sure if I want to put myself out there for the world to read all about my life in such great detail," I said.

"Why not?" Matt replied. "Your life seems boring to me. Hell, it's a good bedtime story that'll put people to sleep, so what's there to worry about?" Matt was being facetious, but there was also a sarcastic edge to what he was saying.

"I don't know," I continued. "I don't want to fall into the stereotype of being another operator who writes a book."

"You know what I have to say to that?" Matt fired back. "Who cares what anyone else thinks? If they don't like it, fuck 'em. It's their loss."

"Yeah, I guess you're right, man. I just don't want to be that guy," I replied.

"Ryan, I'll make this easy for you: If you don't publish this book, I'm going to kick your ass."

And thus the conversation would continue.

Another member of the 7216 was Derrick, who is a lifelong brother along, with Mike Valcq, Tyler Gieck, and Frankie Hernandez. We're always doing something together, whether we're on deployment or at home. Derrick's passion for duck hunting has been something that I've never seen before because I've never met a man who could drink all night, get a couple of hours of sleep, and be completely sober to go duck hunting at four in the morning, but Derrick is that guy. I admire how he puts his heart into being the best operator he can be.

Another good friend, Lucky, and I had many memorable experiences together in combat, which created an ironclad brotherhood between us. Lucky and I were on the same team during my 2017 deployment, and I can say he is one of the toughest guys I've ever met.

Sean Dillon and I have been friends since I was in the navy, where we were roommates going through BUD/S, and we have always kept in touch through yearly family get-togethers.

Bryan Brown and I met while we were in the air force. We are both from Oregon and have gone back to God's country many times together to visit friends and get in a good hike. Bryan ended up hiking the entire Pacific Crest Trail (PCT) in 2018. Someday after I retire, I hope Byran and I can walk the entire length of the Mexico-to-Canada trail together.

I'll never forget how Bryan drove over four hundred miles to see me at Andrews Air Force Base outside of Washington, D.C., after I had returned home from Germany following my IED injury. Unfortunately, Byran arrived at Andrews thirty minutes after my connecting flight departed to San Antonio, Texas, where I was taken to Brooke Army Medical Center (BMAC). After I got settled at BMAC, Bryan visited me multiple times from his base in Alabama to make sure I was still kicking, or at least bitching about my circumstances.

I also want to acknowledge Adam, who started off as my team sergeant. I have always looked up to Adam for answers throughout my career in Special Forces.

Jeremy is a musclebound freak of nature whom I met while going through the Q-Course. After I was injured in Afghanistan in 2010, Jeremy would call me at the hospital to remind me "not to be a pussy" and get back to the fight as fast as I could.

Then there's my boy Jim Gallup, who also went through Q-Course with me. Although Jim and I stayed in Alpha Company together, we usually ended up on different teams but we would always make it a point to meet up to swap war stories or just talk. During my final phase of the Q-Course, Jim and I froze together in the field during one of the coldest Februarys I can remember in North Carolina.

At that time, we were both trying to get water because it had been days since we ate and hours since our last drink of liquid. When we tipped back our canteens, everything was frozen, so we resorted to eating snow.

Thinking back on this experience, I felt at the time that nothing could be worse, but little did I know that many missions in Afghanistan would turn out to be a lot harder, whether it was due to extreme heat, freezing cold, or the steep terrain. One thing is for sure: The Q-Course is hard for a reason, because a combat deployment will test a man in ways that training cannot touch.

Warren Henson, Brian Dwyer, Big Tony Martino, andgPatrick Heffernan (aka Patty P) went through SF training with me from start to finish. Even though we ended up going to different Special Forces Groups, we always seemed to meet up in Afghanistan. As we trudged through training, including the bitterly cold Robin Sage class in February, it seemed like you could find us four together, grabbing a cold beer, studying together for an exam, or relaxing from a long stint of training. After I was wounded, they all made a point to see me and make sure I was going to make it, something brothers do for each other.

Oscar Zamora joined me during my 2017 deployment, when

we became close friends and brothers during the many combat missions we were on together. Will, Dino, Danny, and Juan (the Colombian) were the more senior guys in the company who took me under their wing and helped me achieve the successes I did, along with watching my back throughout many combat missions. I have the utmost respect for their mentorship and leadership.

Enough can't be said about all the men of Alpha Company, 2nd Battalion, 7th Special Forces Group and ODA 7216 who were instrumental in my development as a Green Beret over the years. Not only did these men help my military career, but in the bond created through combat, I will forever consider these men brothers for life.

Last, I want to point out the men who epitomize "heroic courage" and whom I look up to for strength: Ben Harrow, Will Lyles, and Levi Rogers. These three men are the definition of what it means to overcome astronomical odds, to go through hell and back, only to come out stronger on the other side. I will forever be grateful for the lessons I learned from them as well as their strength and determination in putting aside their catastrophic injuries to show me the true value of life. They remind me that no matter what life throws at you or how bad you think you have it, you can always pick yourself up off the ground and kick life in the ass.

For the men in heaven keeping a watchful eye on us, I salute you. May God hold you close and give you the comfort you all deserve. And till we meet again, I will do my best to live the life you all embodied while you were still walking among us.

Interested readers can contact me by writing to tipofthespear@mail.com.